I0799405

IMAGES
of America

CORRY

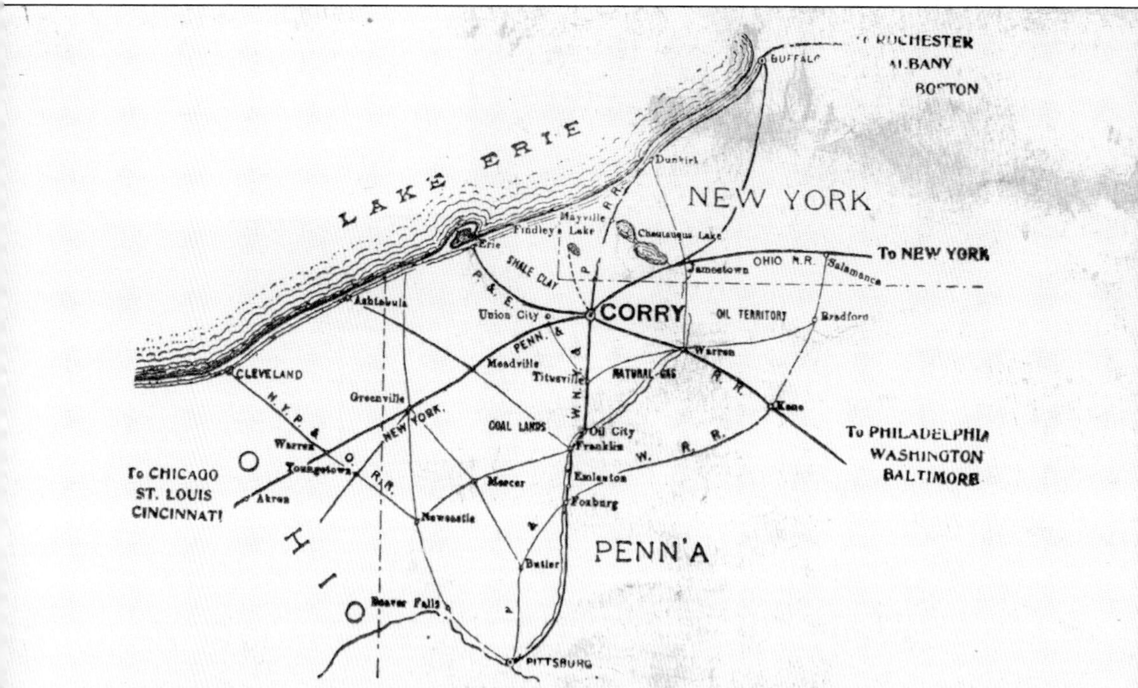

In 1861, when the AG&W Railroad crossed the S&E Railroad, the different widths of the tracks made it imperative that goods were transferred at this point. When oil was discovered in Titusville, Pennsylvania, the Oil Creek Railroad was also built through Corry. Corry grew so fast that in 1863, it became a borough, and in 1866, it received city status. (Courtesy of the Corry Historical Society.)

On the Cover: The depots of Corry were the heart of manufacturing, tourism, and everyday travel to every distant town and city. People, crude oil, materials, circuses, cattle, horses (to be trained for the military), logs that were bigger than the engine itself, and everything imaginable passed through the depots. Everything that was made in the Corry area was shipped from the same depots, such as furniture, brass beds, butter, brooms, leather, and locomotives. (Courtesy of the Corry Historical Society.)

IMAGES
of America

CORRY

Jan Bemis

ARCADIA
PUBLISHING

ISBN 978-0-7385-9260-2

Published by Arcadia Publishing
Charleston, South Carolina

Printed in the United States of America

Library of Congress Control Number: 2011945718

For all general information, please contact Arcadia Publishing:
Telephone 843-853-2070
Fax 843-853-0044
E-mail sales@arcadiapublishing.com
For customer service and orders:
Toll-Free 1-888-313-2665

Visit us on the Internet at www.arcadiapublishing.com

In loving memory of my mom and dad. They taught me to "enjoy life while you can, because you will be old before you know it."

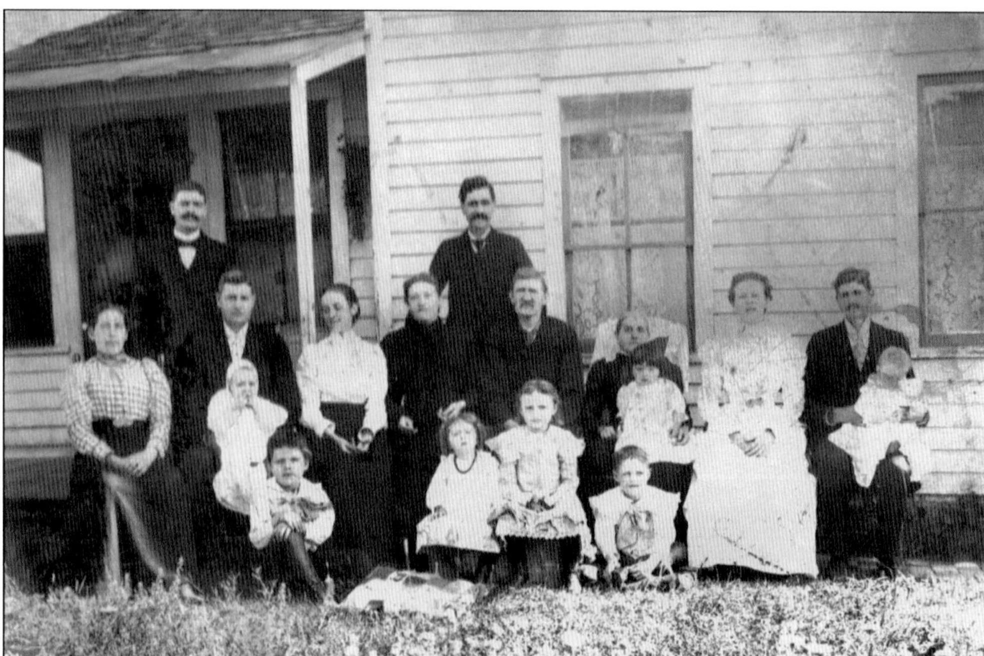

This photograph shows my ancestors that lived in Corry in 1899—three generations of the Young family pictured on Essex Street five years before my dad, Al Young, was born. Four more Corry generations followed after this photograph was taken. Since my roots in this area run so deep, I felt the best gift I could give my hometown of Corry was this book.

Contents

Acknowledgments

I would like to thank the Corry Historical Society for letting me use the amazing collection of Corry historical photographs and information that is stored in the museum's archives. I'd like to also thank Dorothy Jackman for giving me her mother's collection of old Corry postcards and newspapers. I am grateful to the following Corry residents who loaned me their family photographs and shared their personal knowledge: Jim Nelson, Bob Lindsey, Connie Burkhart, Loretta Beckerink, Ann Clark, John Lutz, Bill Hammond, Barb Grape, Tracy Johnson, Albert Young, Mike Magoon, the Corry Fire Department, Audrey Young, Sylvia Royak, Dorothy Jackman, Martha Vincent, Bill Zaphiris, Steve Bishop, Bob and Ruth Ann Grice, Valerie Desmond-Lilley, Joe Royak, and Bob May. I am grateful to Ken Springirth, an experienced Arcadia author, for his words of encouragement. Special thanks to Mark Hulings for countless computer lessons and never ending support.

Unless otherwise noted, photographs appear courtesy of the Corry Historical Society.

INTRODUCTION

Shipping oil from Oil Creek prior to 1862 was a very difficult and inadequate task. When the water was high enough, barrels of oil could be floated down the creek on flatboats, but barrels breaking and boats sinking were a common occurrence. Water was high enough to use this method only about six months out of the year. The rest of the time, barrels of oil loaded onto wagons were hauled by thousands of teams of horses and pulled to the nearest railroad stations: Corry, Union Mills, and Garland. The 20 to 25 miles of dusty or muddy roads on which these teams travelled were littered with deep ruts and swarming with mosquitoes and horse flies.

Another way of transporting oil was the "pond freshet" method. Lumbermen had used this method for years to transport logs when the water was too low. Through a system of floodgates and mill dams, the water could be held back and then let loose to create a surge of water downstream sufficient enough to float the boats loaded with barrels of oil. The boats would be loaded and a toll collected on each barrel. Word would then be sent up the creek to cut the dams. The water would rush down the creek, rising 20 to 30 inches. At the proper moment, the boatmen would cut their lines. In a very short time, 150 to 200 flatboats—large and small—loaded with 20,000 to 30,000 barrels of oil would be floating along endways and sideways on a rushing flood and wildly fighting their way down Oil Creek to Oil City. A third of the oil was lost due to leakage before the boats started, and another third was lost before reaching Pittsburgh. Many men drowned using this method of transport. In 1862, the Oil Creek Railroad was built to Titusville, a distance of 27 miles. Within the next two years, the road was extended down Oil Creek to Shaffer farm and later to Petroleum Centre. The completion of the railroad lessened the necessity of hauling oil over long distances on frightful roads and led to the abandonment of the unproductive and dangerous practice of the "pond freshet" method.

Although not an oil-producing district, Corry was definitely an oil town. In 1859, the area that would become Corry was just a farm covered with trees, stumps, and two or three houses. Through it ran the Sunbury & Erie Railroad, later the Philadelphia & Erie Railroad and then the Pennsylvania Railroad, which afforded the only rail connection for shipping oil prior to May 1861. That month, the Atlantic & Great Western Railroad, which connected with the Erie & Salamanca for New York, extended its line in a southwesterly direction and crossed the tracks of the Philadelphia & Erie Railroad at Corry. By October 1862, the Oil Creek Railroad was completed from Corry to Titusville. With three railroads, Corry grew, and like magic it became the most important transportation center in the oil region. It grew so quickly with a population of 3,000 that there was not enough time to clear the stumps after trees were cut for lumber, so it became known as the "city of stumps."

The reason for the city's remarkable growth and prosperity was the fact that it had one of the largest oil refineries in the oil region, Downer Oil Works. Started in 1861 by Samuel Downer of Boston, the refinery, when it was completed, employed 150 men and had the refining capacity of approximately one million gallons a year.

One

"X" Marks the Spot

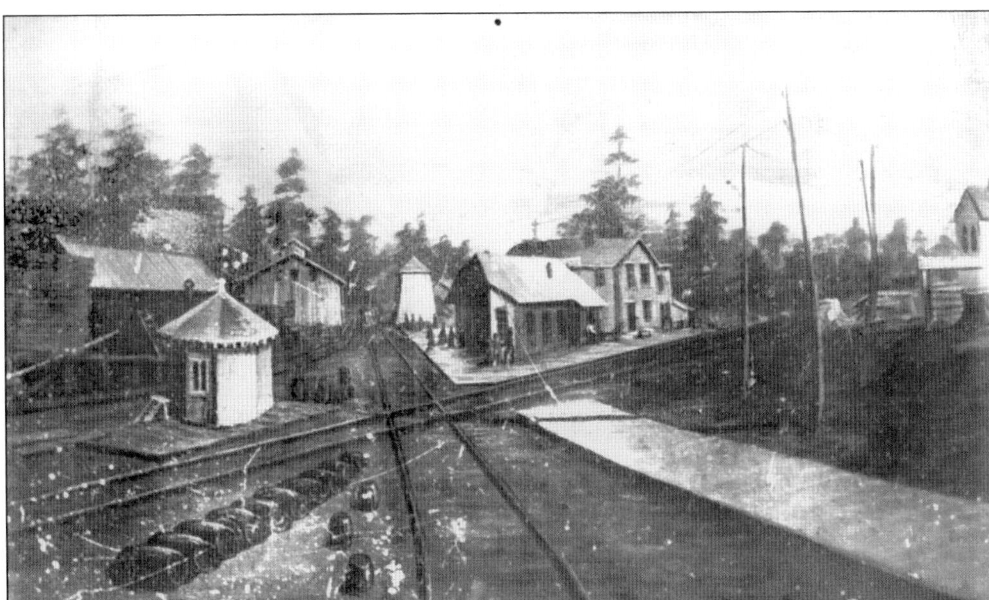

In 1858, Hiram Cory bought 63 acres of thick forests, clean streams, and plentiful wildlife in northwestern Pennsylvania. He built his home in the area that is now west Washington Street between Center and Mott Streets. In 1861, the Atlantic & Great Western Railroad bought a piece of land from Cory for a modest price. The railroad was so grateful for Cory's generosity that they named the station after him. In the paperwork, his name was misspelled with two Rs, but it was easier to leave it spelled incorrectly than to change it, so the station's name remained Corry.

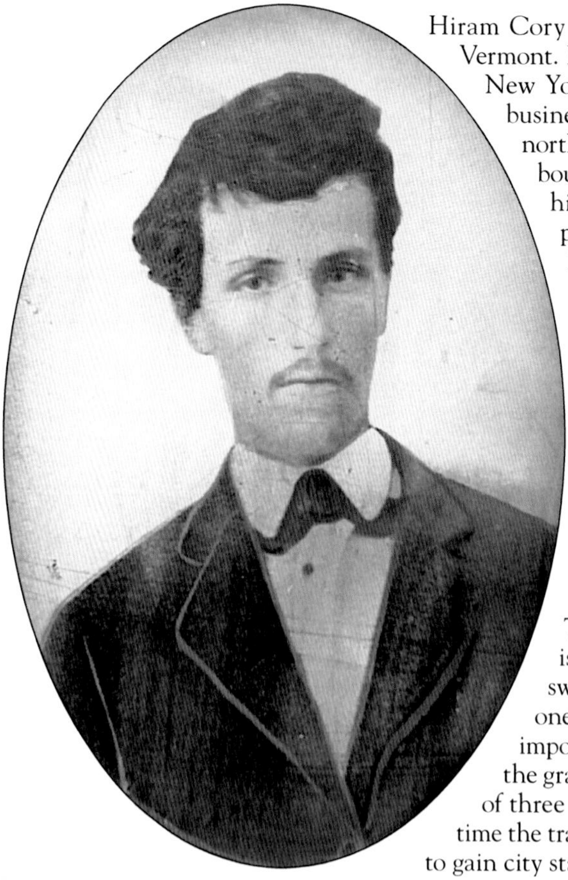

Hiram Cory was born January 1790 in Shaftsburg, Vermont. He owned a tavern at Barcelona Harbor, New York. When the Erie Canal opened, his business became slow, so he bought a farm in northwestern Pennsylvania. After the railroad bought his land, they named the station after him and the area became increasing more populated. Cory moved to the Spartansburg, Pennsylvania, area and died there in 1875. He is buried in Forest Lawn Cemetery.

There was no planned reason why Corry is located where it is, considering it was a swamp. When railroads lay their tracks, a one foot or less per mile grade was the most important issue. Corry happened only because the grade of surrounding land caused the tracks of three railroads to cross at one point. From the time the tracks crossed in 1861, it took only five years to gain city status.

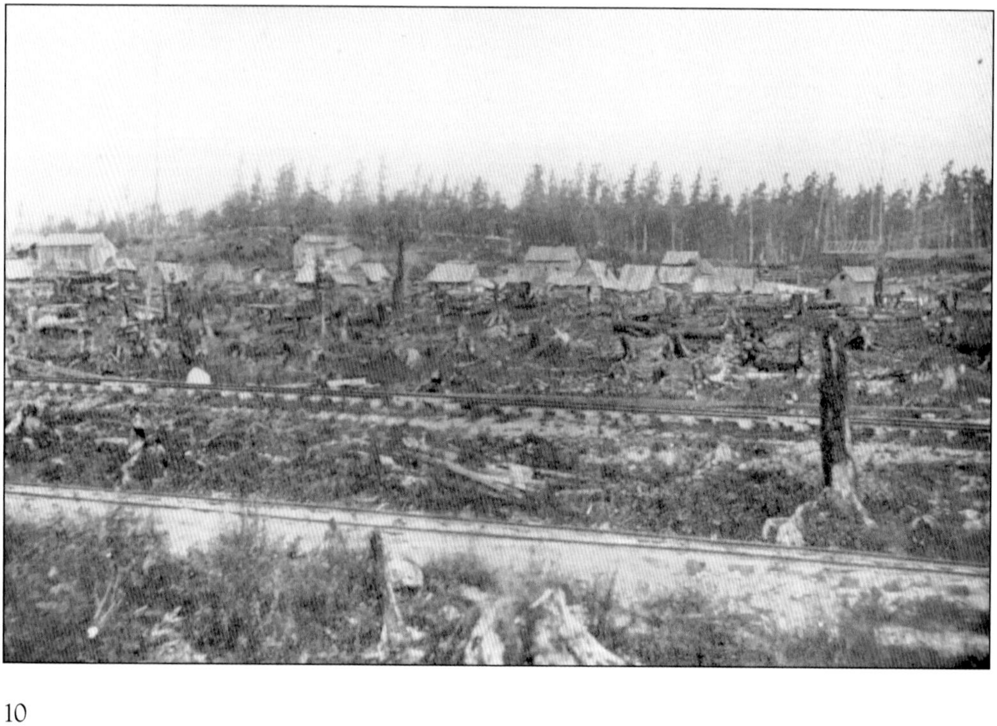

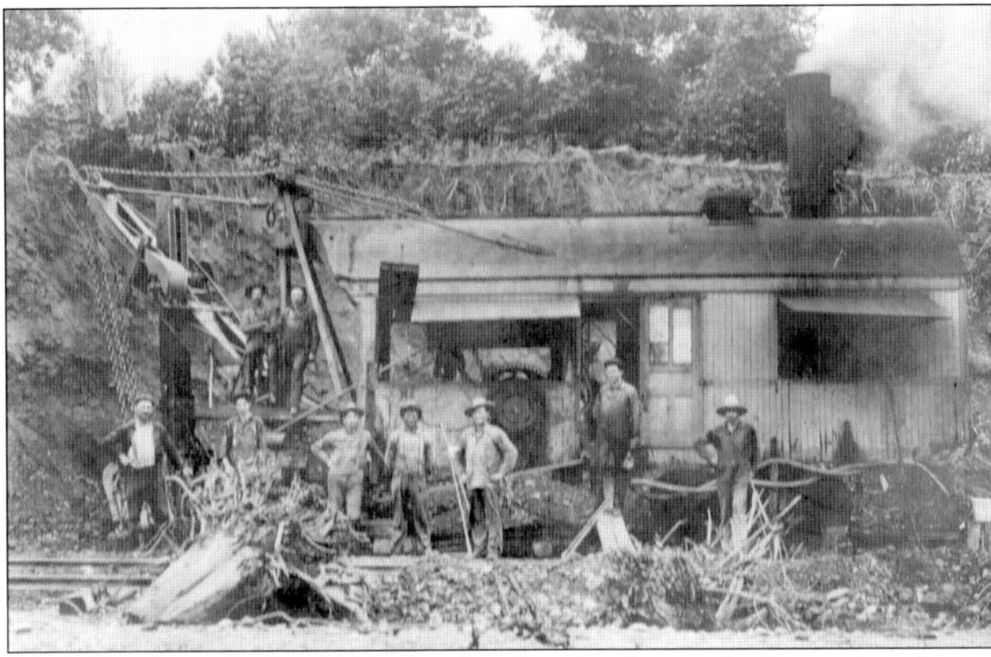

Clearing a path in which to lay a railroad was brutal, tedious work. Cutting through trees, removing stumps, and digging into hillsides to make a path level and with wide curves took a lot of planning and scouting of the area. The roads had to be stable enough so a train hauling hundreds of barrels of oil would not sink into the ground and derail.

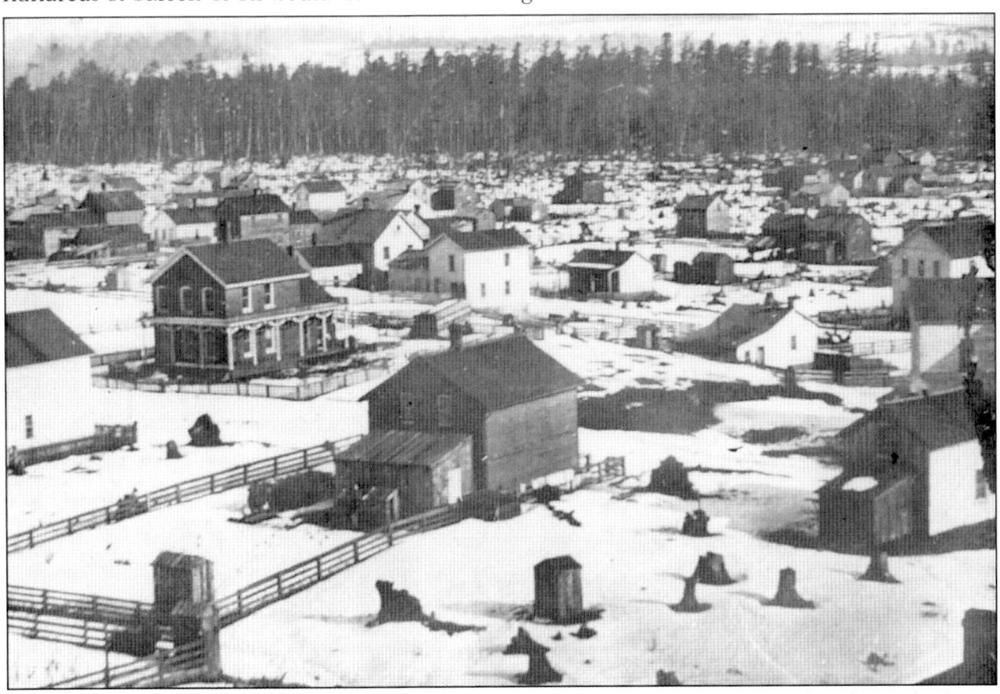

This is an early photograph of Corry looking east. When the railroads were first being laid out, the workmen tied so many strings around the trees to plan the path of the tracks that Corry's early nickname became "city of strings."

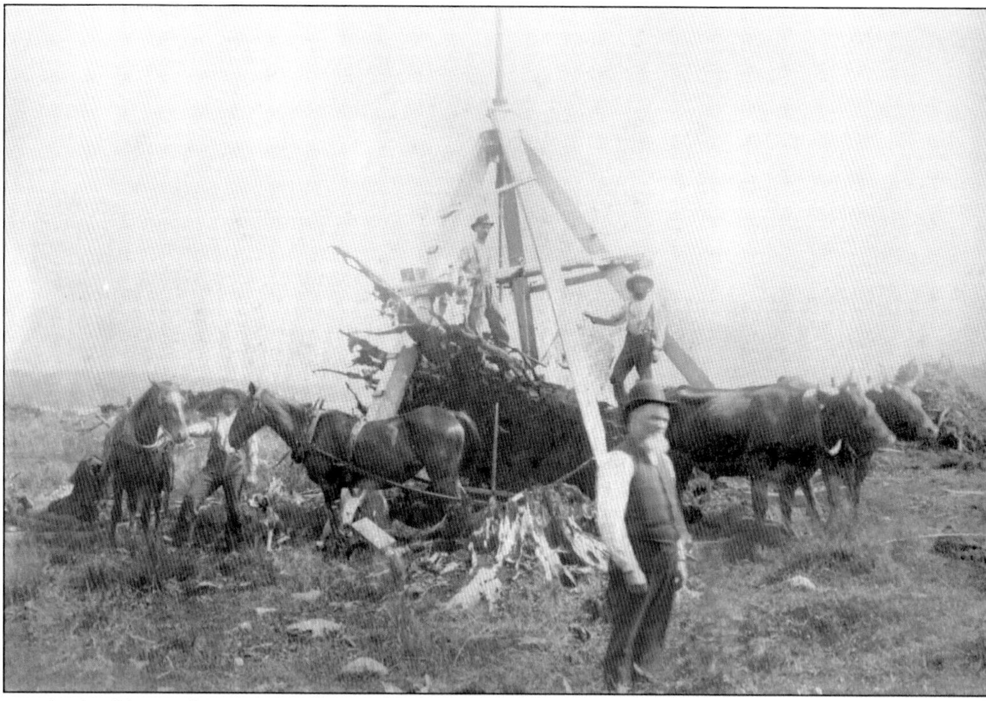

As the building of factories, shops, and houses expanded the city, more trees for lumber as well as open lots were needed. The biggest problem was removing the tree stumps fast enough. New inventions were tested to make the work more efficient. This stump-pulling machine, invented by E.D. Hyde, is shown in use at the Butterfield farm. Pictured from left to right are Butterfield, J. Logan, A. Whiteley, and Barney Hill. (Courtesy of Al Young.)

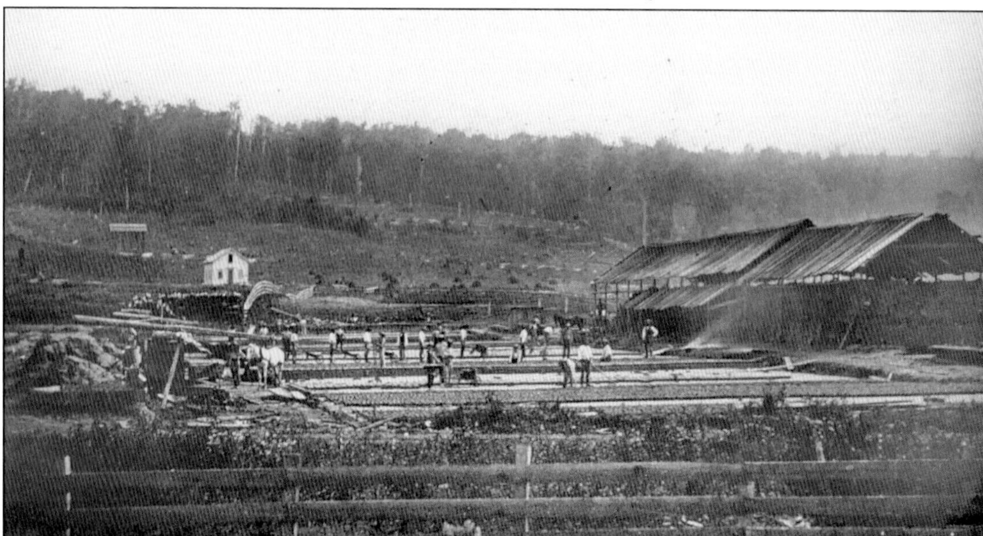

There were three brickyards in Corry: Red Star Brick, Corry Brick, and Corry Brick and Tile. Millions of bricks were molded and fired at the brickyard behind the Boston Hotel in the area of Main Street and First, Second, and Third Avenues. Using these bricks, by the fall of 1862 the largest refinery up to that time had been completed. Corry had dozens of brick buildings, and many of the roads that were paved with brick are still in use today.

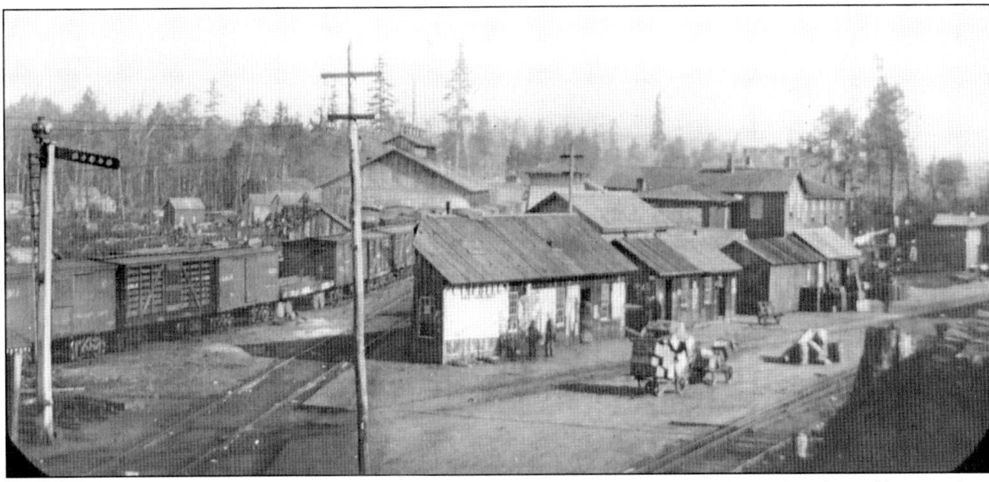

In 1861, the only building in the valley by the railroad was a triangle-shaped ticket office wedged between two tracks. The major importance of this crossing was that the two railroads were of two different gauges—AG&W had a six-foot width, and S&E had a four-foot-by-eight-inch width. The different widths made it imperative that goods be transferred to the different cars at this point. After oil was discovered in Titusville, Pennsylvania, this fact was even more important and Corry became a major exporter. In 1862, the Oil Creek Railroad was built, making three railroads accommodating two rail widths. Corry grew so fast that in 1863, it became a borough, and in 1866, it received city status.

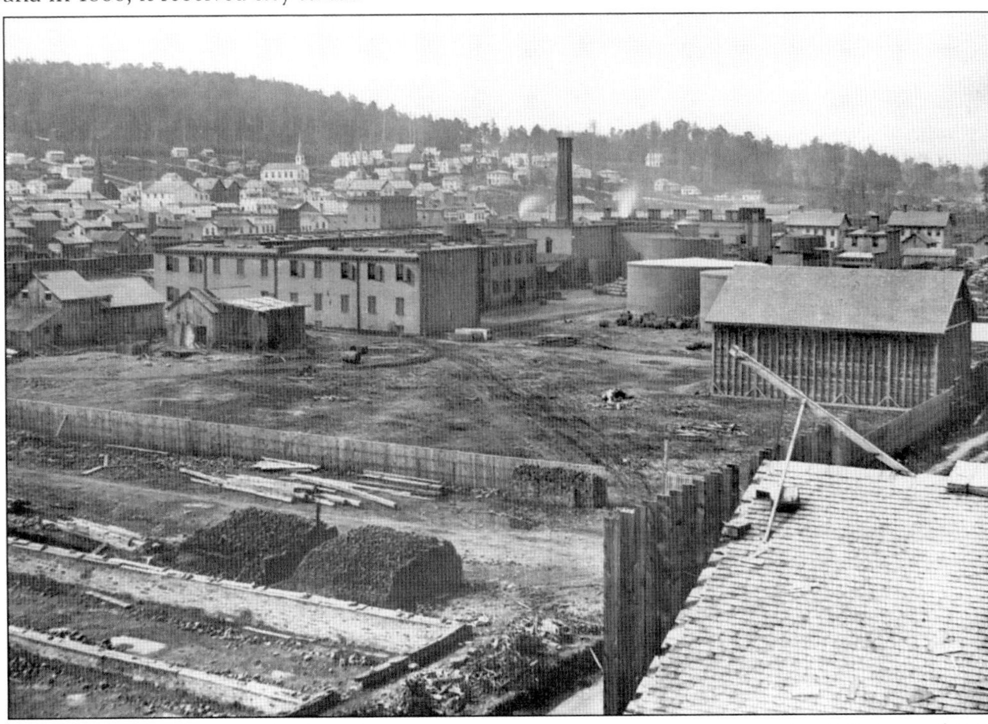

Indians and early settlers had used oil, or petroleum, as medicine for years. In 1850, Samuel Kier of Tarentum, Pennsylvania, developed a still to refine oil into kerosene and improved the oil lamp to efficiently burn oil. It still smelled terrible, however, and could not be used in lamps in a house. Kier also was the first to use a mechanical pump to obtain oil out of the ground.

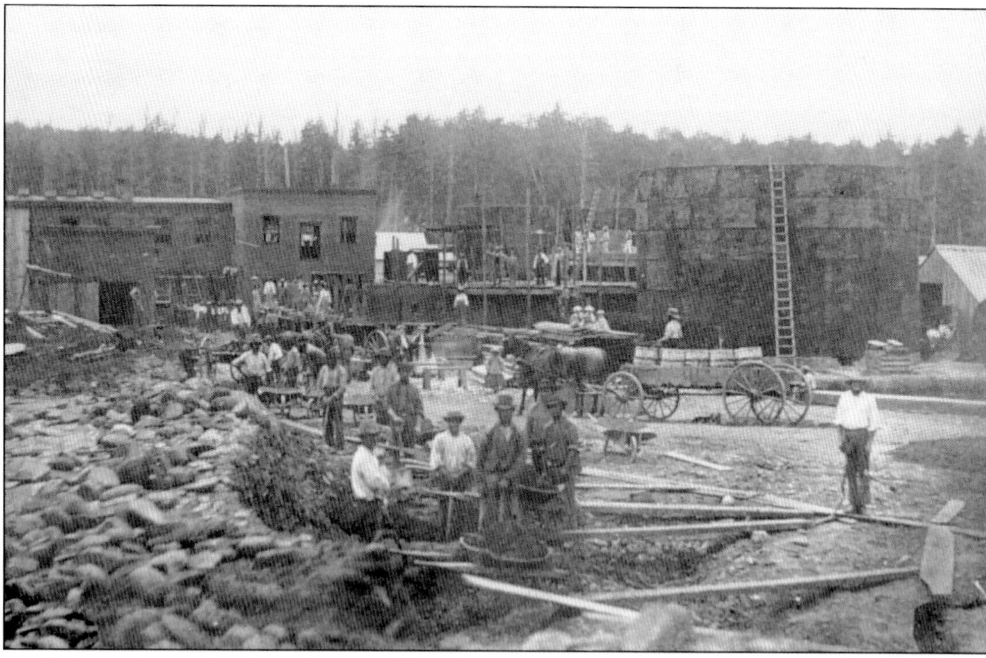

In 1860, a spice dealer, A.C. Ferris of New York, found a way to remove the terrible smell from burning kerosene in oil lamps by adding caustic acid. This made it a very marketable product around the world. The best work in distillation was done at Downer Oil Works, the first modern oil refinery in the world. They used "fractional distillation," a combination of inventions of three individuals: Abraham Gesner, Luther Atwood, and Joshua Merrill. Gesner and Atwood had perfected methods of extracting oil from coal.

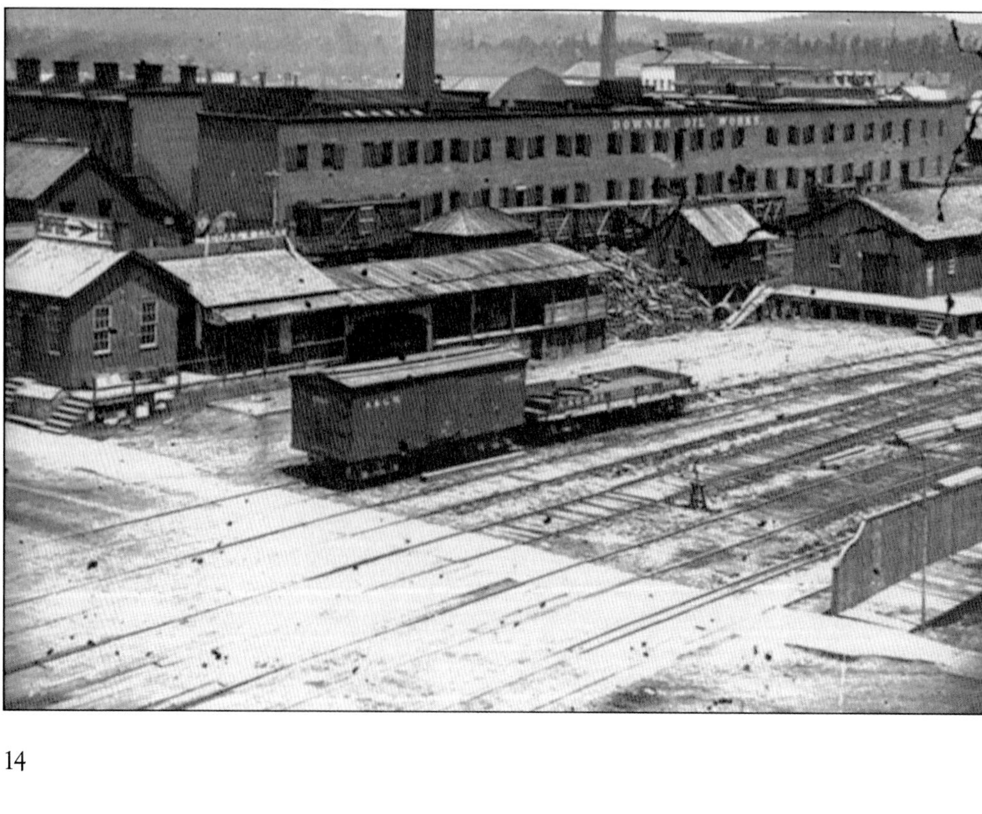

Joshua Merrill (1828–1904) was a young man around the time the other two men, Abraham Gesner and Luther Atwood, had retired. Merrill was therefore able to spend more years working with petroleum during the discovery period and subsequent years. Merrill became the foremost oil chemist of his time—possibly in history. He experimented with petroleum, coal, and asphalt. All the modern methods he developed were used at Downer Oil Works.

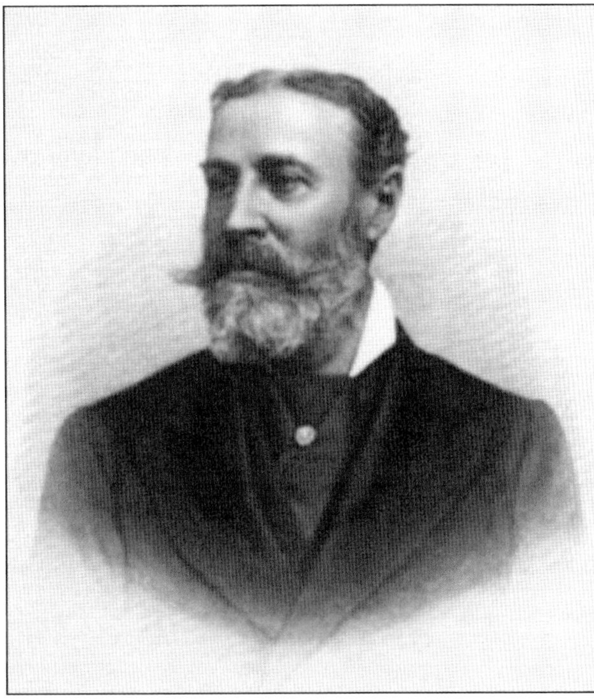

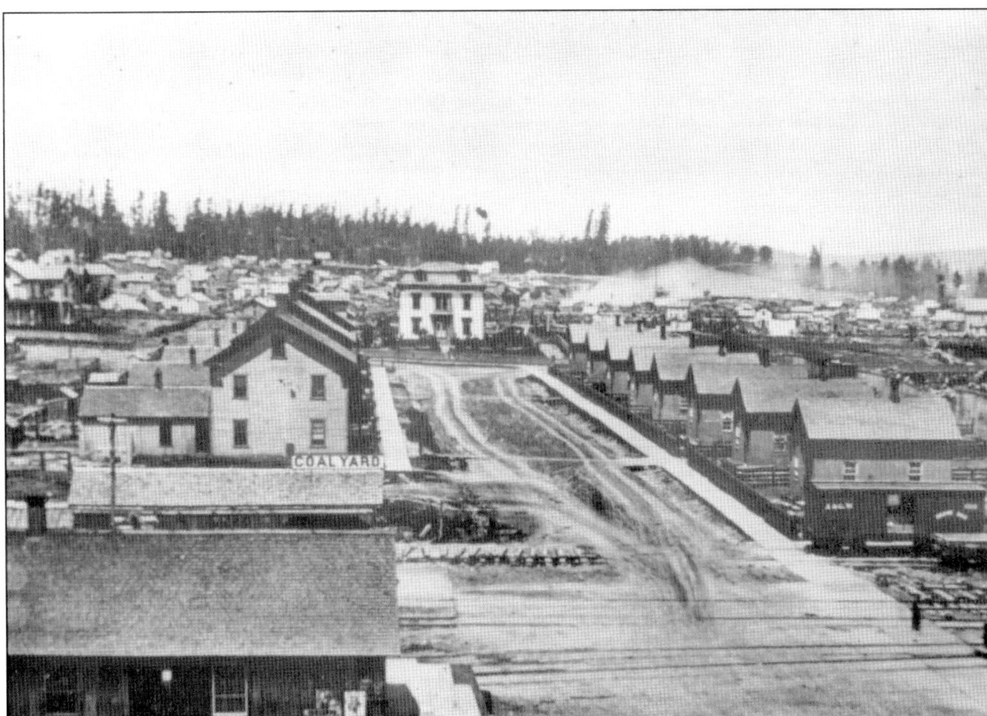

This is a very early photograph of First Avenue looking north from South Street. The huge house at the end of the street was built for the superintendent of Downer Oil Works, W.H.L. Smith. The refinery also built the row of little buildings on the right and rented them to the workmen for $25 a month.

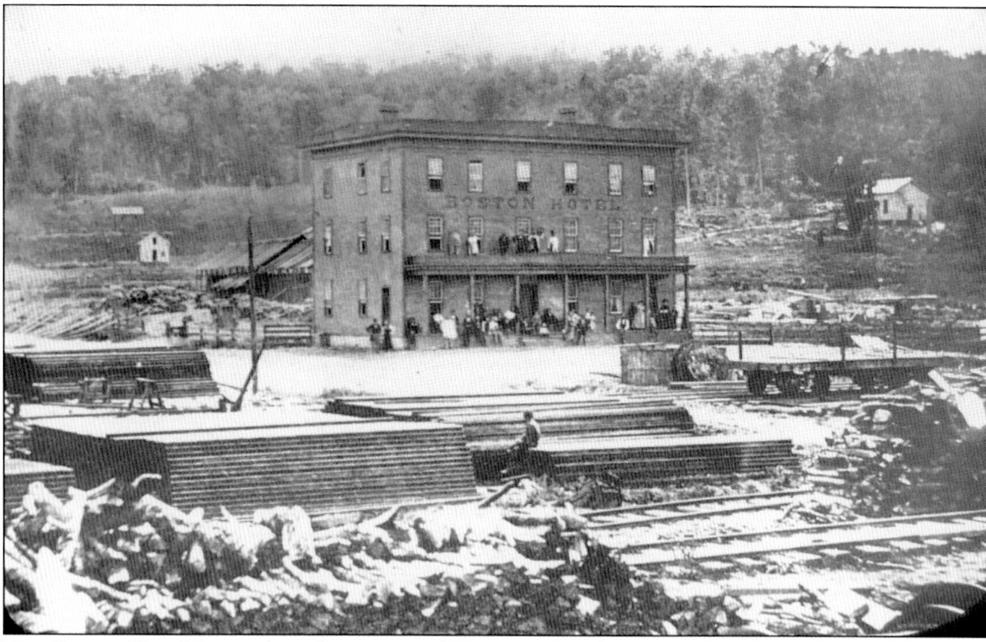

The Boston Hotel, located on the corner of West Main and First Avenue, was the first hotel to be built in Corry. W.H.L. Smith (who was from Boston) and others who were interested in Downer Oil Works built the hotel in 1862. It was put up to make quarters available for their employees and to provide accommodations during the oil boom days.

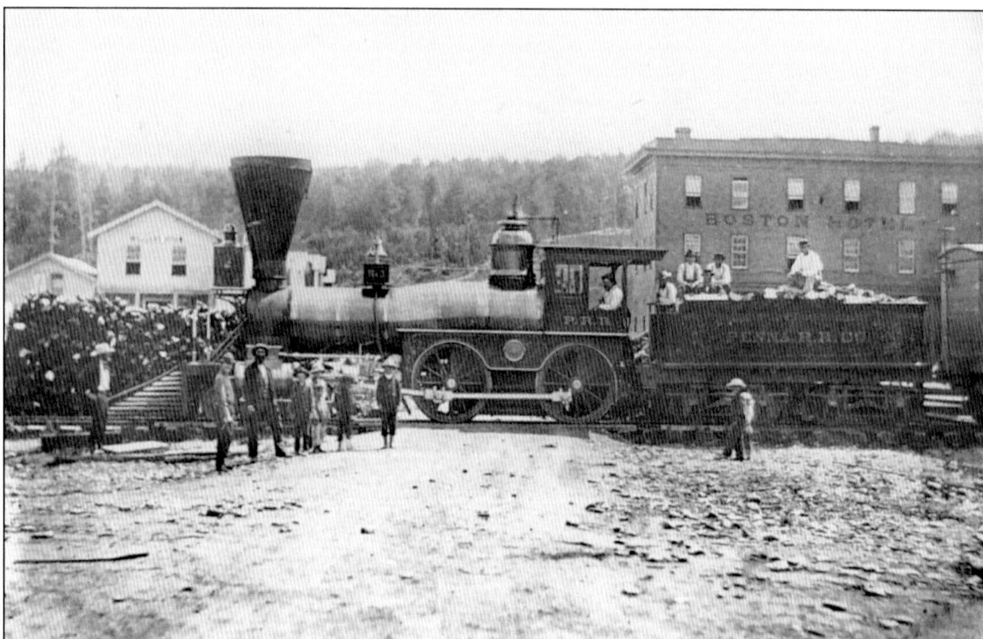

The Boston Hotel had several owners or managers over the years, including Andrew Griffith, Frank Koleher, and A.F. Messenger, who were the earliest ones. When it was the principal hostelry in the city, the Boston Hotel boasted 40 rooms. In its later years, a wing extending along First Avenue was added and leased for commercial use.

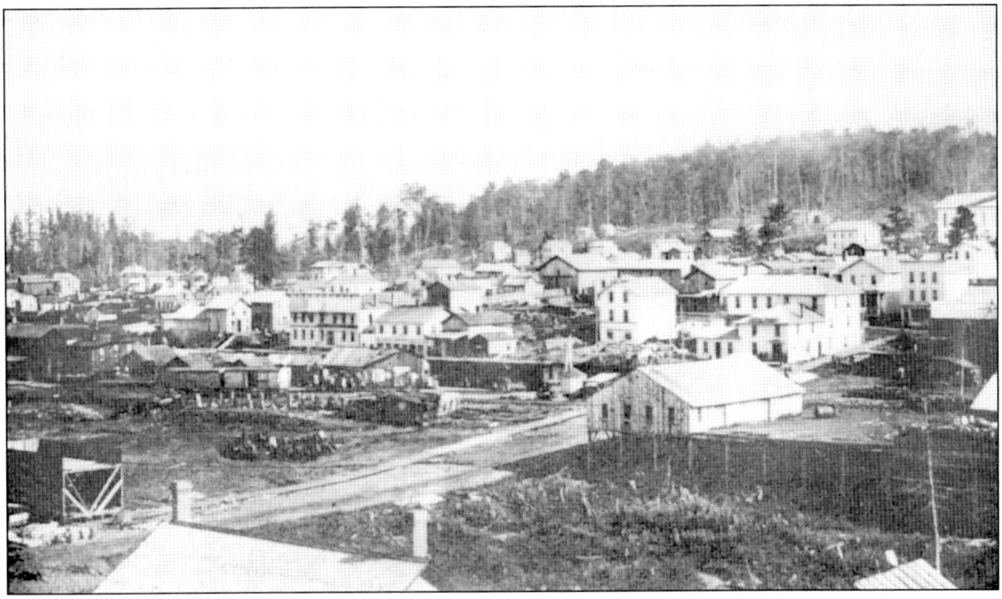

The city was growing fast. Pictured is Main Street intersecting with Cross Street before it was renamed Maple Avenue in the 1860s. In the distance are the wood-frame structures of the first Concord School and Methodist church, which had been built as the families settled into a new location. Along Main Street are the Empire House, St. Nicholas Hotel, and a dining hall.

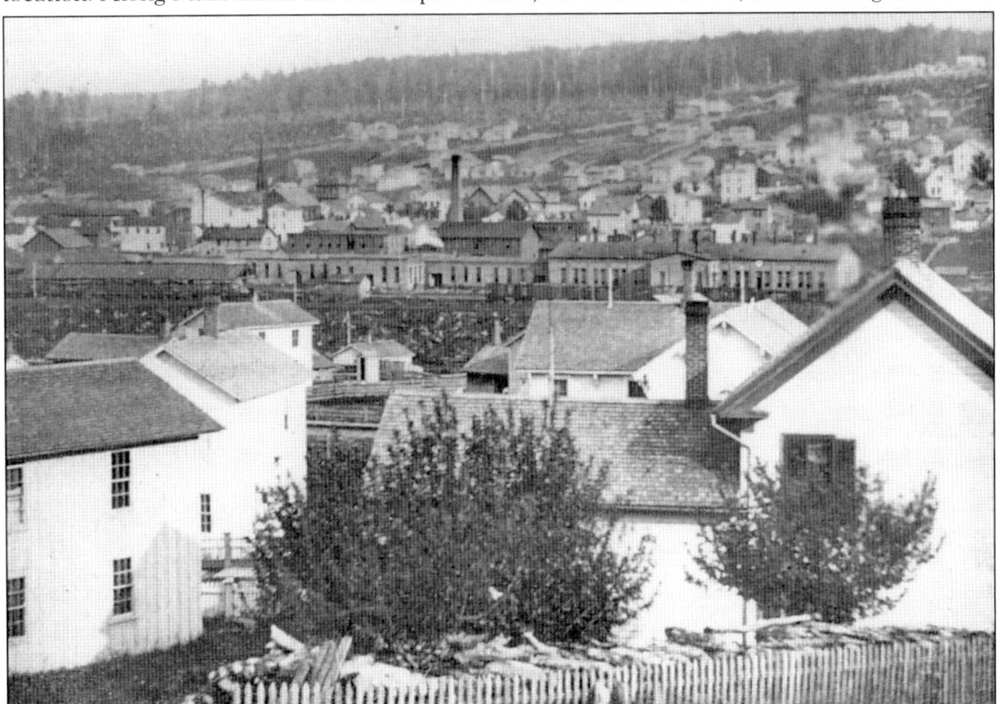

This photograph was taken from a point near the Cook, Leach & Davis sash factory on the corner of West Washington and West Wayne Avenues (now Mead Avenue). The long brick buildings of the Climax Manufacturing Company were located between West Main Street and the railroad tracks and extended from Second Avenue to Fifth Avenue.

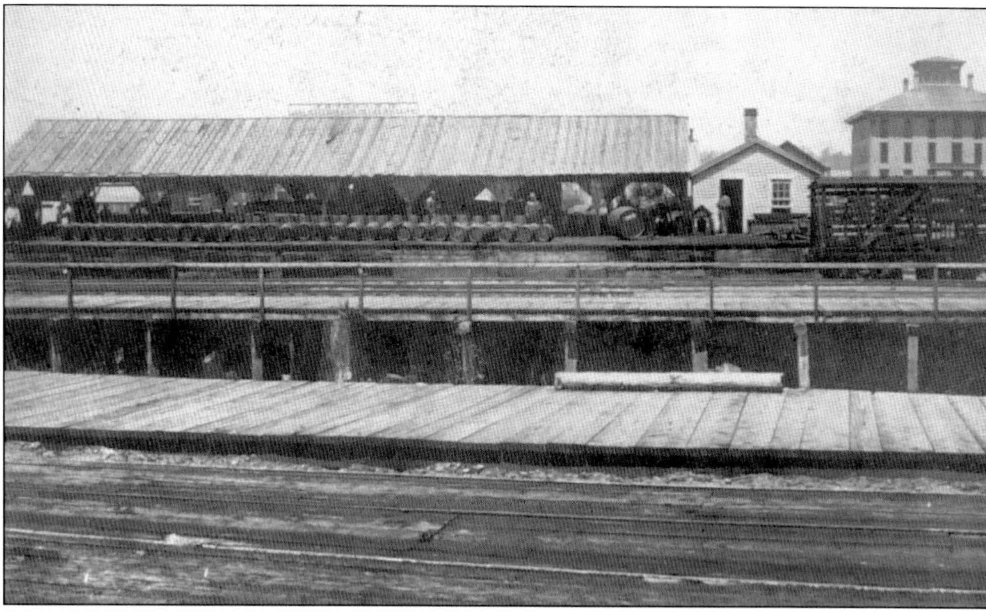

In 1865, a train car containing 62 barrels of crude oil became unhooked from its train and raced down the grade of the P&E railroad west of Corry and toward the depot. After gaining speed, it ran into a westbound locomotive. On impact, the headlight broke and oil barrels burst open, immediately catching fire. There was a fear that Colman's platform, which contained a large quantity of oil, would ignite.

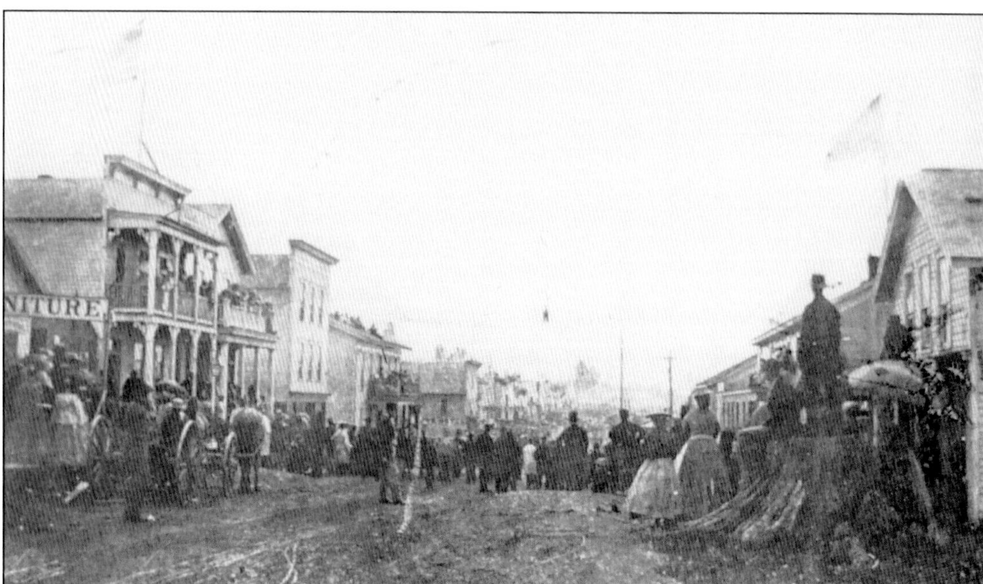

On August 22, 1877, George A. Olmstead wrote, "Ettie and I went to Corry to see the show and parade. We saw a woman walk the rope, she performed very well. She would stop occasionally and perform some feat such as to stand on one foot and stick the other out and then again stop and get down on one knee then sit down on the rope, etc."

Two

MADE IN CORRY

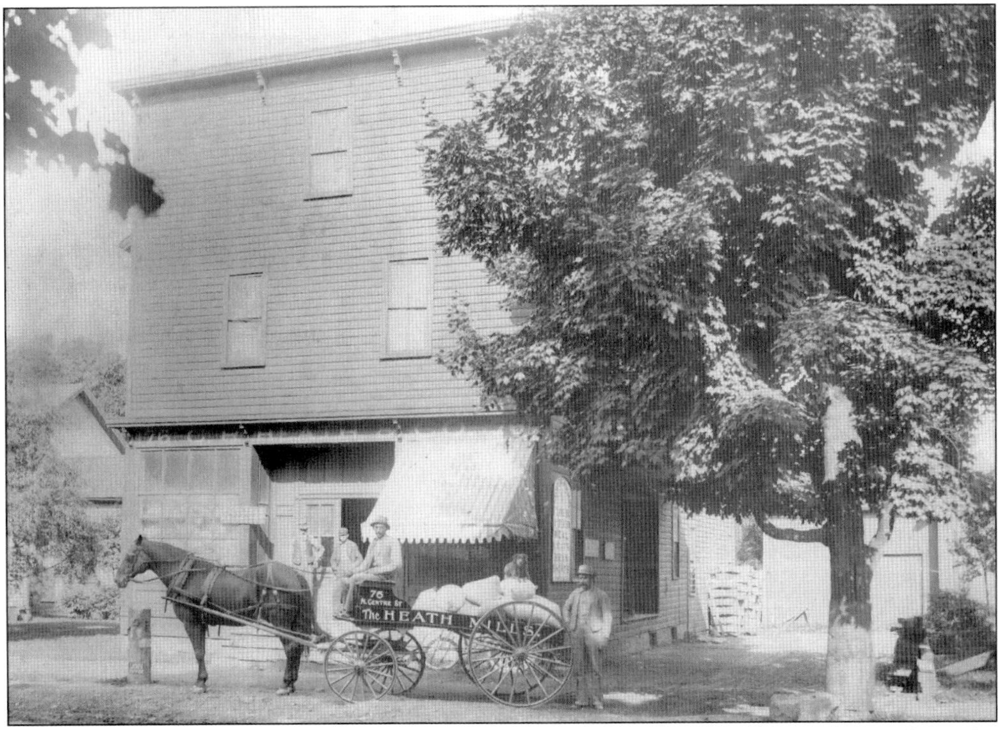

Corry had both large and small industries. Everything that a person needed was made in the area, such as condensed milk, cheese, wooden pails, baby jumpers, typewriters, brooms, furniture, brass beds, wagons, candy, horseshoes, saddles, harnesses, and even explosives. Mineral water, beer, and milk were bottled in Corry. Chickens, sheep, cattle, and horses were raised here, and oats, wheat, and buckwheat were grown and brought to the mills, where they were made into flour and feed.

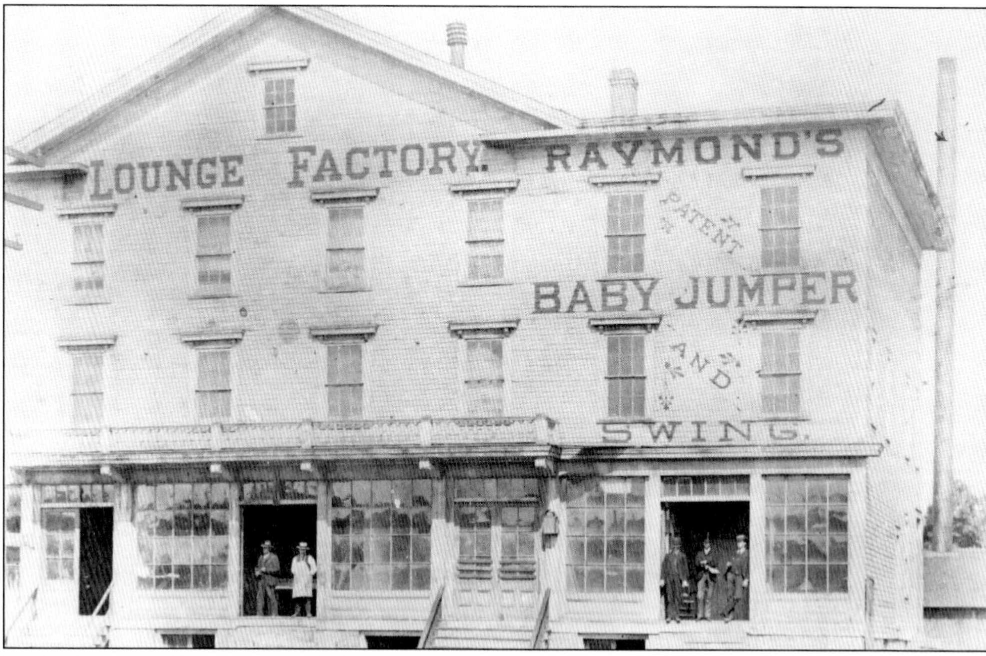

In 1883, George Barnes started the Corry Lounge Factory in the basement and first floor of the opera house. Fifteen to eighteen workmen manufactured around 100 lounges of various patterns per week. In the same building, Murray Raymond invented and started manufacturing the baby jumper and swing, and soon, 150 jumpers were being manufactured each week.

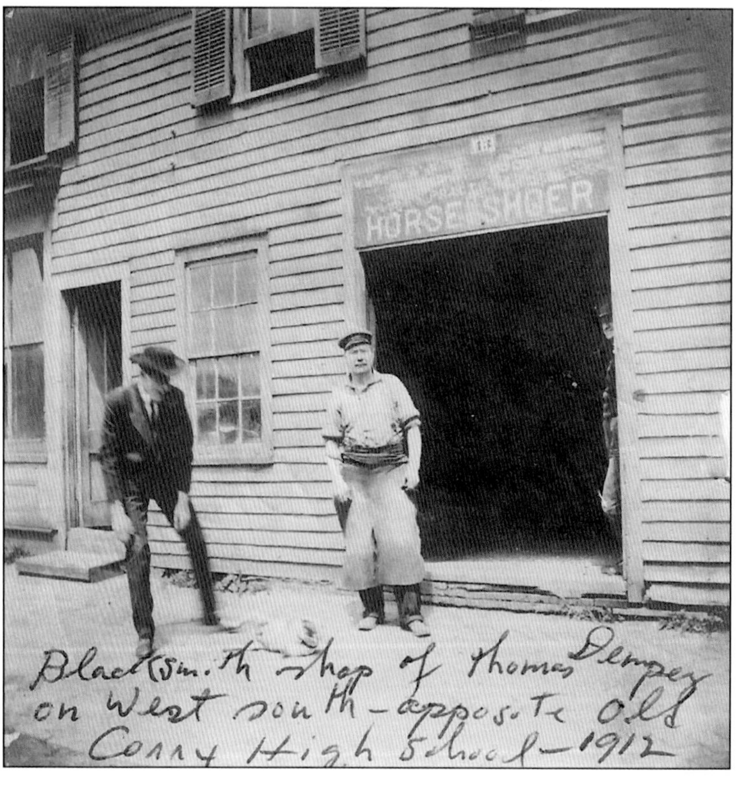

There were dozens of blacksmiths in the city in the 1800s and early 1900s, and they were usually located near the hotels and boarding stables. A.G. Albro was in the business for over 20 years and was well known to the trade. F.C. Fields opened a horseshoeing and wagon repair shop on First Avenue in 1911, having previously been engaged in the same business on the north side of town.

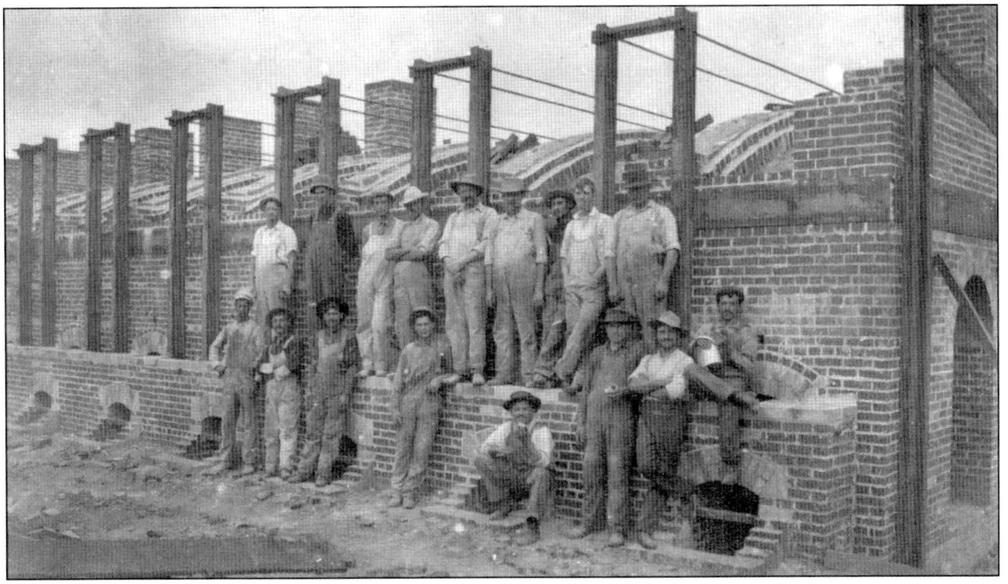

Corry Brick and Tile was organized in 1908 and then purchased the Red Star Brick Company, which had been unsuccessful due to the inferior goods it manufactured. Many people were skeptical whether or not Corry shale was suitable to make first-class bricks. Corry Brick and Tile proved that the quality of Corry shale is second to none in the state, "when handled by one who knows," according to an unidentified worker.

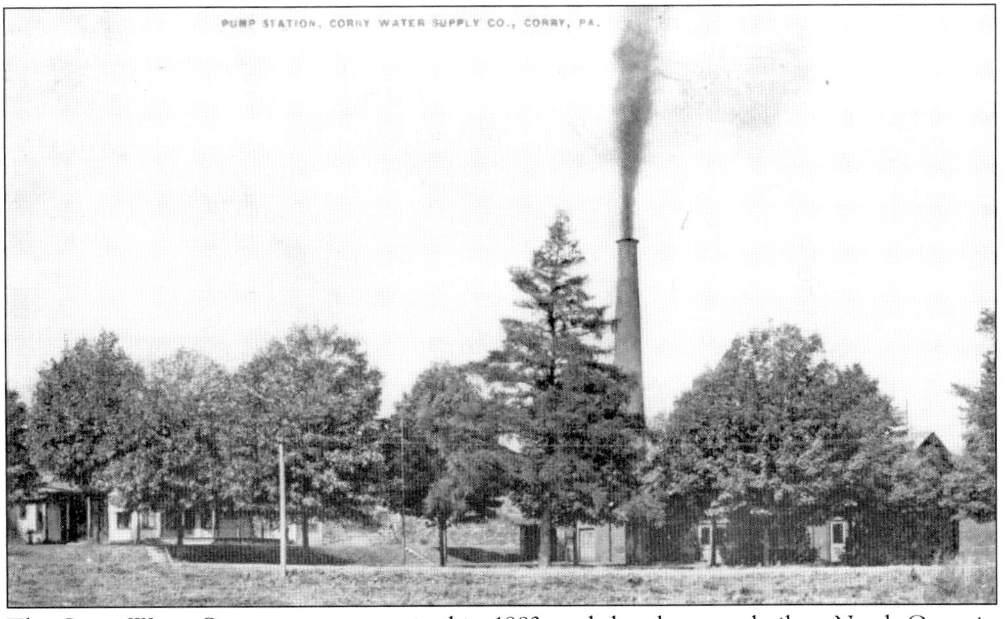

The Corry Water Company was organized in 1883, and the plant was built at North Corry in 1886. Up until that time, private wells had been the chief source of water, and wooden water tanks placed at various locations about the city were Corry's only fire protection. The plant consisted of a pumping station in north Corry, where the pure water supply was derived from 26 artesian wells and pumped by a battery of steam pumps through the city's 40 miles of mains, supplying the city directly when they were in operation. At the same time, any surplus was taken care of at the reservoir built in 1886 on a high hill in the southwestern portion of the city.

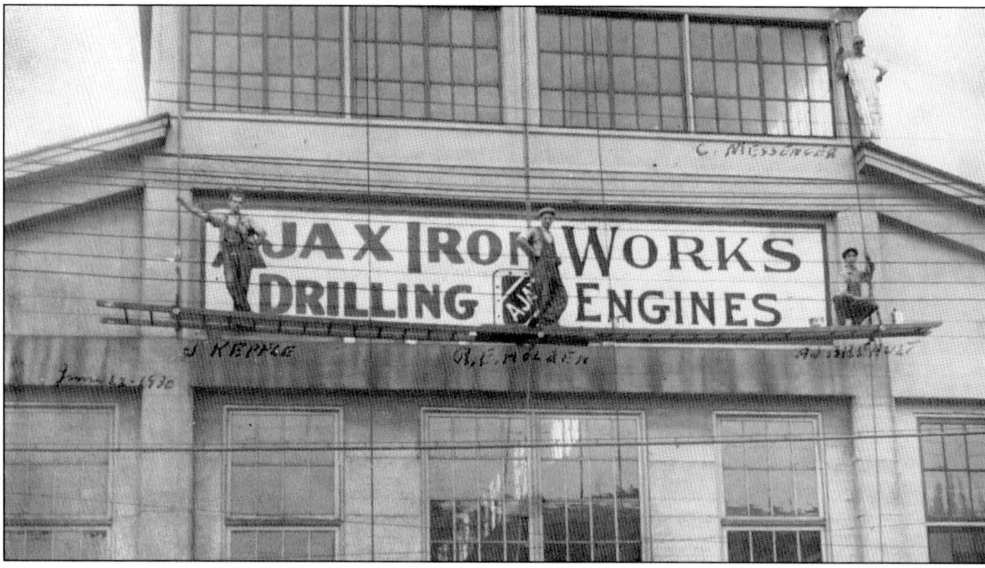

Early in 1876, a partnership was formed between George Gibbs, C. Harmon, and Lewis Bliss for the purpose of engaging in a general machinery-manufacturing business. Particularly, they were interested in the manufacture of a new drilling and pumping steam engine for the oil country. The Ajax Drilling Engine was well known and could be found in all the oil- and gas-producing fields in the world. It was found in Mexico, South America, Russia, India, Burma, South Africa, and Canada. Large numbers of the Ajax engine were sent to California, Oklahoma, Kansas, Texas, and Louisiana. In 1892, the business was incorporated under the title of Ajax Iron Works.

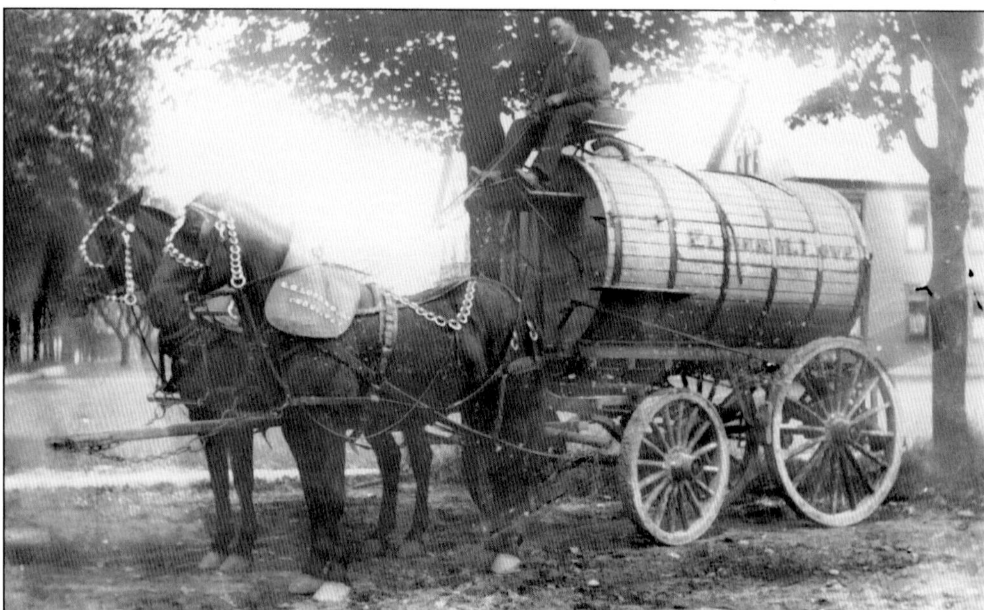

E.M. Love & Son was one of the largest contractors in the area for road building and brick or concrete paving. Most of the paving done in Corry between 1905 and 1913, including East Main Street, South Street, South Center Street, Maple Avenue, and Pleasant Streets, was done by the Love concern. The company was well equipped to handle all kinds of road work, with four huge steam rollers and two big power concrete mixers.

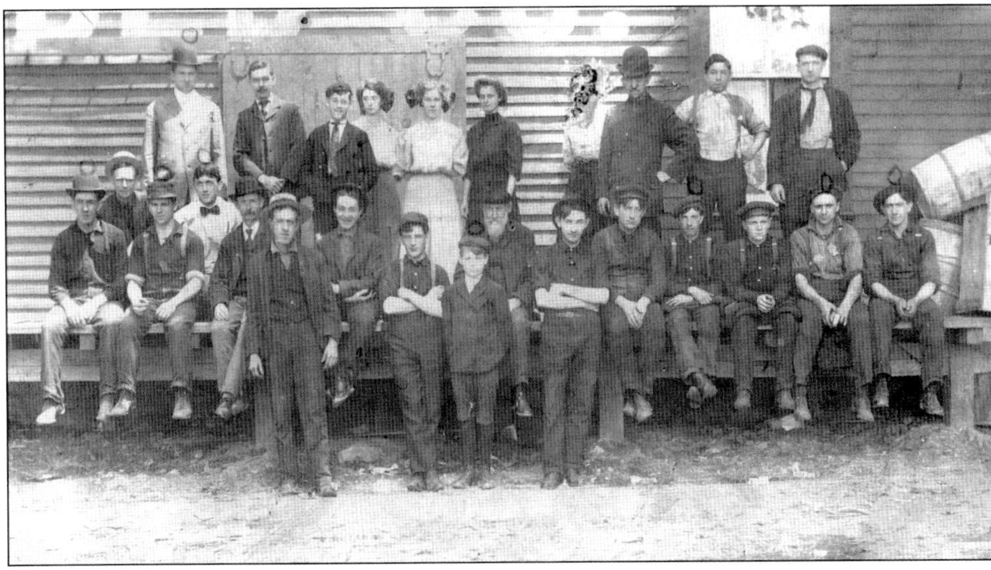

Corry was home to the largest brass bed factory in the country. Kurtz Brass Bed Company started at the old Methodist Church property on the corner of Concord and East Pleasant Streets and manufactured about 40 beds daily for eight years. In 1911, the company built a huge plant that measured 300 feet by 110 feet on the east end, which was adjacent to the Erie Railroad. By then, Kurtz was turning out more than 200 beds daily.

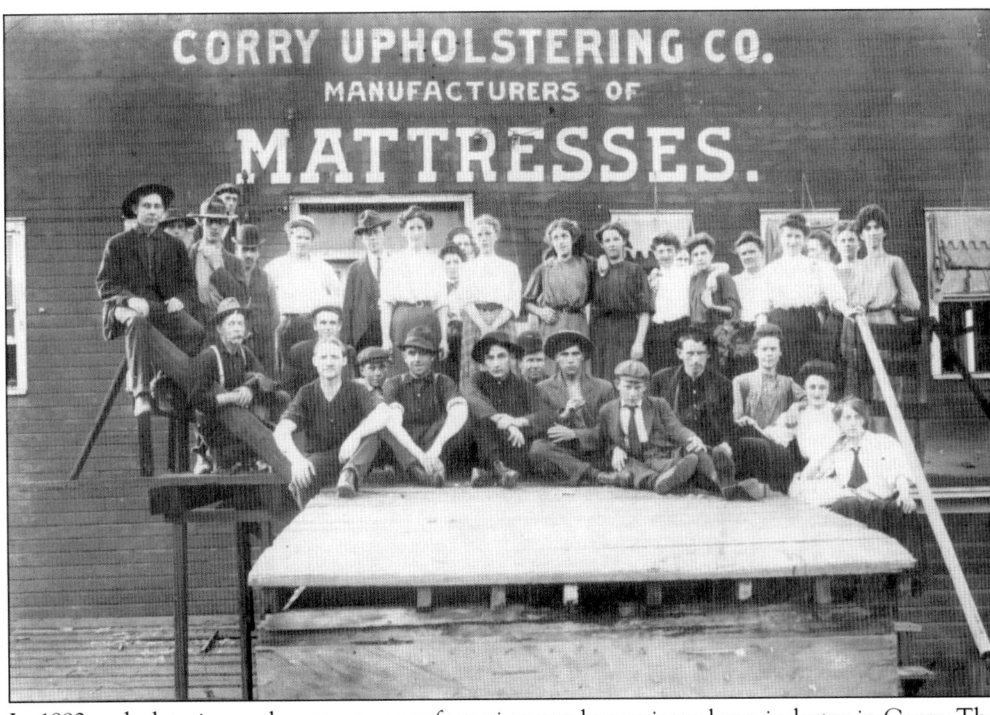

In 1892, upholstering and mattress manufacturing was becoming a large industry in Corry. The Corry Upholstering Company made superior grades of mattresses because they employed skilled mechanics. Their furniture and mattresses were made with animal hair from the tannery, straw, excelsior (wood shavings), and Spanish moss from the Southern states.

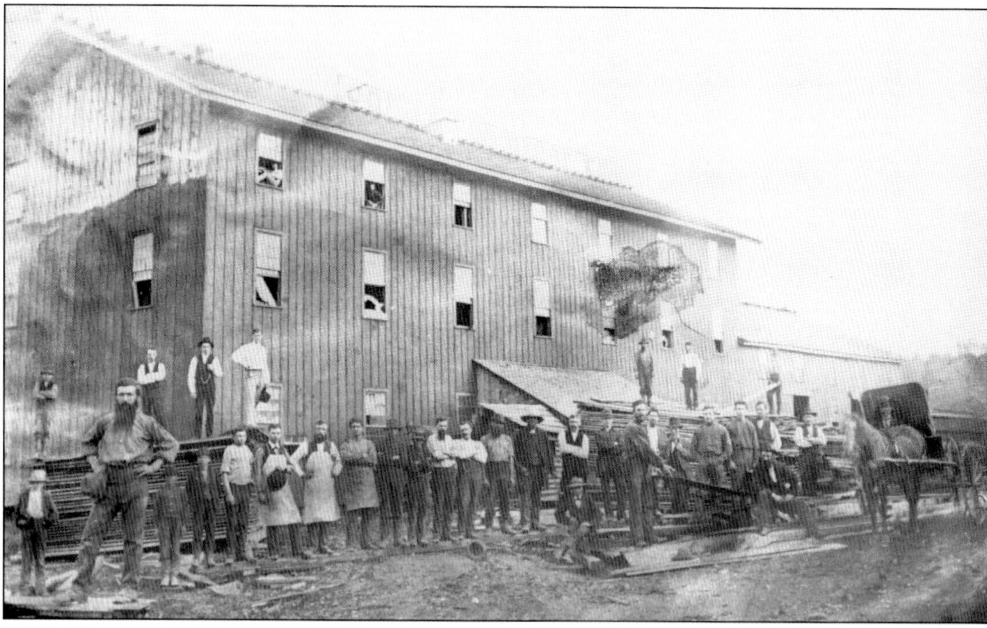

K.P.L. Furniture Company, owned by Keppel, Patterson, and Lippman, occupied the entire block on Williams Street between East Main and South Streets. The bedroom furniture was manufactured with quartered oak, mahogany, and birds-eye maple. They supplied distributors in Chicago, New York, and Pittsburgh. The plant was magnificently equipped and employed 30 to 40 men in 1913.

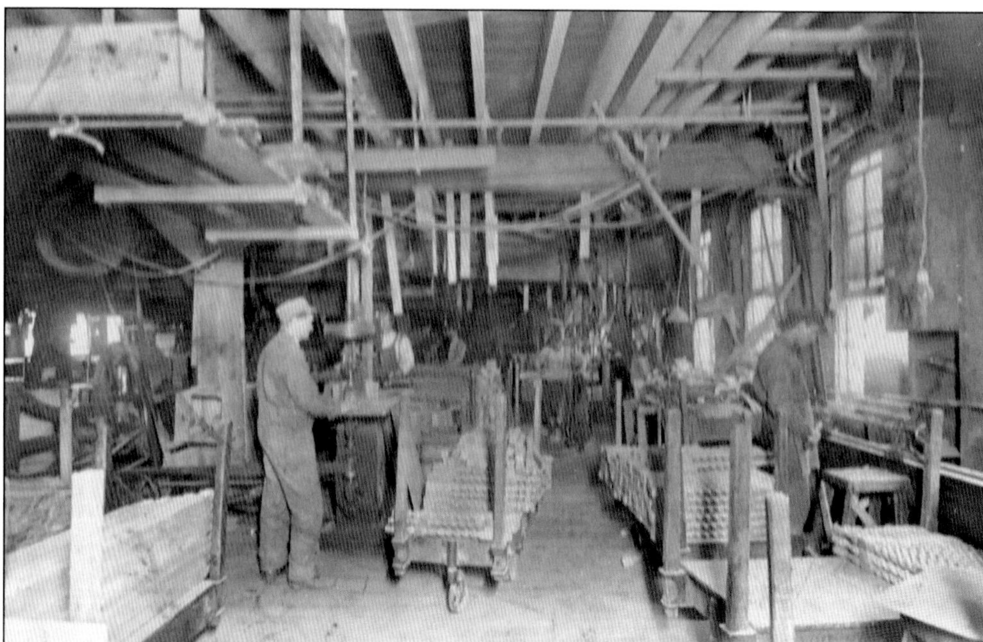

Corry Chair Company, located on East Washington Street, manufactured plain and fancy wood chairs—cane and wood bottomed—and also manufactured every style and design of upholstered chairs and rockers. Their advertisement boasted, "Our line of goods can be compared with all competitors in artist designs, durability and cheapness."

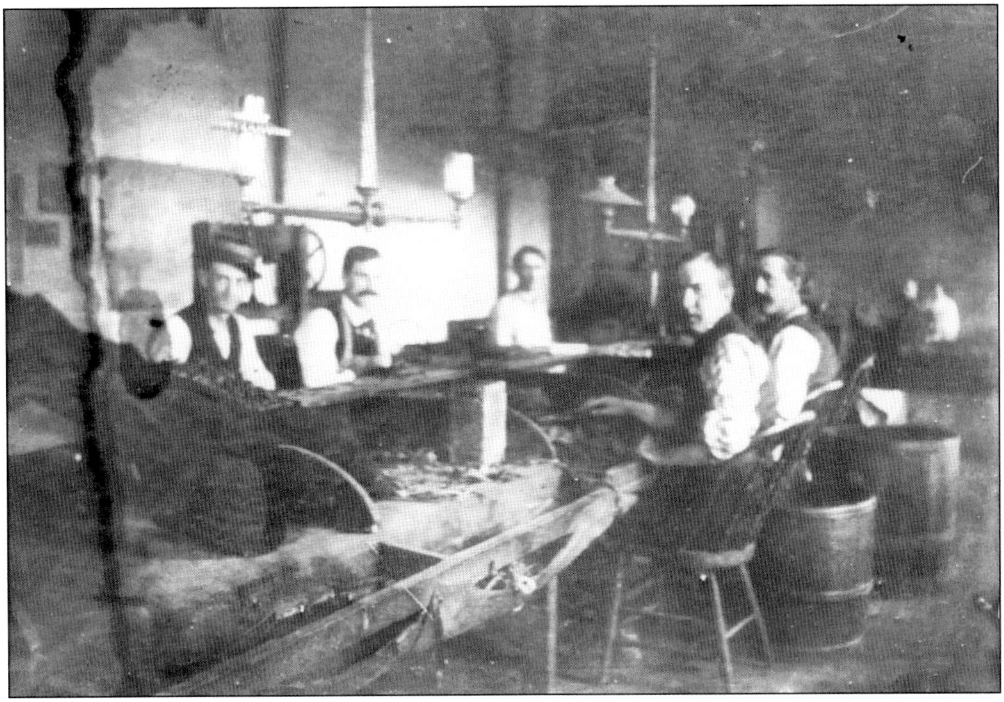

Corry had several cigar manufacturers in the early 1890s. N.W. Hull & Company had 40 workers making 15 million cigars annually. Keleher's employed nine people who made 2,500 per day at 13 and 15 Spring Street. Nantes made 200,000 to 300,000 cigars and cheroots annually at 42 East Main Street. The Solitaire Cigar Factory made 20,000 cigars a month at 14 South Center Street, their leading sellers being the "Solitaire," "Geranium," "Pet Pug," "Daisy," and "Comforter."

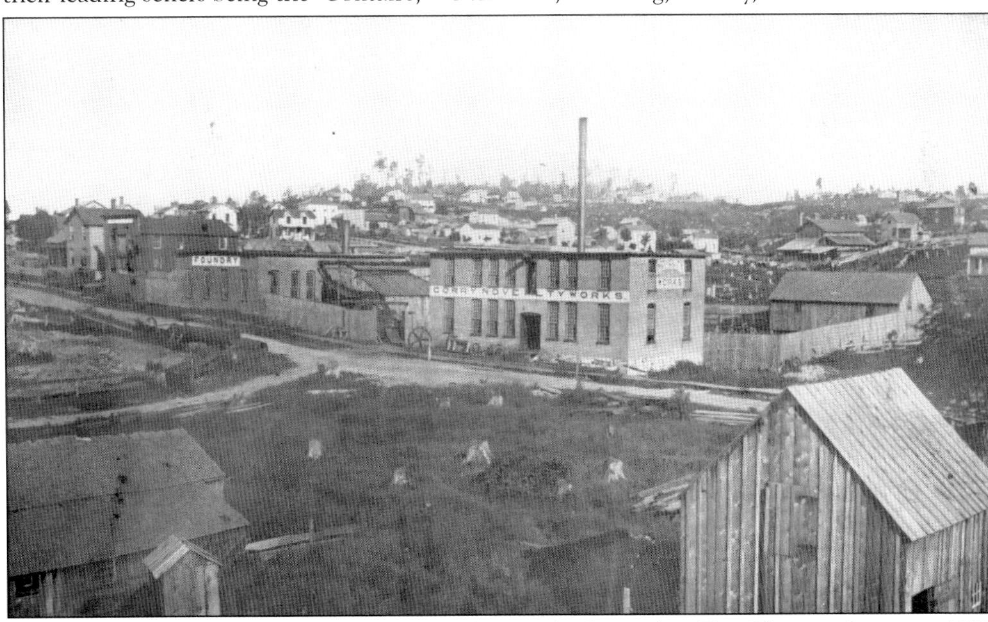

King, Shafer and Company built Corry Novelty Works, located on East Pleasant Street, in 1870. For several years, it was a general machine and repair business, and then manufactured King's patent portable engine with great success. (Courtesy of Barb Grape.)

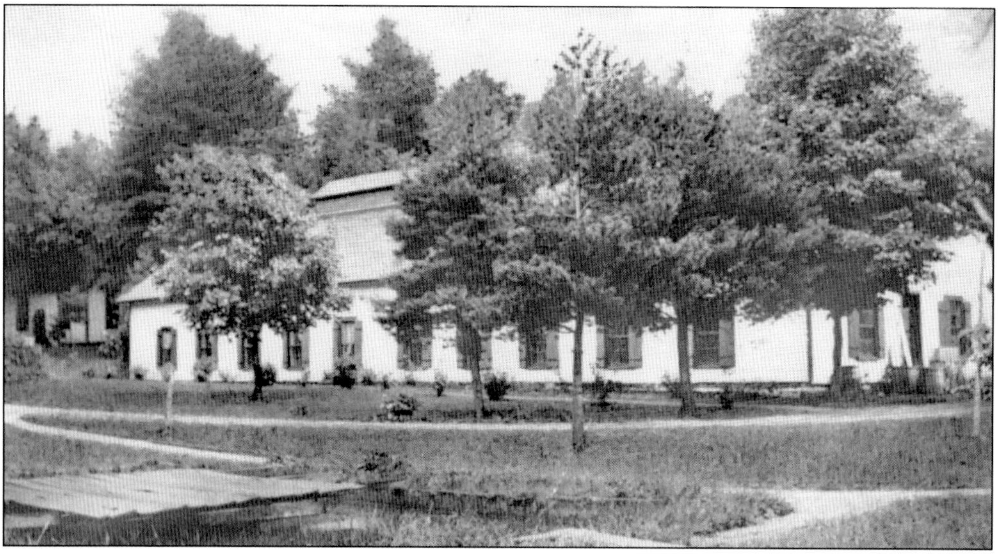

The Pennsylvania Fish Commission established the Corry Fish Hatchery in 1876. It is the longest continuously operated hatchery east of the Mississippi. It is supplied by the abundant springs around Corry, which have uniform flow and temperature. For years, people viewed it as a park where they could walk around, enjoy the trees and fountains, feed the huge carp, and observe the tiny newly hatched fish.

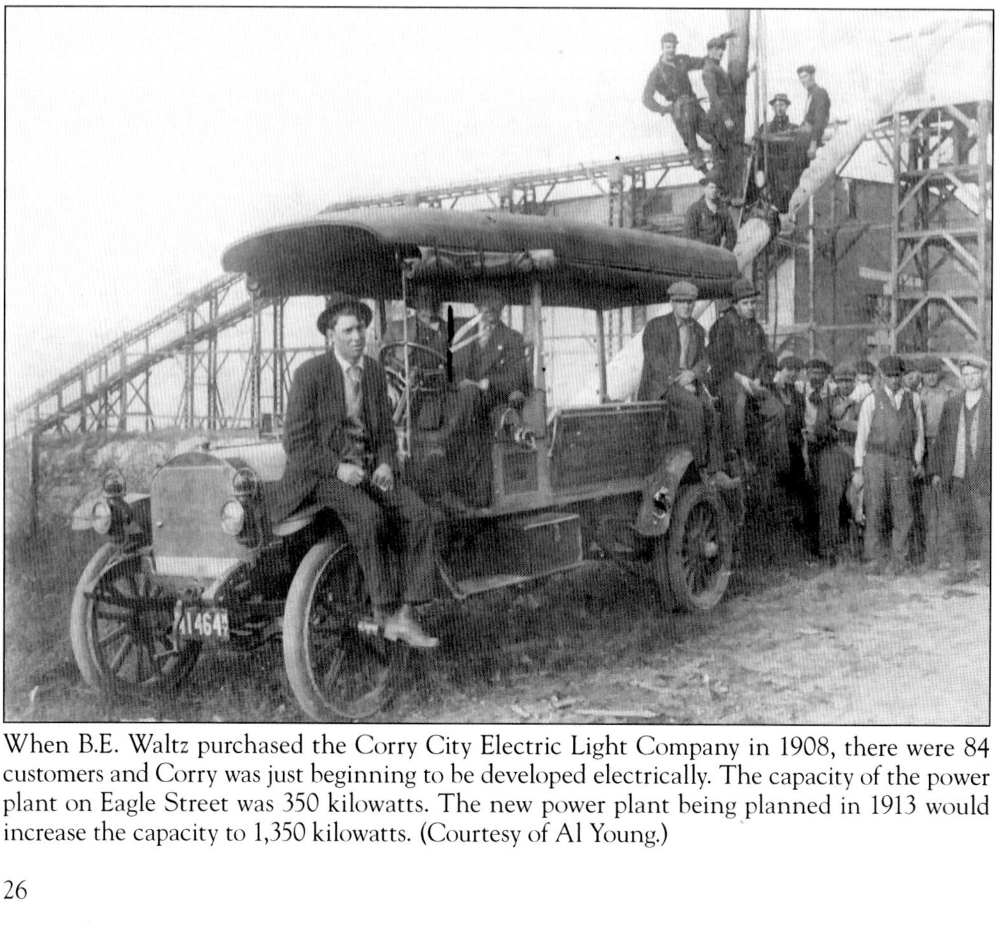

When B.E. Waltz purchased the Corry City Electric Light Company in 1908, there were 84 customers and Corry was just beginning to be developed electrically. The capacity of the power plant on Eagle Street was 350 kilowatts. The new power plant being planned in 1913 would increase the capacity to 1,350 kilowatts. (Courtesy of Al Young.)

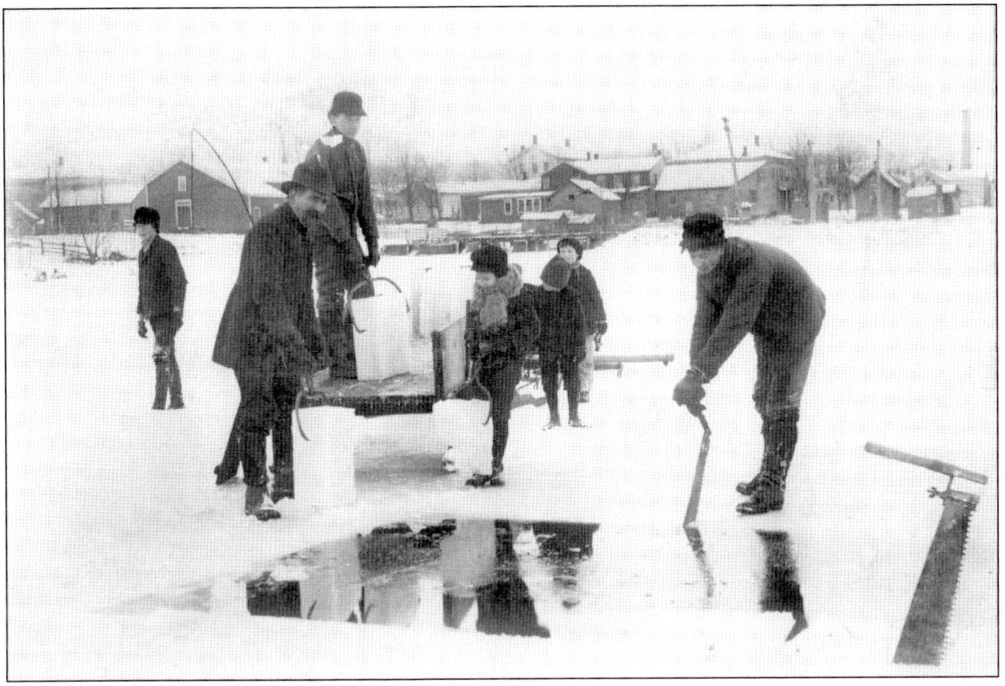

Shannon Natural Ice Company was located on West Columbus Avenue, where Thomas Shannon had a large natural ice pond and commodious storage buildings. An additional icehouse was maintained in the central portion of the city. The ice was delivered by horse-drawn wagon to their customers. It was also conveniently located by the "Big Corry Fair" grounds and racetrack, where tons of ice were consumed each summer.

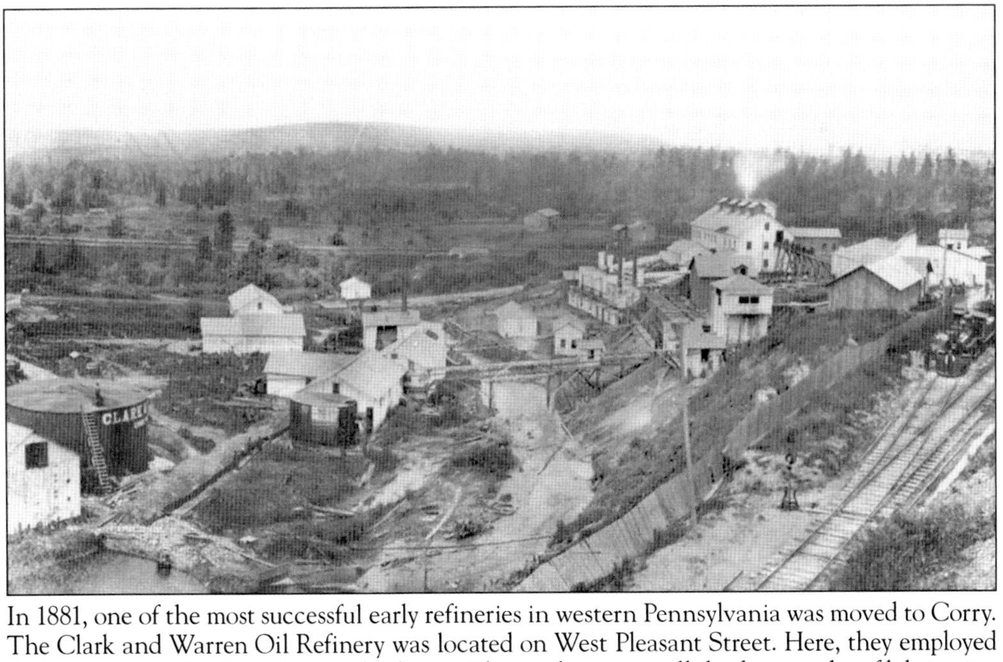

In 1881, one of the most successful early refineries in western Pennsylvania was moved to Corry. The Clark and Warren Oil Refinery was located on West Pleasant Street. Here, they employed their new methods of distilling and refining. The products were all the finer grades of lubricating oils, coal test filtered cylinder oils, and illuminating oils of 120, 150, and 300 degrees.

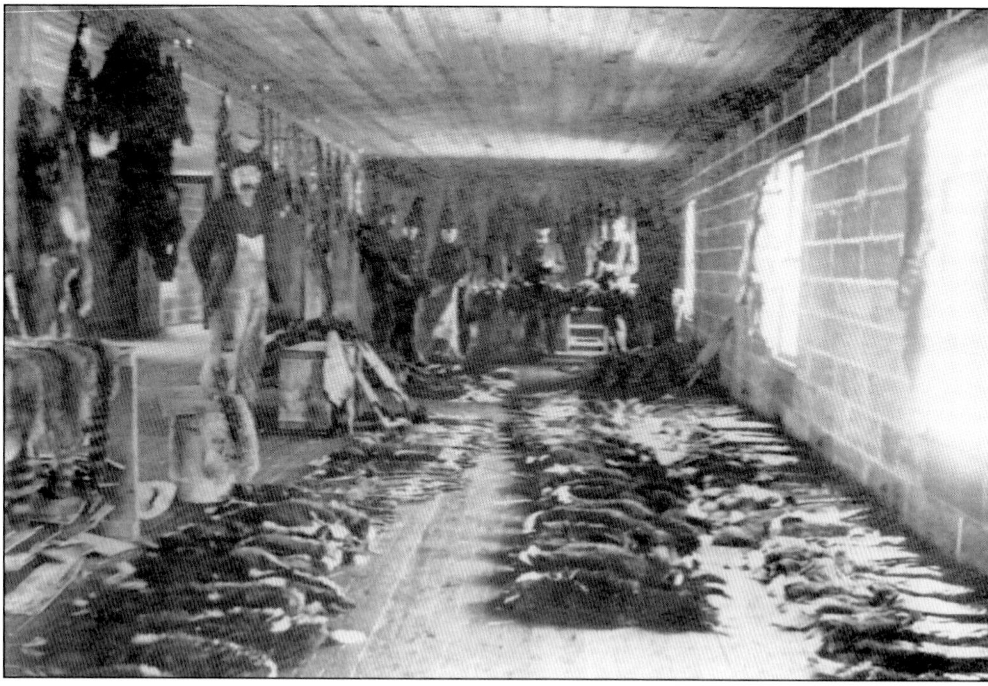

In business since 1906, John Drought & Company was located along the tracks between Pennsylvania Avenue and Cross Street and was one of the largest firms of its kind in the country. J.P. Drought, E.L. Morrow, and O.H. Whetson bought and sold all sorts of hides, pelts, rare furs, wool, and tallow.

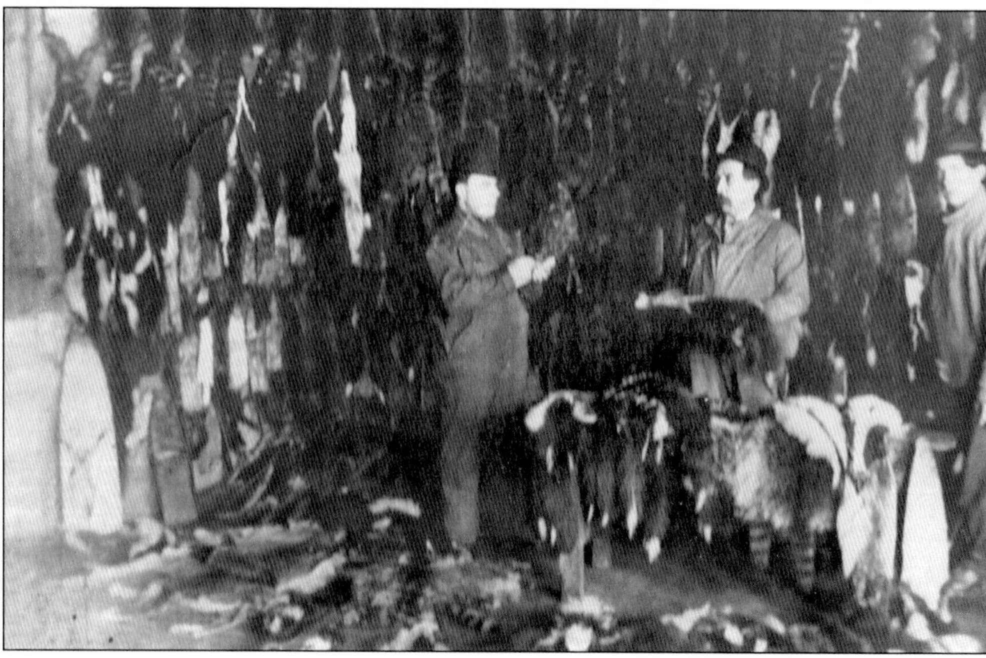

John Drought & Company's big warehouse property in Corry is the most advantageously located for business, with shipping facilities along the tracks and vast areas of storage room. Purchasing agents from the largest consumers of hides and furs in the business made regular trips to Corry to buy stock, and shipments were immense.

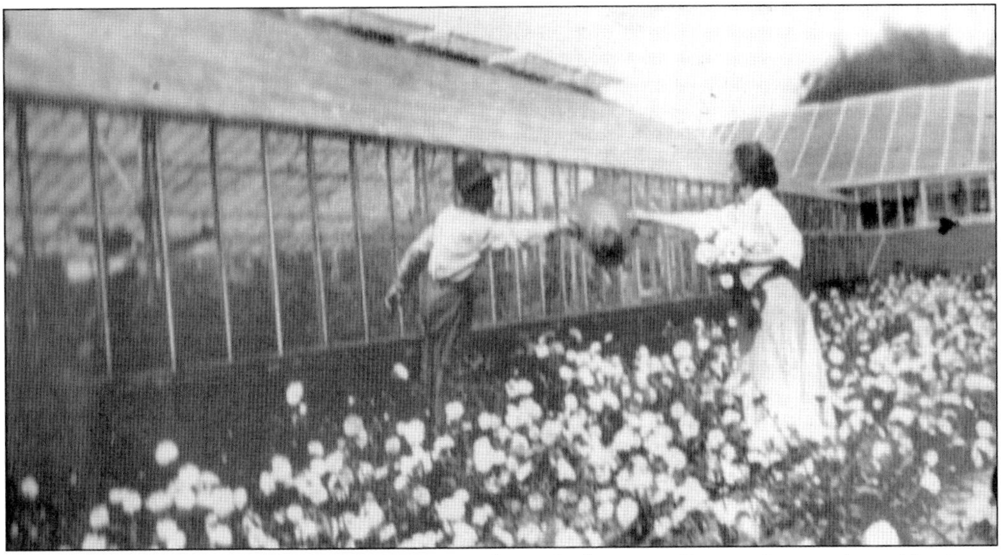

Mary Rhodes, located at 74 Mott Street, was the only florist in Corry who conducted business all season. Her greenhouses were constantly filled with rare and choice plants, tropical as well as native. Cut flowers, hardy fruit trees, and shrubbery were also available, with special attention given to floral arrangements.

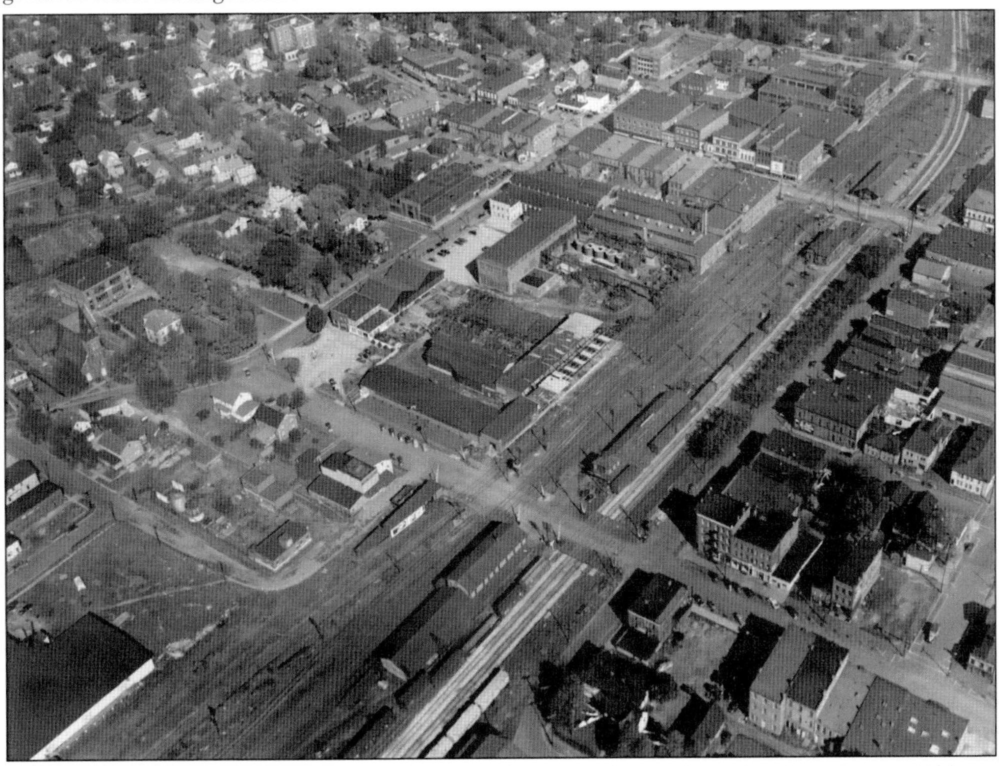

In this 1939 aerial view of Corry, many factories that started near the railroad tracks are visible, as are the family-owned stores along First Avenue. The Boston Hotel, Imperial Hotel, Corry Hotel, and the Catholic priest's house were familiar landmarks at the time. Downtown was a beehive of activity, as the railroads were still in use.

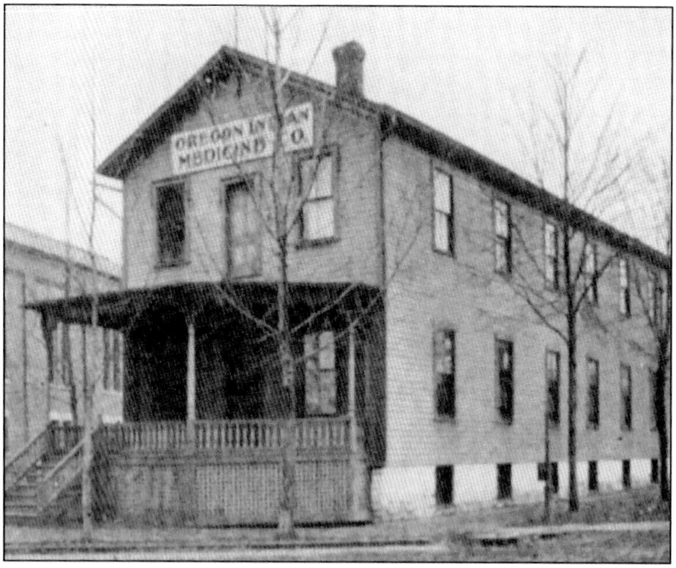

The Oregon Indian Medicine Company moved to East Washington Street from Pittsburgh in 1883. Col. T.A. Edwards, along with a group of Indians, prepared home remedies made from formulas. Edwards claimed to have been taught by the Indians about herbs, Aloe Vera, and alcohol. Ka-ton-ka, Indian cough syrup, Modac Oil, Nez Perce Catarrh Snuff, War Paint Ointment, Quillia Soap, and other products were sold through at least 50 "traveling medicine shows."

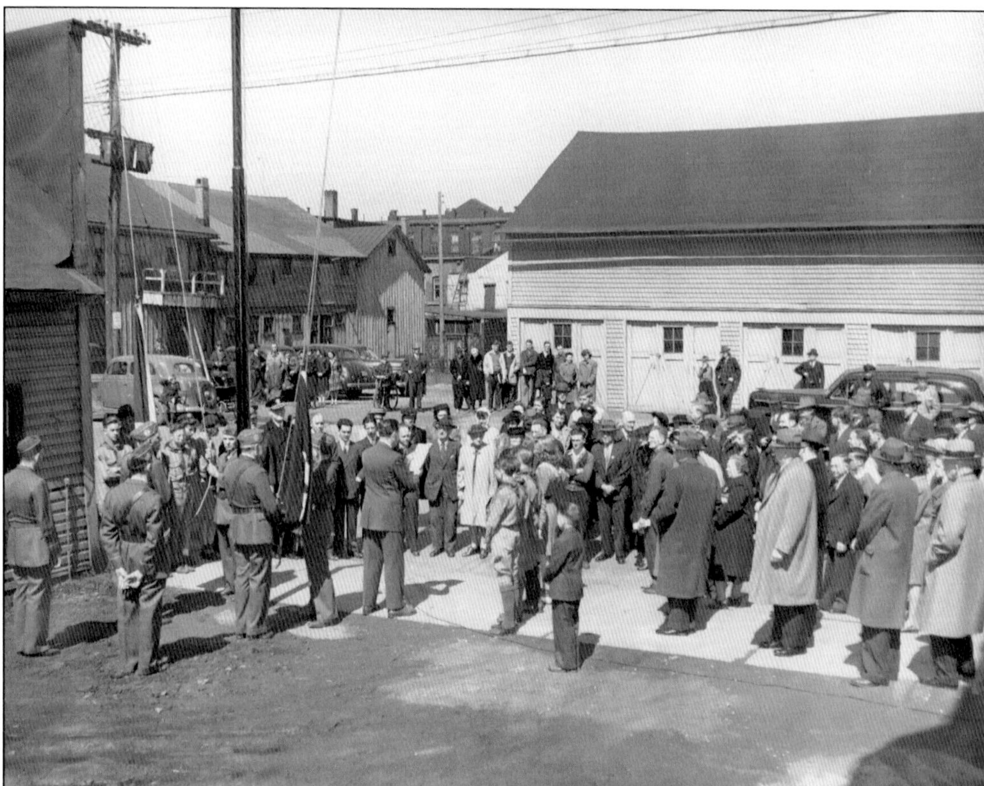

Trill Indicator Company was founded in 1901 by William L. Trill. The US Maritime Commission honored the company for good work in war production, presenting the Maritime "M" Award on April 9, 1943, with an impressive ceremony at the plant. The company also received the Gold Star Award. The indicator was an important part of every engine for the fleets of cargo ships during World War I and Liberty ships in World War II.

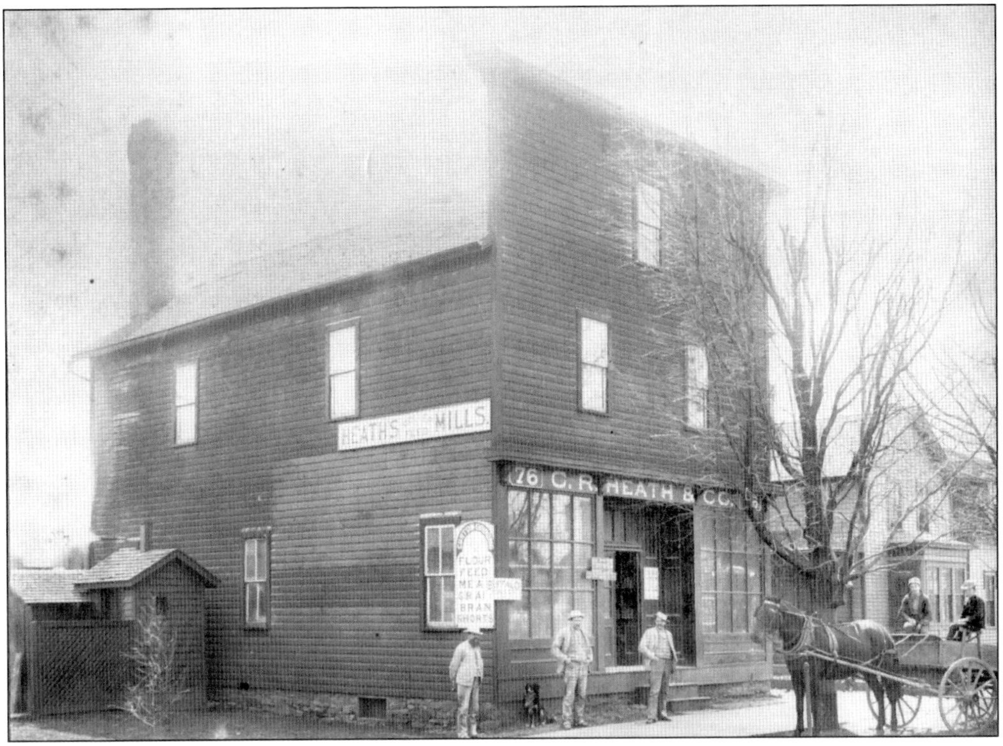

Heath's Mill, located on the corner of North Center and East Park Place, was built in 1887. The mill was one of the neatest and most modern mills in the area. Various grades of feed, flour, poultry, and stock feed, along with large quantities of fertilizers and baled hay, were sold. The mill also provided custom grinding. A mysterious fire all but destroyed the mill in 1913, but it was rebuilt in better shape than ever.

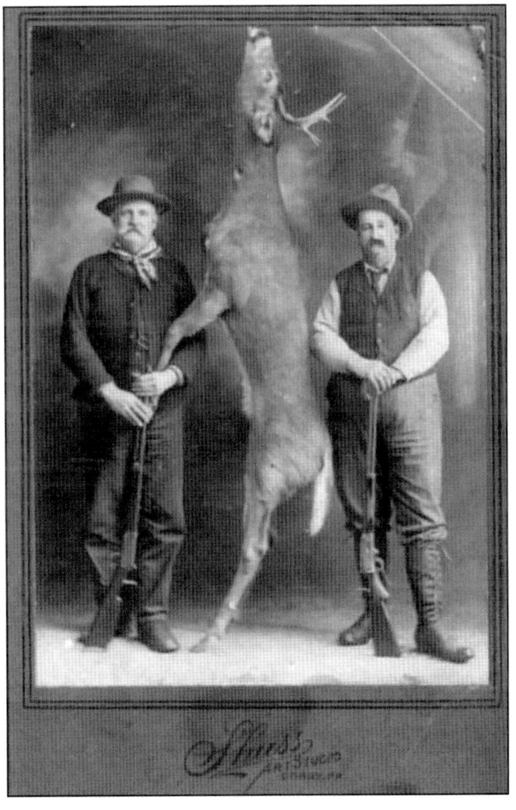

By 1913, the studio of Walter Shuss—formerly the Brooks Studio on North Center—was one of the best-equipped photographic establishments in the area. An innovation that was original in this Corry studio was the use of electricity in making night photographs possible. A series of incandescent lamps were arranged to burn for an instant at twice their normal voltage, resulting in a remarkable effect.

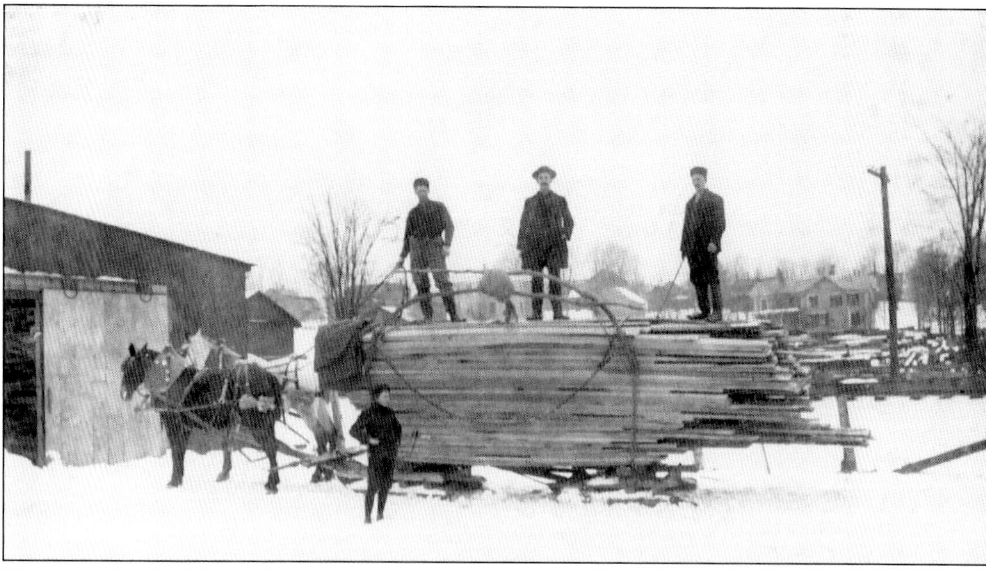

H.H. Kepple, Will Ploss, Tom Mooney, and J.H. Miller are pictured unloading lumber for Mahle Brush Block factory, on Grace Street, in 1905. Blocks of hard wood were bored with rows of holes to be made into all types of brushes. A very large amount was consumed in the manufacture of brushes made in the convict-operated brush factories of big penal institutions, including Sing Sing Prison of New York.

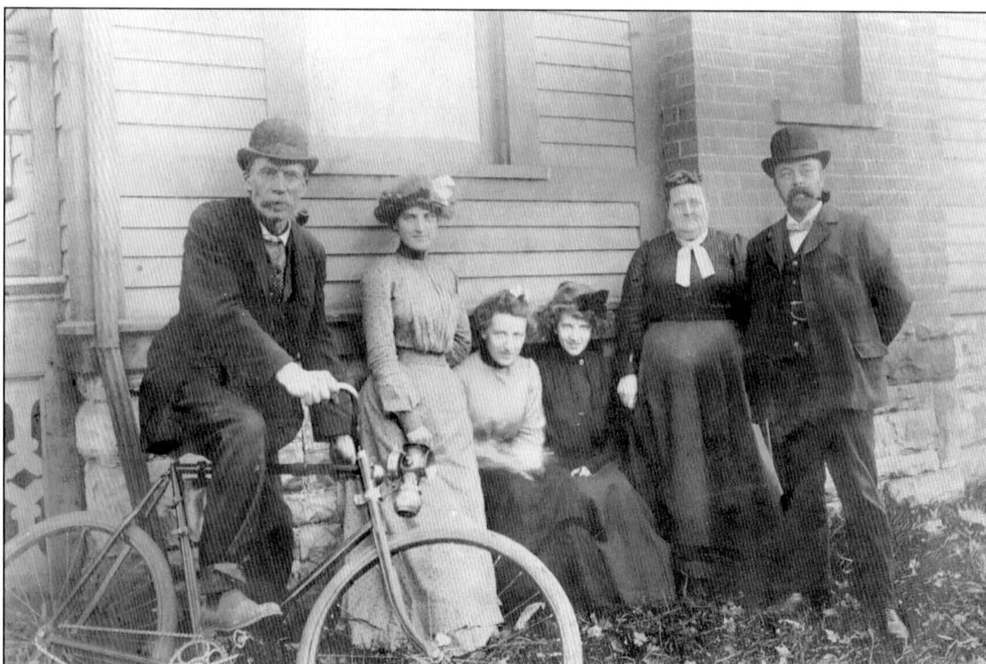

Alexander McInnes Sr. was originally from Scotland and founded McInnes Steel in 1895. He moved the business to Corry in 1901 because of the railroads. This was the first plant in the United States to make "molybdenum steel," which won an award at the St. Louis Exposition in 1904. In the 1960s, the company became one of the major suppliers of forgings for the aerospace, turbine, and nuclear industries.

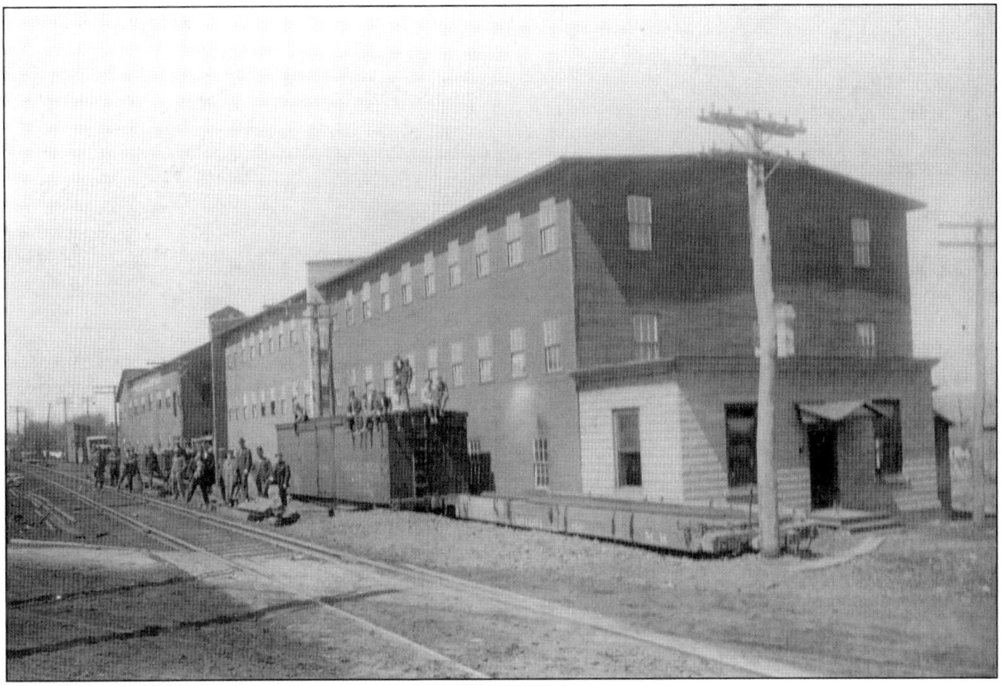

Perry Collier developed a bleacher system that could be assembled and knocked down in less than an hour and a half. Manufacturing started in Collier's shop on Maple Avenue then moved to a large building on Railroad Street in the 1920s. Seating with a footrest was a vast improvement, making them much more comfortable over old bleachers. The Collier Trestle was also used for scaffold supports.

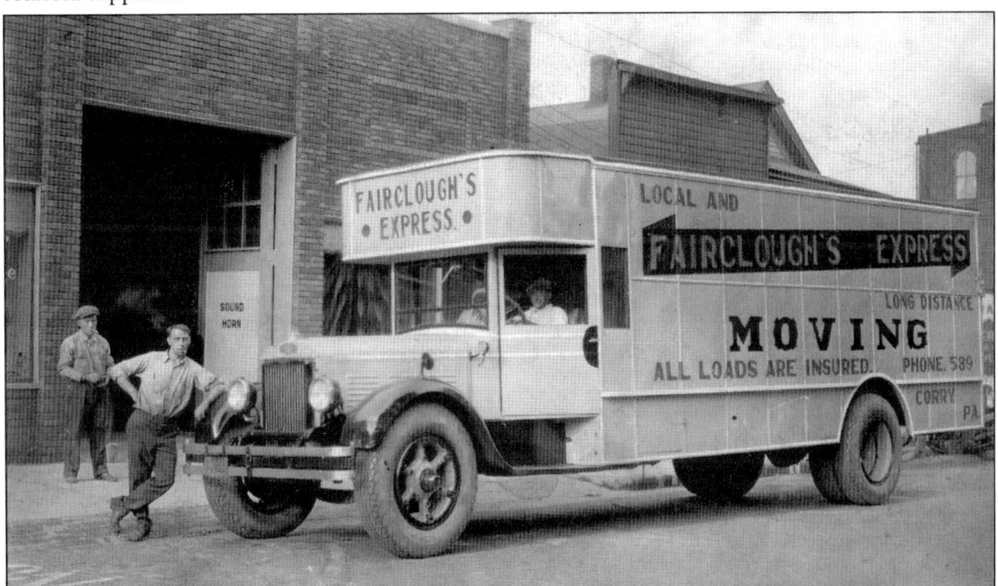

Perry Collier was a master of remanufacturing trucks. He rebuilt a vehicle for a specific purpose, making them strong enough to carry heavy loads or adding a large box to make it into a moving van. He built refrigeration trucks, buses, and delivery vans. The Collier Garage was located in the alley between Main and East South Streets in the 1920s and 1930s.

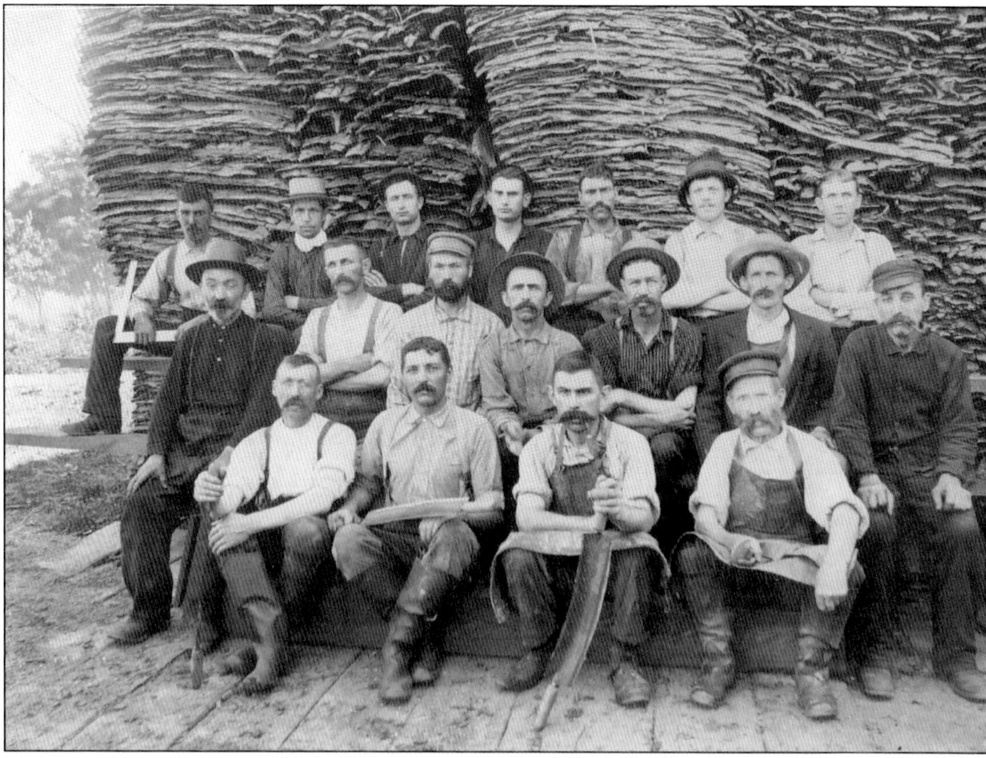

The tannery of the J.W. and A.P. Howard Company, located on East Main Street, started in 1863 and could tan 50 hides a day. It became one of the largest in the country after J.J. Desmond and F.A. Loveland purchased the plant in 1899. Hides were purchased in volume from North America, continental Europe, Africa, South America, and China. In 1913, the capacity was 1,000 hides a day. In addition, the company controlled tanneries in Spring Creek, which had a capacity of 300 hides daily, and Corry Chrome Company, which had a capacity of 200 hides a day. Tanning materials, such as Myrabolam nuts, Valonea cups, and mangrove bark, were shipped in from Argentina, India, northern Africa, and Central America. Everything was tanned, from polar bears to skunks. (Below, courtesy of John Lutz.)

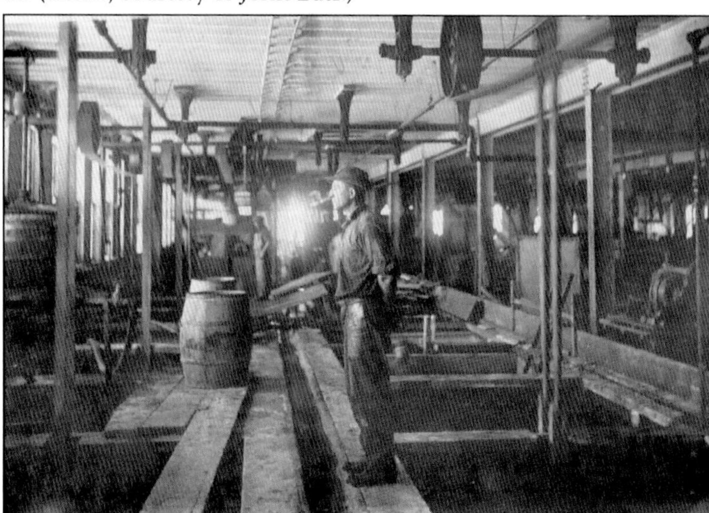

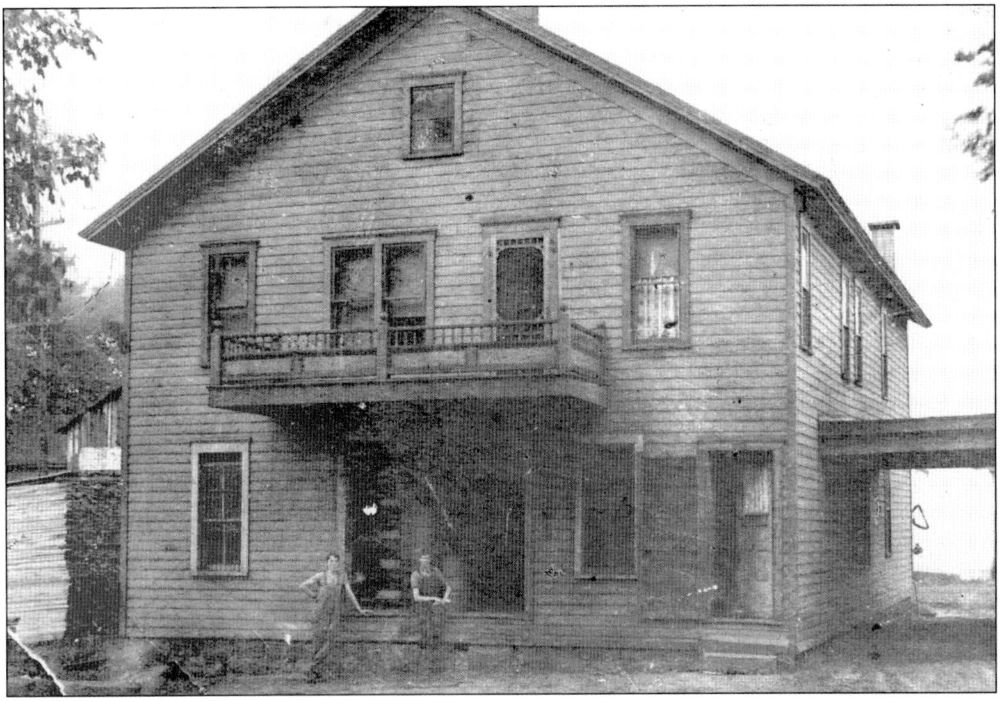

The Corry Wrench Company, located on Eagle Street just south of Washington Street, started in the early 1900s. Their products consisted of a high-grade line of agricultural wrenches in 6-, 8-, 10-, 12-, and 15-inch sizes. The plant employed 15 to 20 workmen who produced 1,200 to 1,500 wrenches daily.

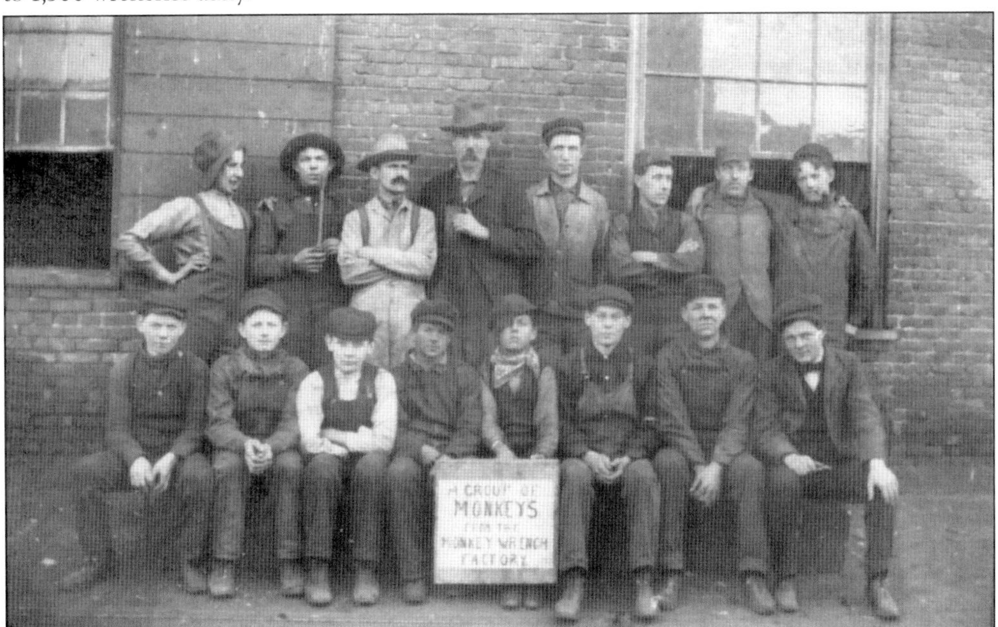

In 1873, there were so many jobs available that factories were using children to extend the labor force. Boys and girls, ages 10 to 15 years old worked for about 60¢ a day. Hundreds of children were employed doing small, tedious jobs that were easy to learn.

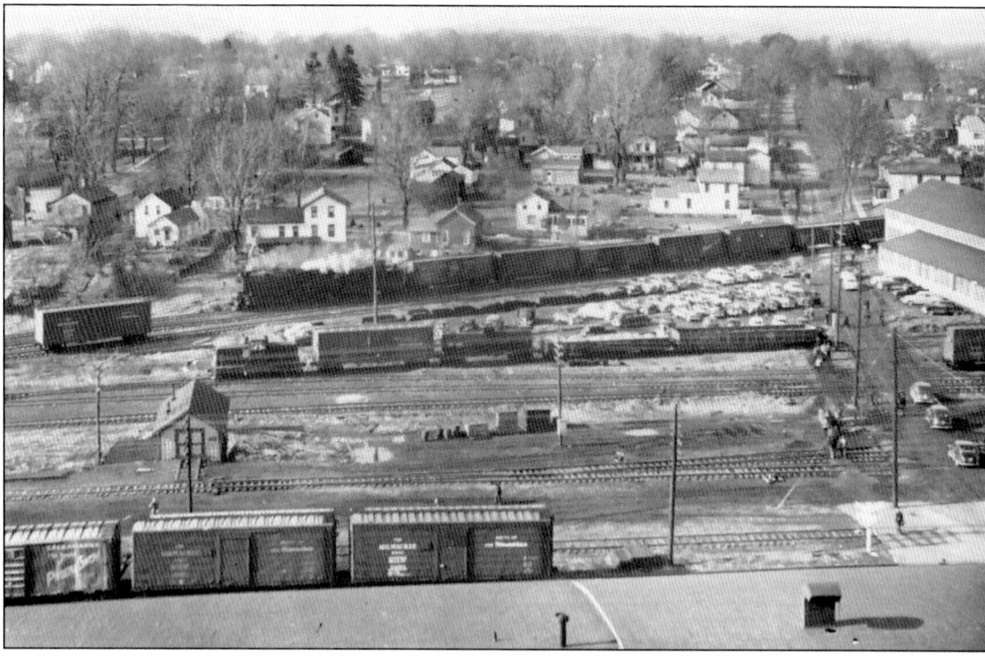

The Rogers Structural Steel Company was incorporated in 1909 and supervised by Clarence Rogers. Their concrete and steel warehouse and steel working plant was built in 1911 on Eagle Street. One of their first accomplishments was the erection of the Ajax machine shop and fireproof foundry. Rogers also built the Shreve Chair Factory in Union City, the Mohawk Milk condensing plant in Sherman, New York, and the United States Brake Shoe Company plant in Corry.

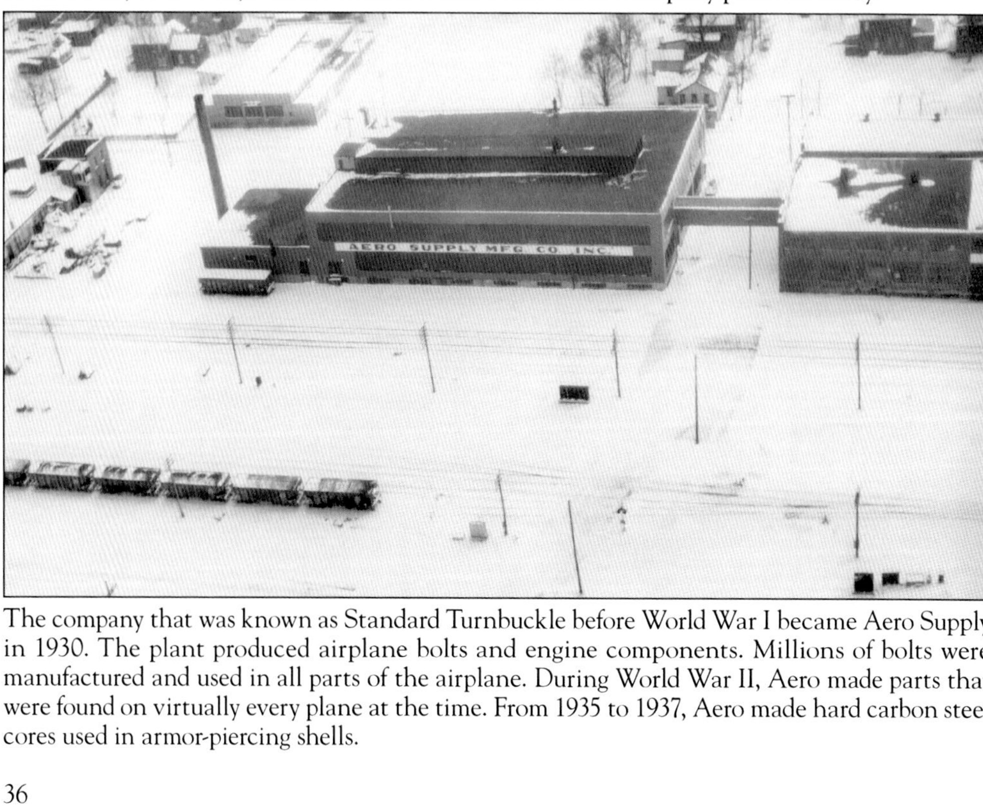

The company that was known as Standard Turnbuckle before World War I became Aero Supply in 1930. The plant produced airplane bolts and engine components. Millions of bolts were manufactured and used in all parts of the airplane. During World War II, Aero made parts that were found on virtually every plane at the time. From 1935 to 1937, Aero made hard carbon steel cores used in armor-piercing shells.

Three

SOLD IN CORRY

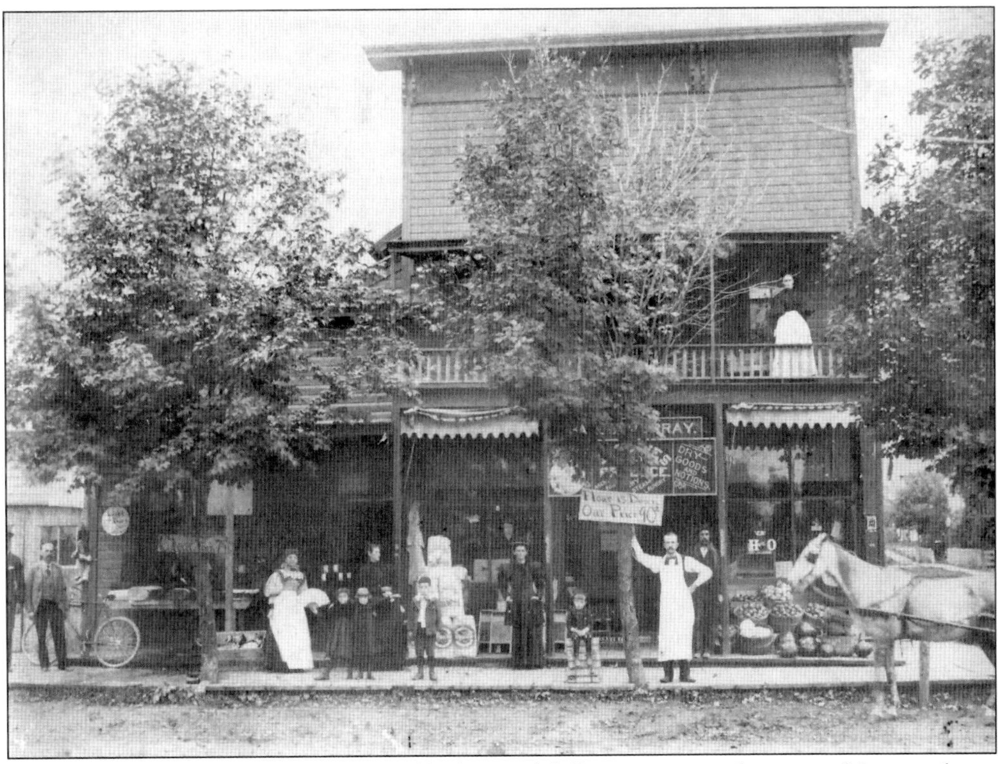

J.D. Murray started business in 1883 and had several different stores and partners. He moved into his own store on the corner of North Center and Irving in 1911. He carried an excellent line of "fancy" as well as staple groceries and provisions. Among the lines handled were Heinz, Edwards, and Beechnut. Occident flour was another leader in the Murray store, which was known for its special sugar and other bargains.

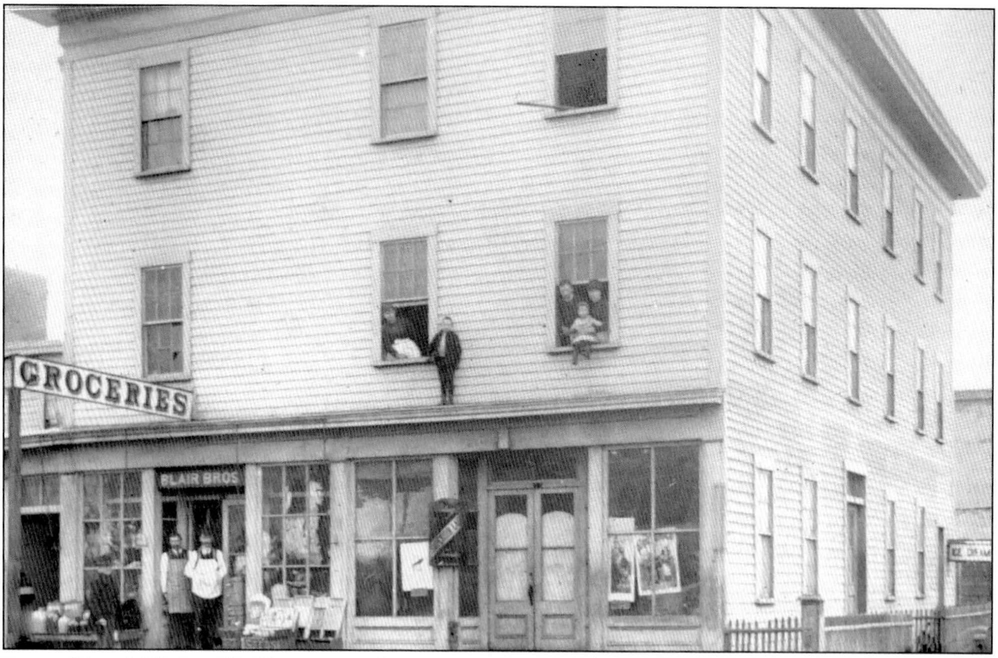

James T. and Walter W. Blair opened a grocery store in the just-completed Darling Building on First Avenue in 1897. The establishment was one of the best-known groceries in the city. Ceresota flour, Campbell fancy goods, confectionery, cigars, and tobaccos were carried at all times in connection with the grocery business, with fresh produce carried in season.

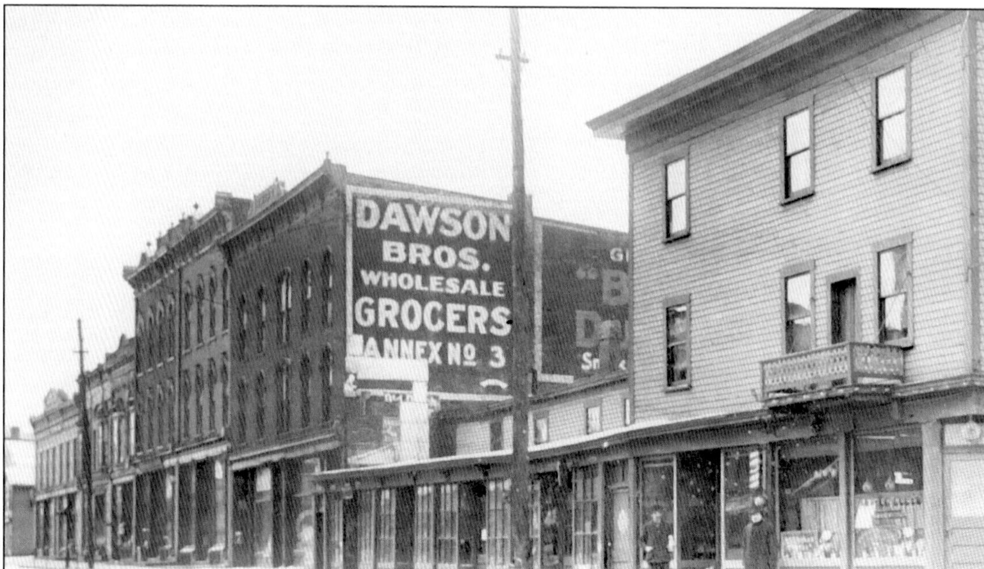

The Dawson Bros. store was built on the land where the brickyard once operated. The Dawsons started with a newsstand and went into the grocery business in 1876, moving their grocery store from Center Street to First Avenue. In 1906, the firm went into the wholesale business exclusively and were represented by several traveling salesmen and shipping throughout western Pennsylvania and east along the Philadelphia and Erie division.

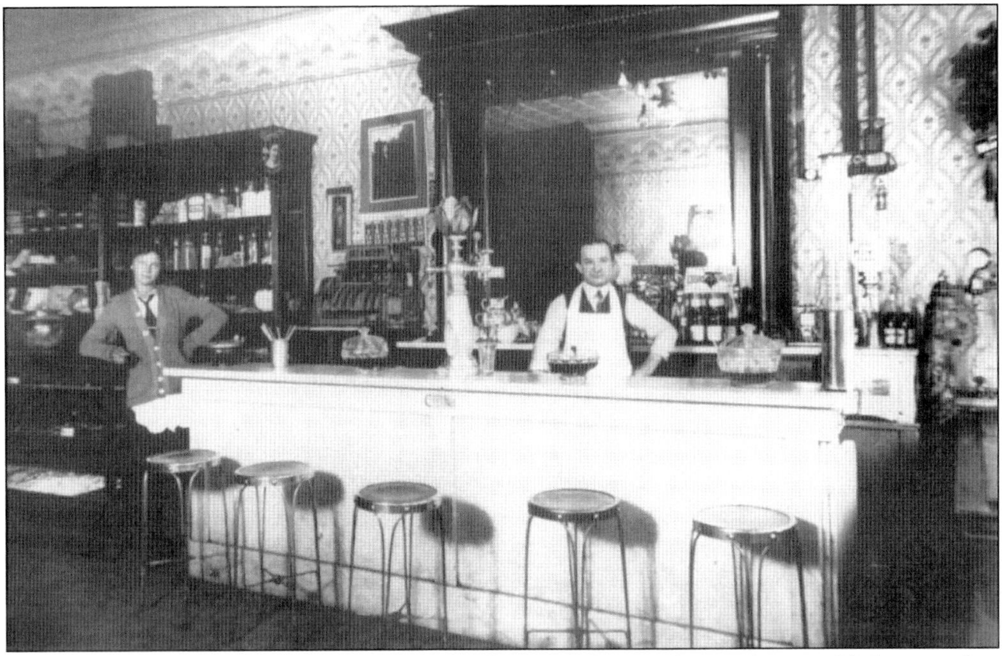

Tony A. Paver was a confectioner at 118 North Center Street. A complete establishment of its kind included an excellent fountain for dispensing all kinds of soft drinks and ice cream made in Corry by Geiger and Son. The large trade of confections at the candy shop was maintained with sweets made in its own candy kitchen.

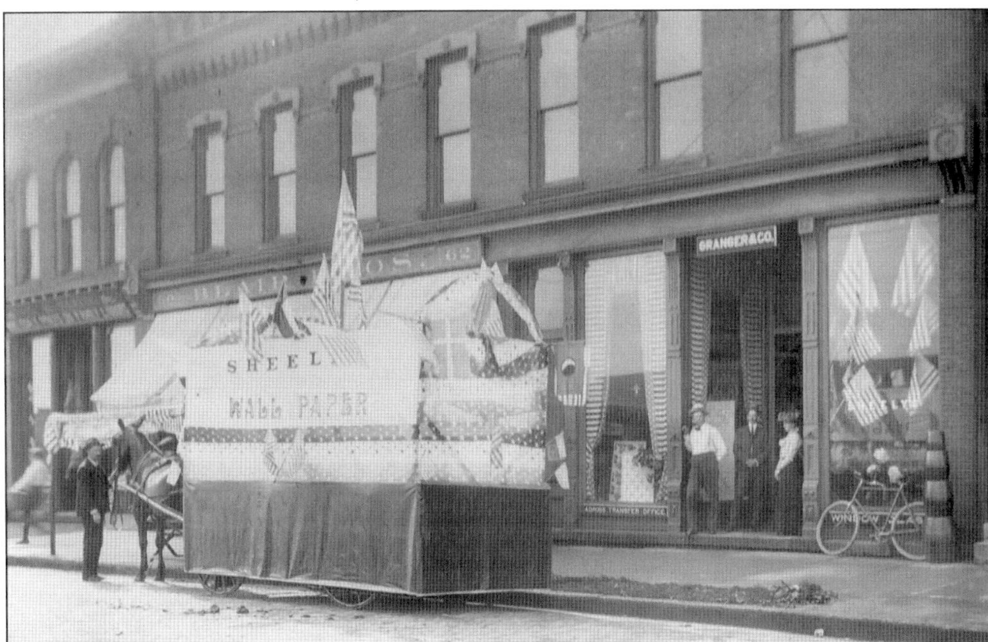

J.M. Sheely started in the paint and paper business in 1883. It was originally located on First Avenue and then on West South Street, eventually moving to West Main Street in 1906. The store carried a complete line of house paints, wallpaper, floor finishes, and supplies for various kinds of artwork, including pyrography, watercolors, and oil paints.

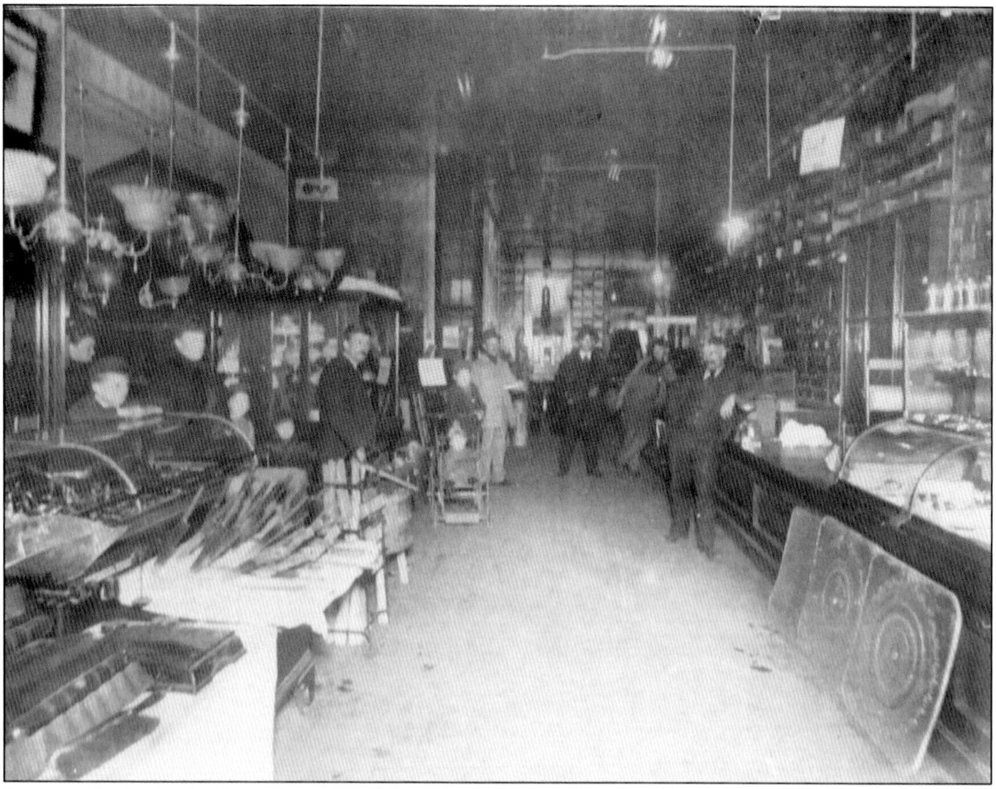

Barlow Hardware built and occupied the magnificent main building on North Center Street in 1890. The basement and three floors were filled by their immense stock, which included plumbing, harness, horse blankets, tools, farm supplies, sporting goods, guns, ammunition, and all sorts of stoves and lighting supplies. They handled everything from a carpet tack to an automobile. In addition, there were two large warehouses and a yard in the rear of the building for wagons, buggies, cutters, building supplies, and coal. Barlow Hardware supplied much of the material used for building the town and was a successful business for years.

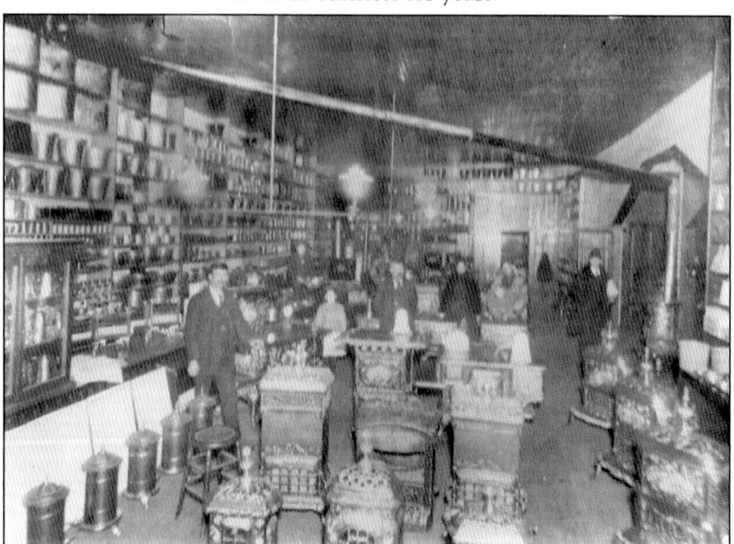

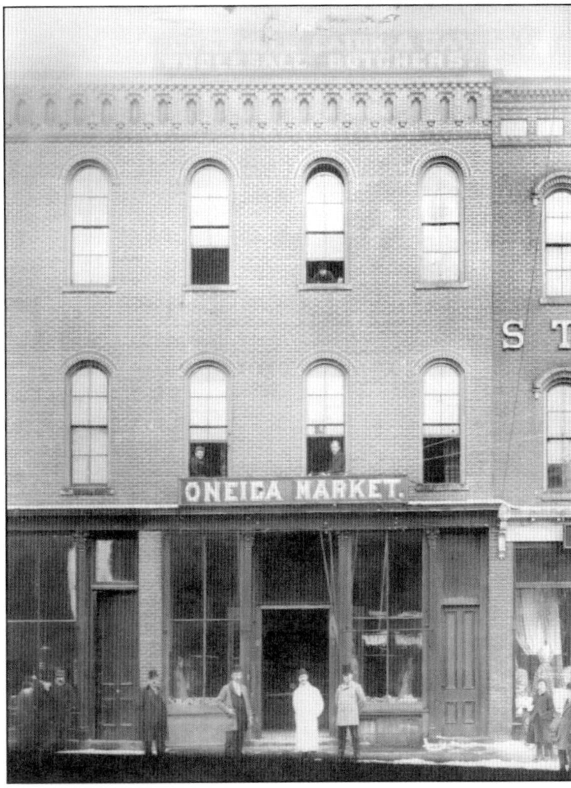

James Hassett and Son started their meat market business in 1907 with a shop on First Avenue and remained there until they purchased the Oneida meat market in 1911. A year later, they purchased the Washington meat market. By 1913, they maintained two big retail establishments on the north side. The Hassetts also sold their products wholesale and shipped a large amount of local dressed meats. The former Steely slaughtering establishment, located east of the city, became part of the Hassetts' properties in 1913. The Oneida and Washington establishments specialized in Swift and the Hassetts' own dressed Western meats. They also handled excellent hams, bacon, and sausage.

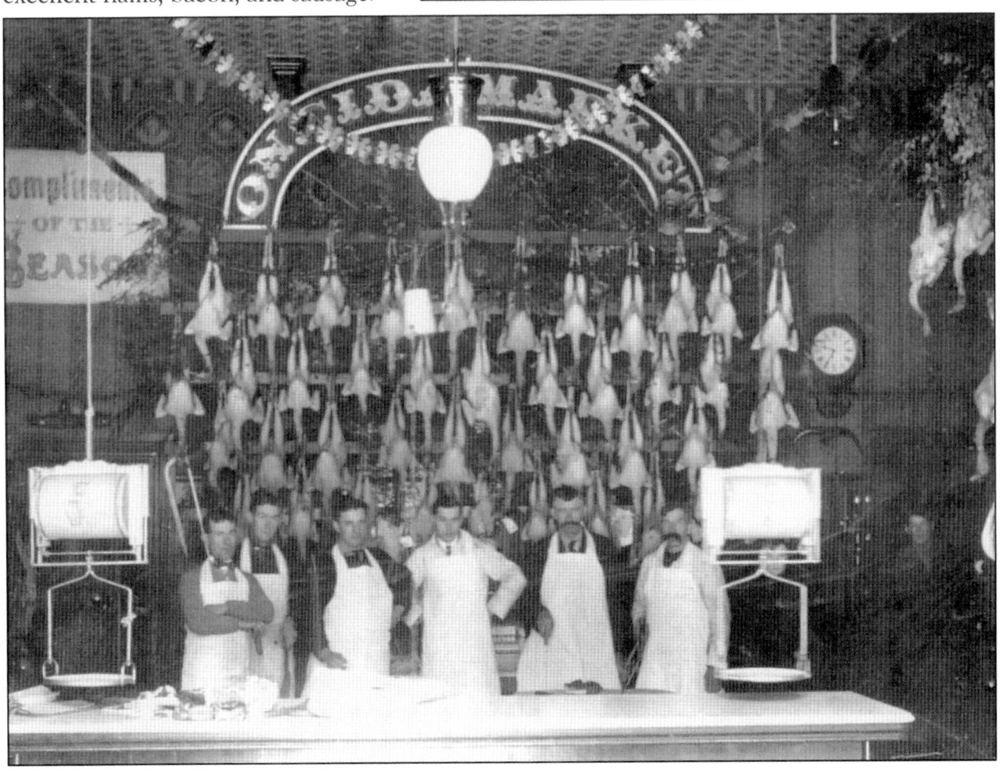

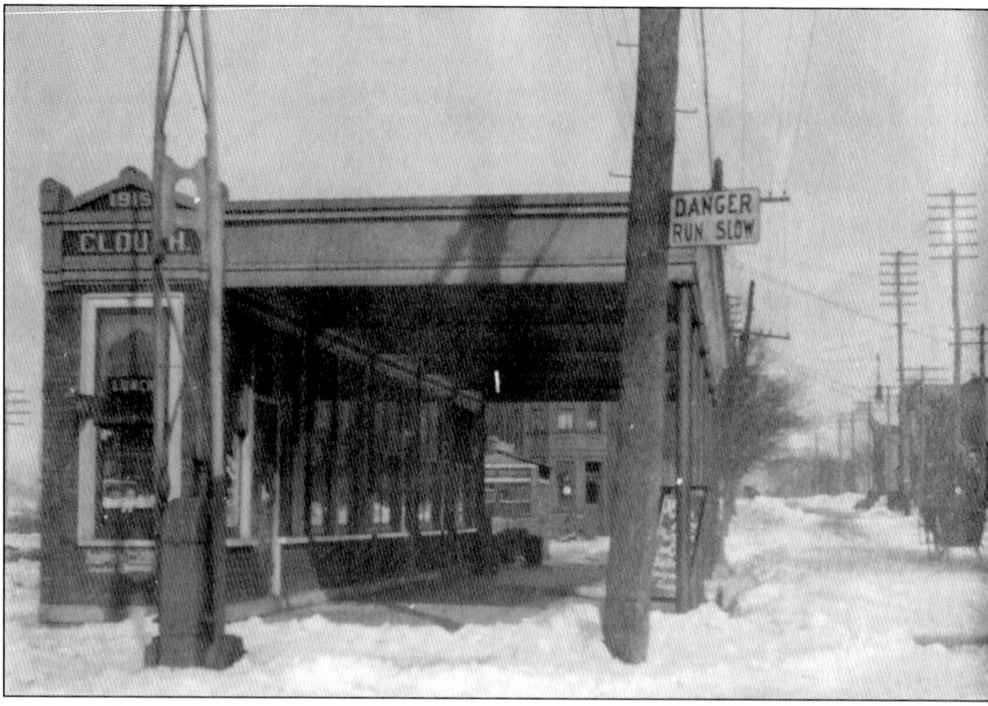

In 1902, John Clough started selling peanuts, popcorn, and knickknacks from a wagon between Main Street and the railroad tracks. This minor business venture grew to big proportions when he started manufacturing corn fritters and other products for wholesale. He constructed a building with a basement and a second floor extending over the sidewalk. It was big enough to provide room for other enterprises.

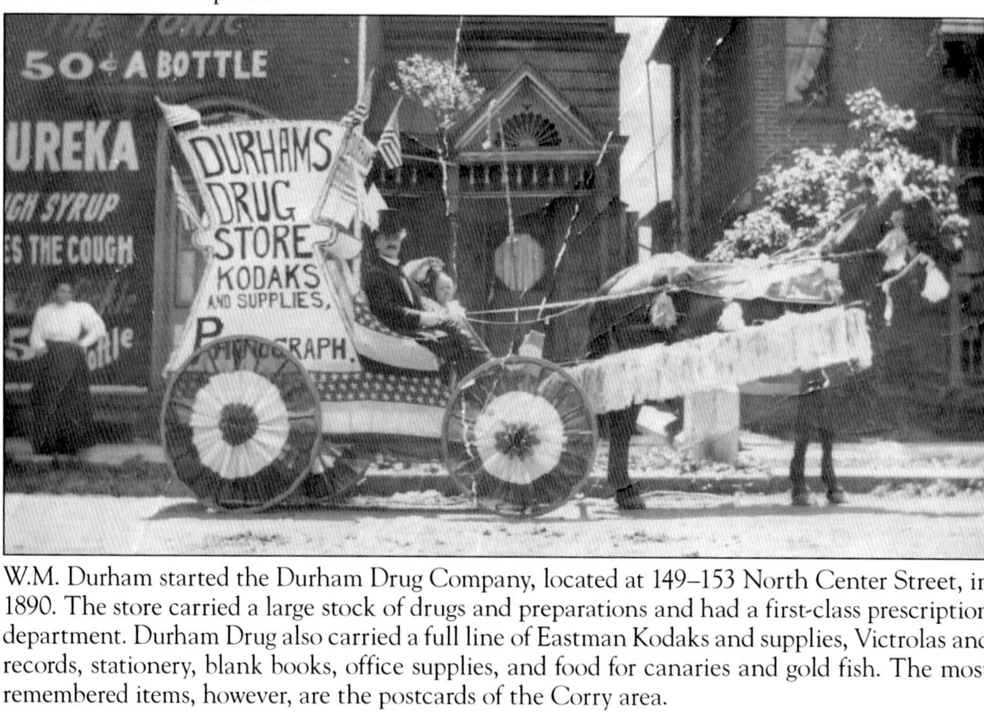

W.M. Durham started the Durham Drug Company, located at 149–153 North Center Street, in 1890. The store carried a large stock of drugs and preparations and had a first-class prescription department. Durham Drug also carried a full line of Eastman Kodaks and supplies, Victrolas and records, stationery, blank books, office supplies, and food for canaries and gold fish. The most remembered items, however, are the postcards of the Corry area.

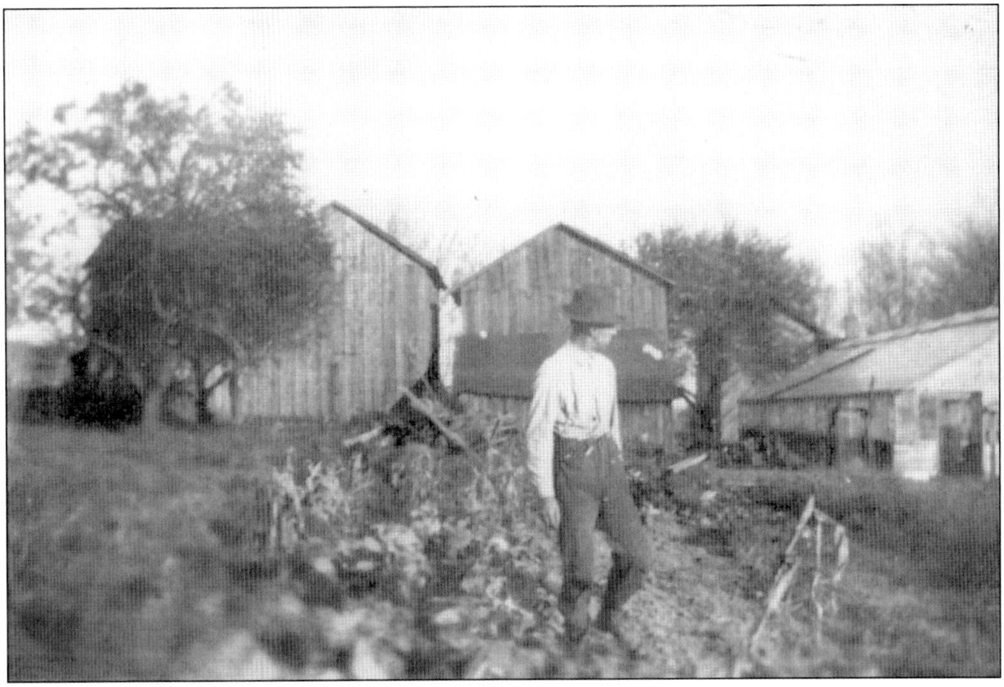

In the early 1900s, florist William D. Rowe's extensive greenhouses on East Wayne Street were devoted chiefly to the production of small vegetables and green produce, which he raised for the wholesale market. He was able to provide them in seasons when the usual crops were not available for sale. Rowe specialized in the reproduction of immense quantities of tomatoes and other garden plants. He was very successful because his two large greenhouses of modern pattern were equipped with first-class heating systems and other facilities. He supplied restaurants in Corry as well as those out of town with the freshest vegetables that they needed for salads, sandwiches, and side dishes.

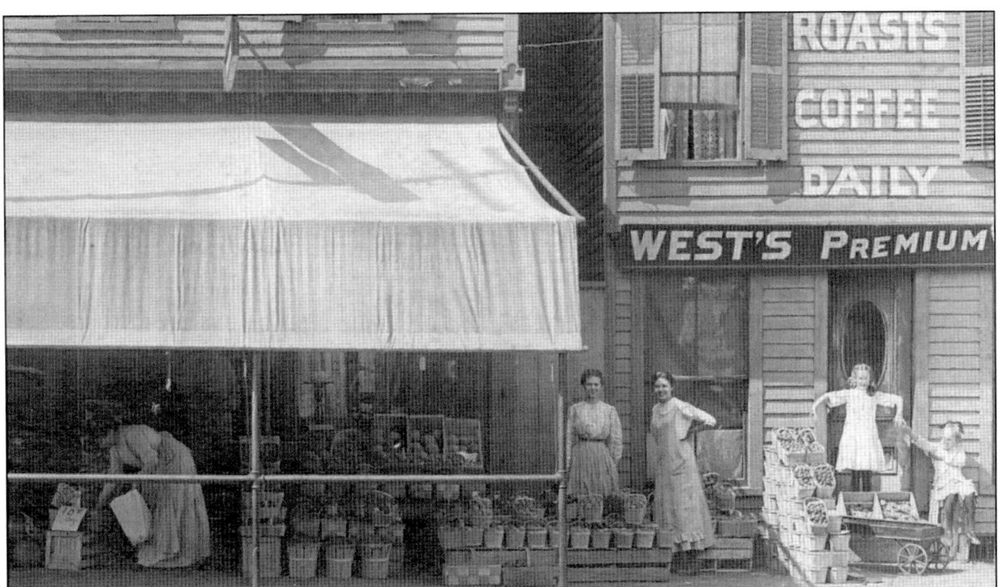

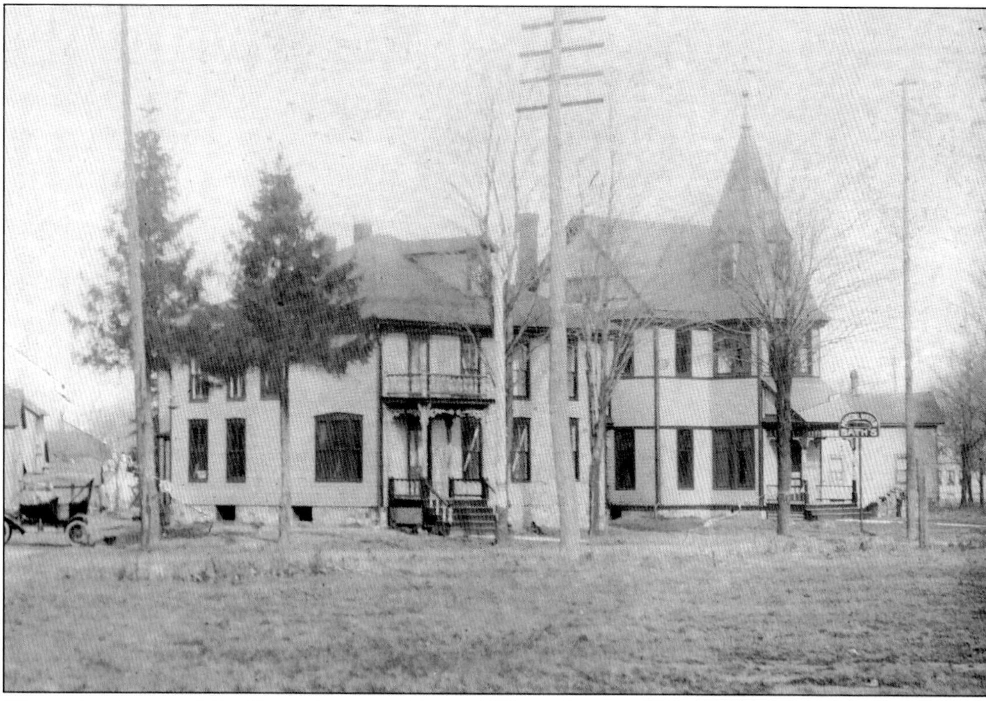

The spring house of the Corry Artesian Mineral Water Company was located on East Washington Street. People flocked from miles away to sample the "health giving" mineral waters. Some drank the mineral water from the flowing well or bought bottles of it at $3.50 per case, while others preferred bathing at the house for 35¢. The house burned in 1914, ending the business.

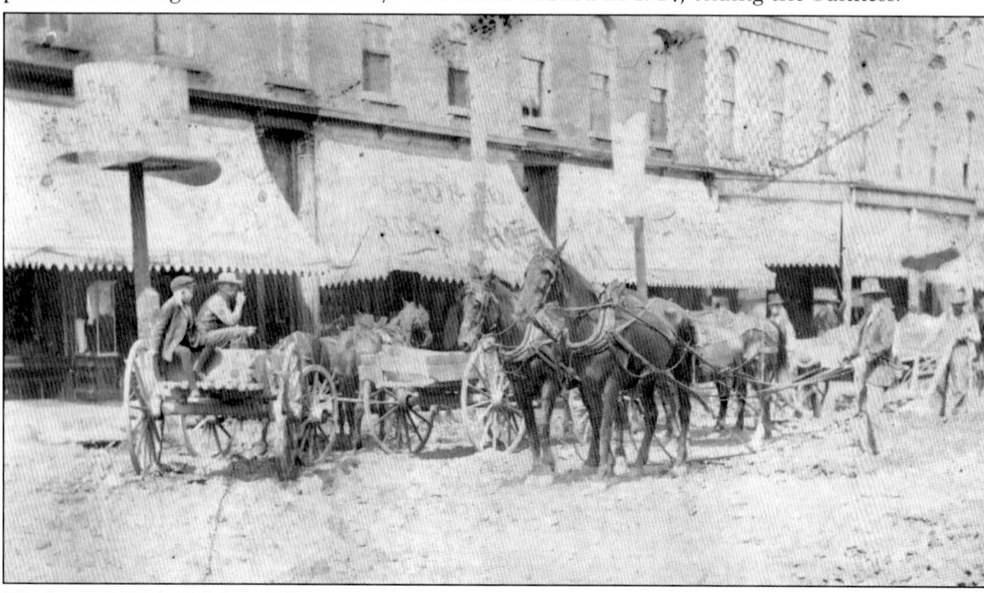

Weeks and Wakefield, well-known painters and paperhangers, opened a store on Park Street in 1885. In 1902, they moved to an elegant new store on Center Street. In 1905, Wakefield sold his interest to Breadon, another well-known expert in the business. The store had a complete supply of wallpaper, paperhanging supplies, paint, varnish, and decorating supplies. The store also had an art-framing department.

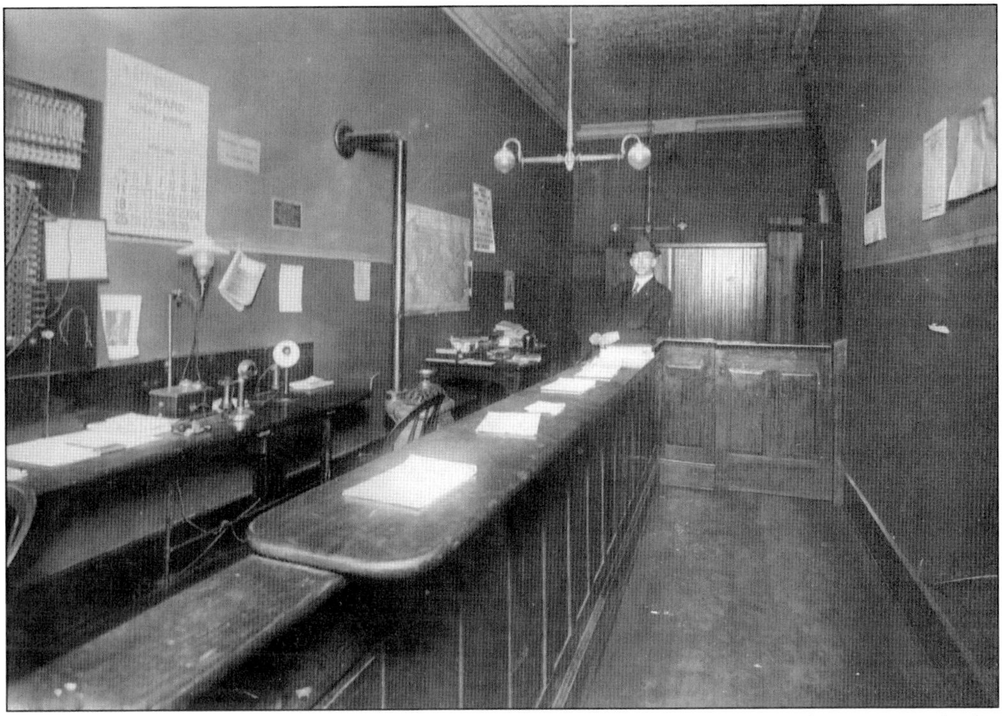

Postal Telegraph and Cable Company, started in 1907, was a means of quick service with the outside world, both in business and other communication. The office, under the management of P.J. Webber, did a remarkably large commercial telegraphic and correspondence business. The service was appreciated by the general public and especially by the businessmen of the city.

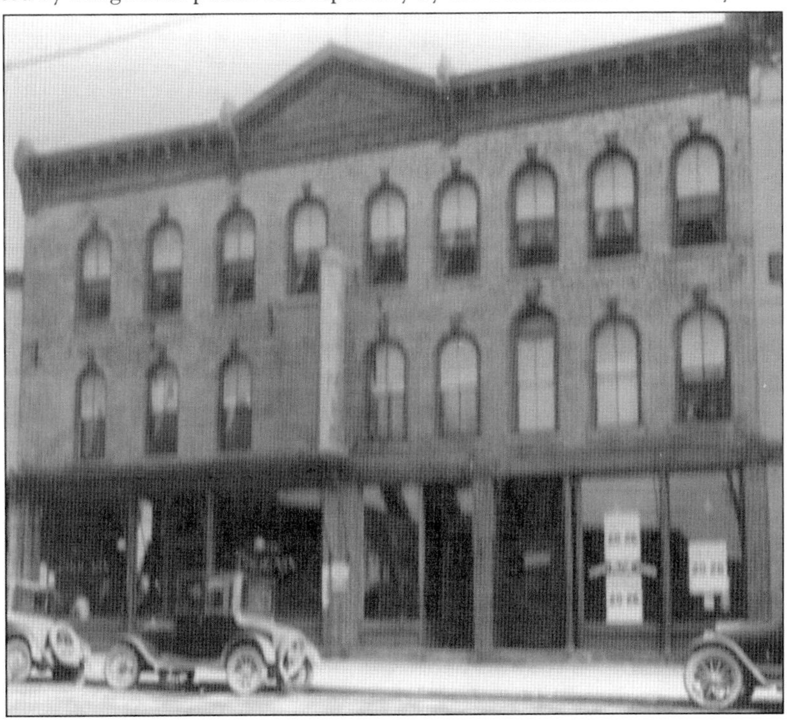

The Phoenix Hotel saw 37 passenger trains stop in Corry every day. Many of the passengers stayed the night to wait for the next train or were salesmen selling their wares in the area. It was an elegant hotel with 40 rooms boasting running water, steam heat, and a telephone system. The vehicles date this image to around the 1920s.

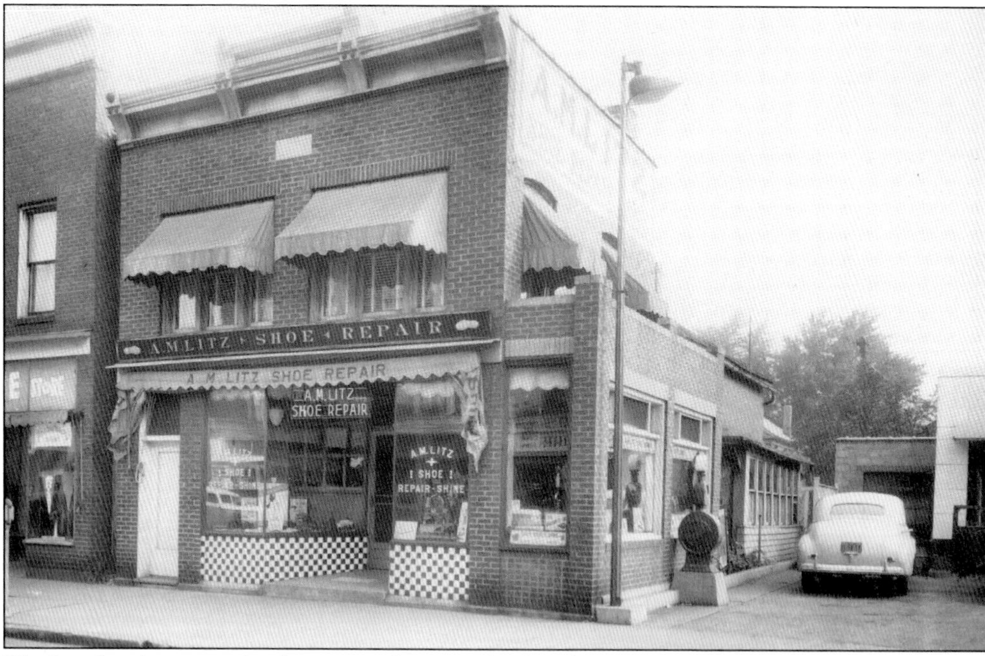

The Litz family was in the shoe repair business for decades. In 1912, Frank P. Litz started business on West Main Street with shoe shining and shoe repair. He also sold cigars, tobacco, and fancy groceries and Italian produce, specializing in Italian olive oil. Tony Litz had a shoeshine and repair shop on Center Street, and Mike Litz had the same type of business on South Street.

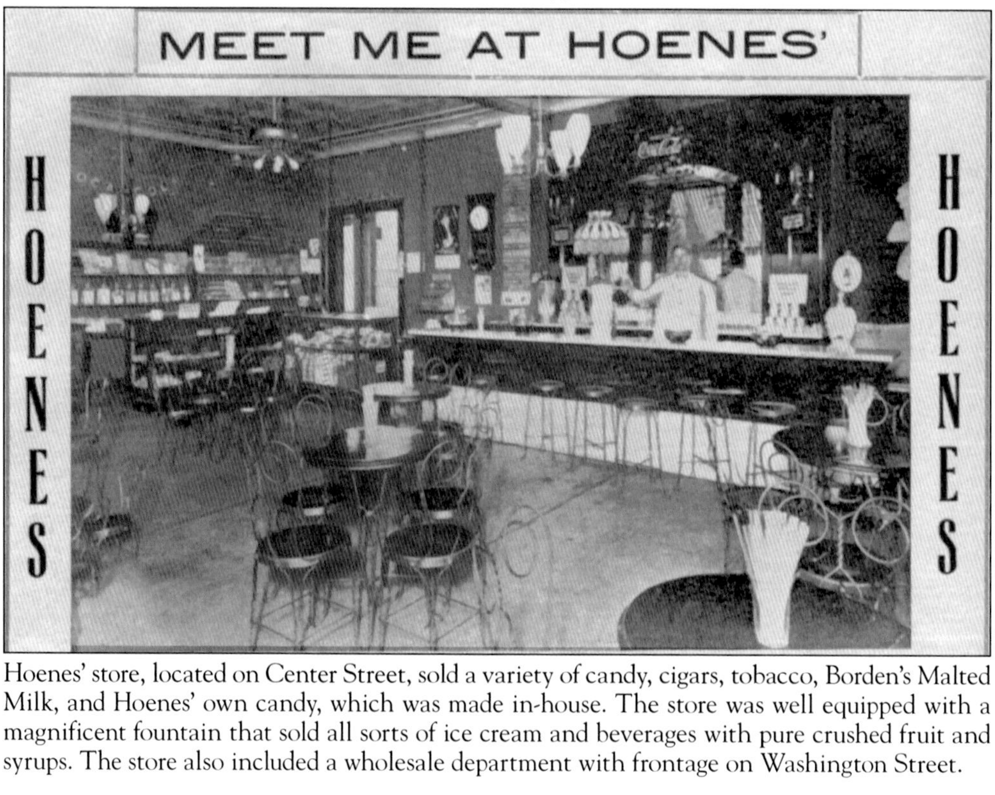

Hoenes' store, located on Center Street, sold a variety of candy, cigars, tobacco, Borden's Malted Milk, and Hoenes' own candy, which was made in-house. The store was well equipped with a magnificent fountain that sold all sorts of ice cream and beverages with pure crushed fruit and syrups. The store also included a wholesale department with frontage on Washington Street.

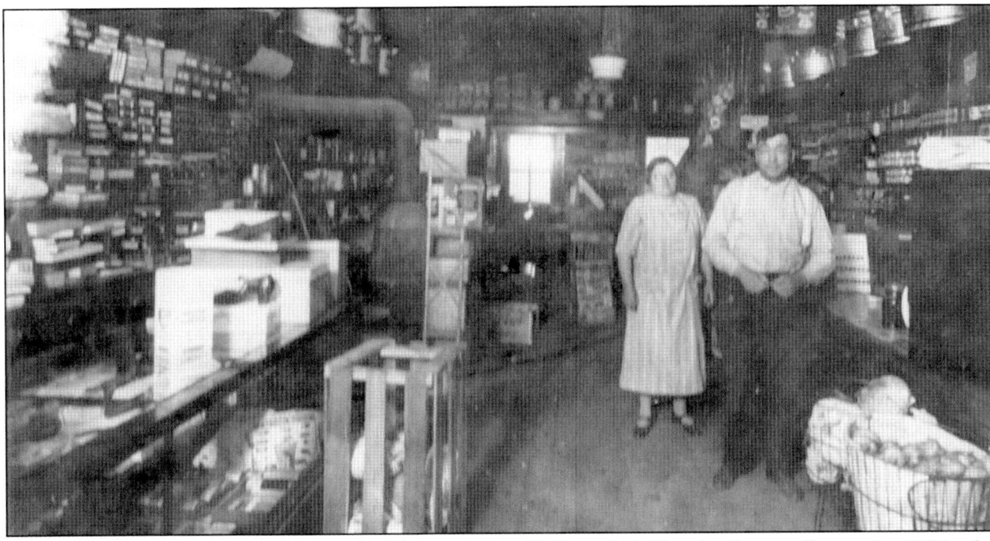

B.W. Sennett & Son crockery started business in 1880 at 113 North Center Street. In 1913, the main floor was filled with dry goods, dresses, silks, Elliott's table linens, Warner's rust proof corsets, notions, undergarments, hosiery, and Butterick patterns. The basement was filled with crockery, china, Fostoria fine glassware, Johnson's English porcelains, and all sorts of home furnishings.

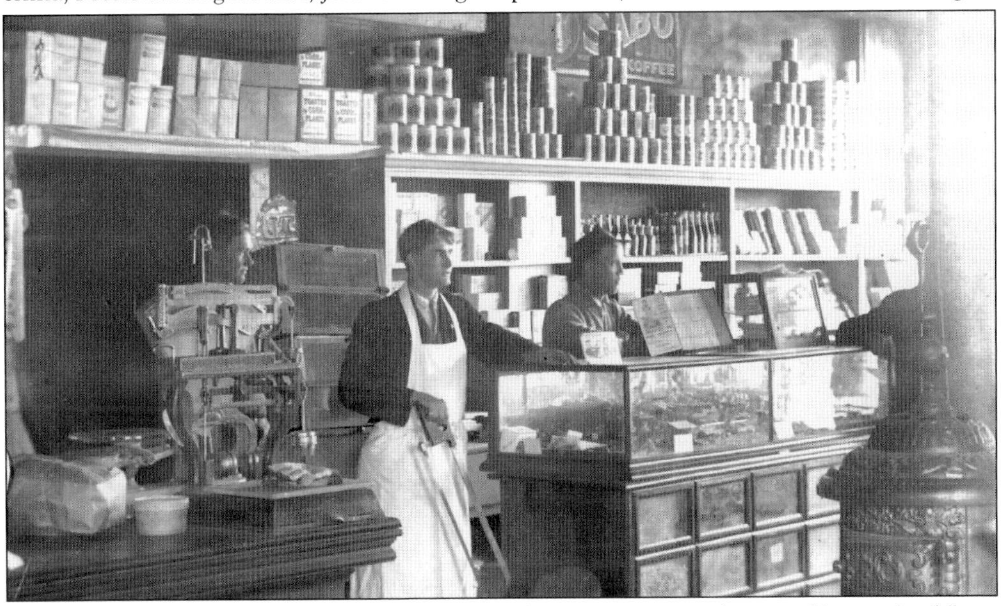

As Bob Lindsey remembers, in the 1800s grocery shopping meant picking up 50 pounds of flour, 50 pounds of potatoes, and 25 pounds of sugar along with a list of other essentials, such as thread to mend socks and borax to wash hair. The cloth sacks that animal feed came in were made into aprons and dresses. The grocery stores did not let customers go down the aisles as they do today—rather, the grocer would take the customer's list, go get the items, and bring them to the cash box. The grocer would have them added up in his head by the time he returned with the groceries. In the 1940s, there was a grocery store on the corner of Main Street and First Avenue that was very tiny; however, products on shelves reached clear to the ceiling. A rolling ladder ran down the aisles so the grocer could climb up and retrieve the items. He also had a long pole with squeezers on the end for cereal boxes and such.

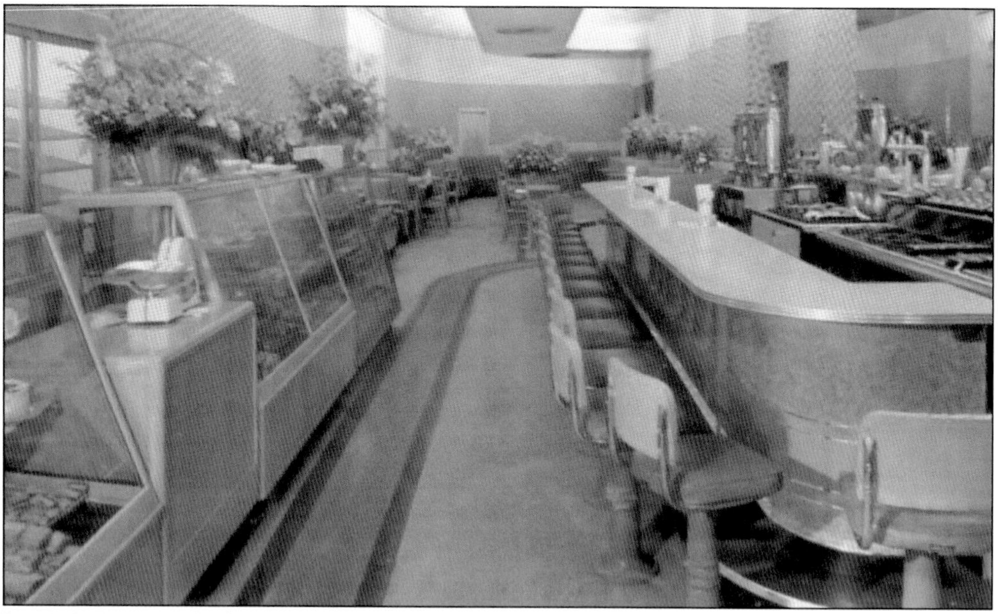

In 1912, Peter and Thomas Chappenikis purchased the Arcade Confectionery, and in 1919 William H. Zafiropulos joined his cousins in the business. William opened the Ritz Restaurant and Soda, Pastry, and Candy Shop in 1941 at 22 North Center Street. In 1947, the Ritz Chocolate and Candy Company became incorporated, and the restaurant was part of the corporation. The products were marketed as William and Mary Famous Pennsylvania Candies. The restaurant closed in 1976, and the Ritz Chocolate and Candy Company moved to 46 North Center Street. A new building was constructed at the present location at 1221 North Center in 1995. The Ritz went online in 2006 and, along with the store, is still in business today. It is currently owned and operated by William's son William J. Zaphiris.

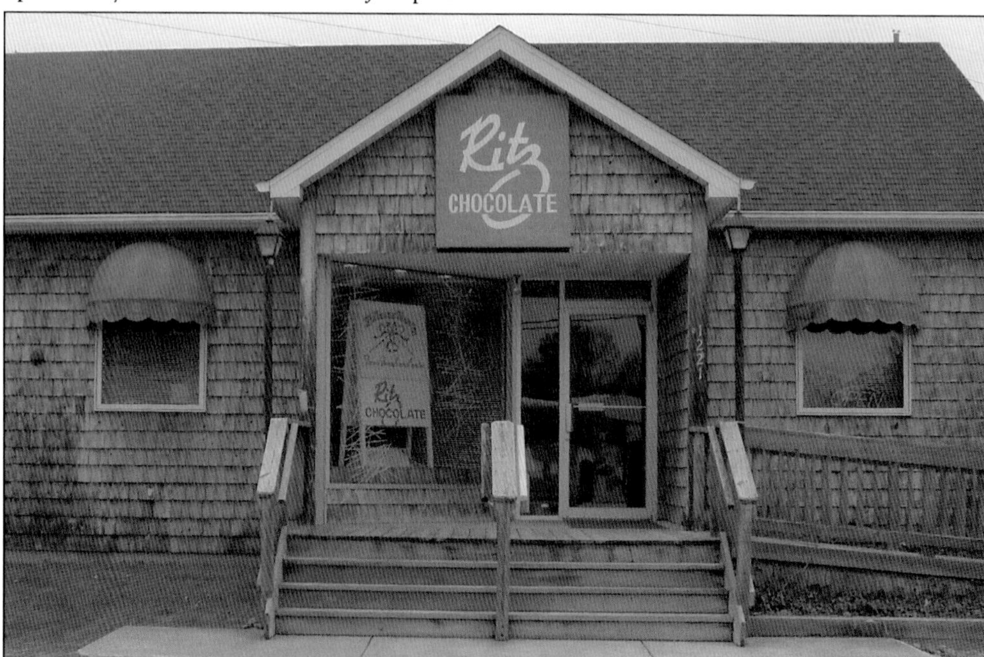

Four

DESIGNED BY A.P. MOUNT

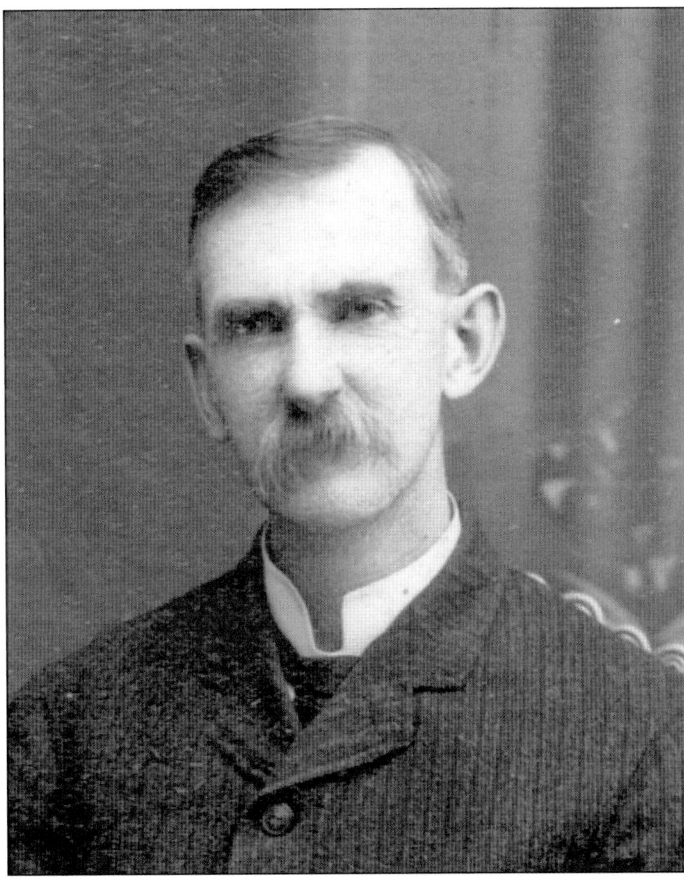

Born in 1851, Aretas Patterson Mount—better known as A.P. Mount—was Corry's most successful architect around the turn of the century, with his office in the Traction Building. Having a thorough knowledge of his profession, he kept busy drawing plans for houses, stores, churches, and large public buildings. The state board awarded him the contract to design the armories in Corry, Warren, and Grove City. (Courtesy of Martha Vincent.)

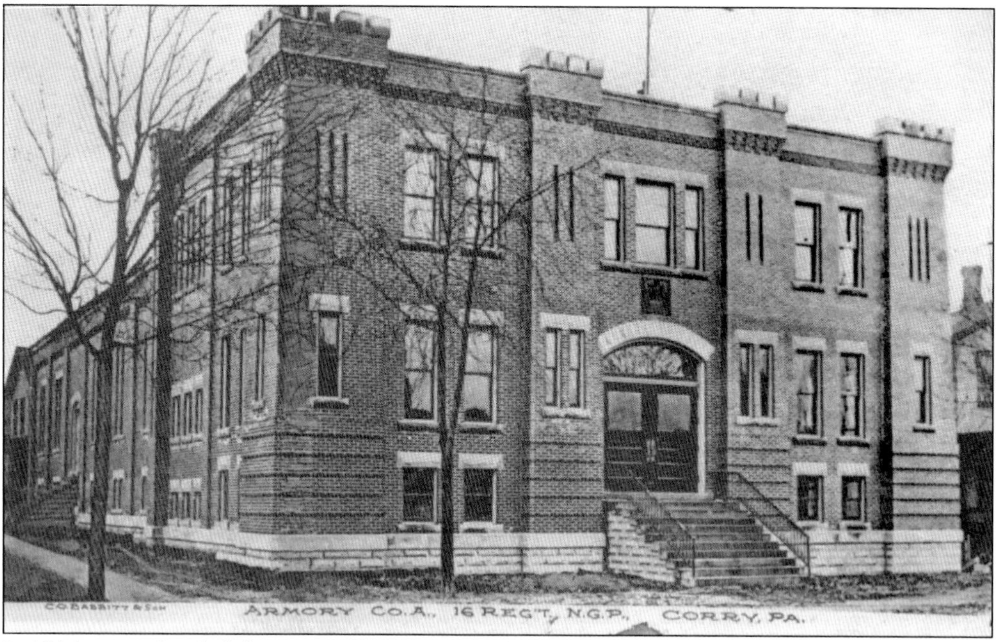

In 1906, it was decided that an armory was needed to house Company A, 16th Regiment Infantry, Pennsylvania National Guard. The state armory board purchased a lot on the corner of Washington and Maple Avenues from the estate of Thomas Edwards (of the Indian medicine company). A.P. Mount drew plans in the Romanesque style, and the contract was awarded to G. Thomas of Corry.

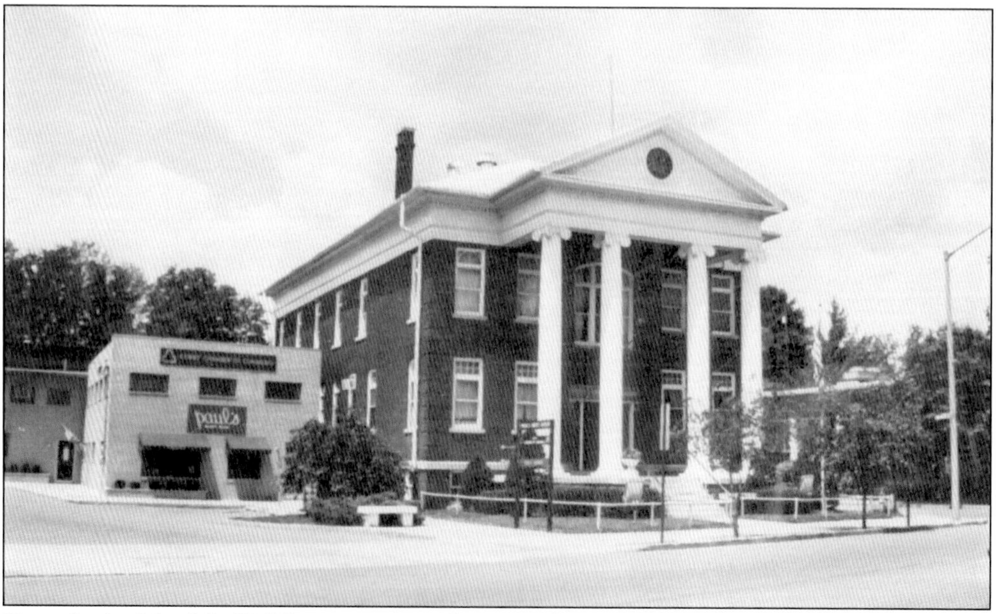

Corry Lodge No. 769, BPOE, was organized on March 26, 1902 with 36 charter members. The first meetings were held at Knights of Pythias Hall in the city building and the Maccabee Hall until their new home was completed on the corner of North Center and Clinton Streets, where the roller-skating rink once stood. The new building was dedicated on December 27, 1912. (Author's collection.)

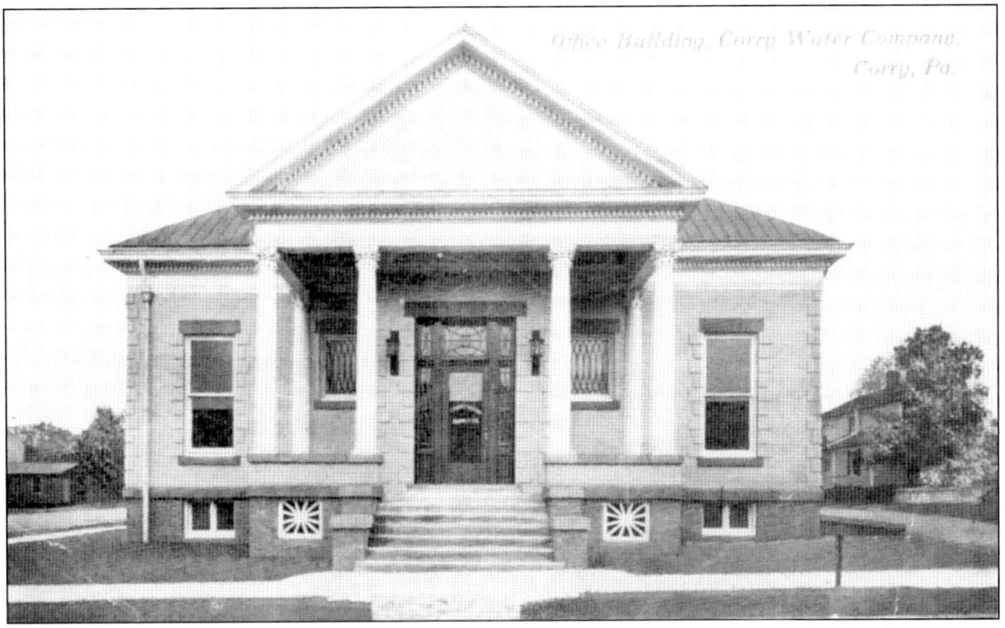

Pure water was pumped from 14 artesian wells north of Corry and forced through the city in a 12-inch main for three miles to the reservoir on the hill south of the city. The city was supplied directly from the pumps when they were in operation. The surplus goes to the reservoir, which holds five million gallons. The office building, which Mount designed, was built in 1908 on Pleasant Street.

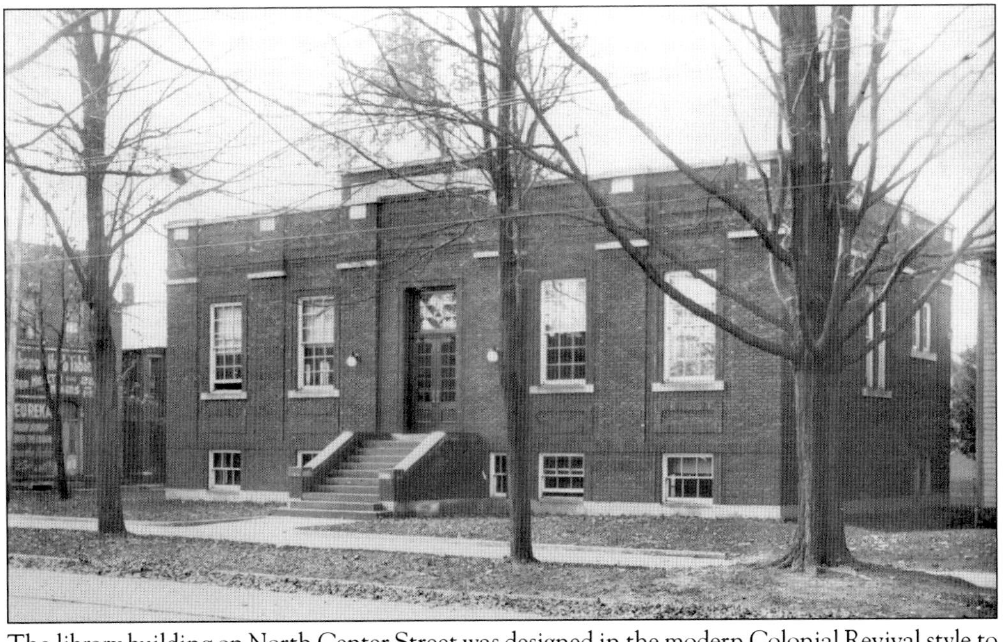

The library building on North Center Street was designed in the modern Colonial Revival style to reflect stability and importance. The project was funded by a grant from the Carnegie Foundation of Pittsburgh, Pennsylvania. The building served the community as a library from January 1919 until 1996, when a new library was constructed on Washington Street. It then became the home of a bar and restaurant.

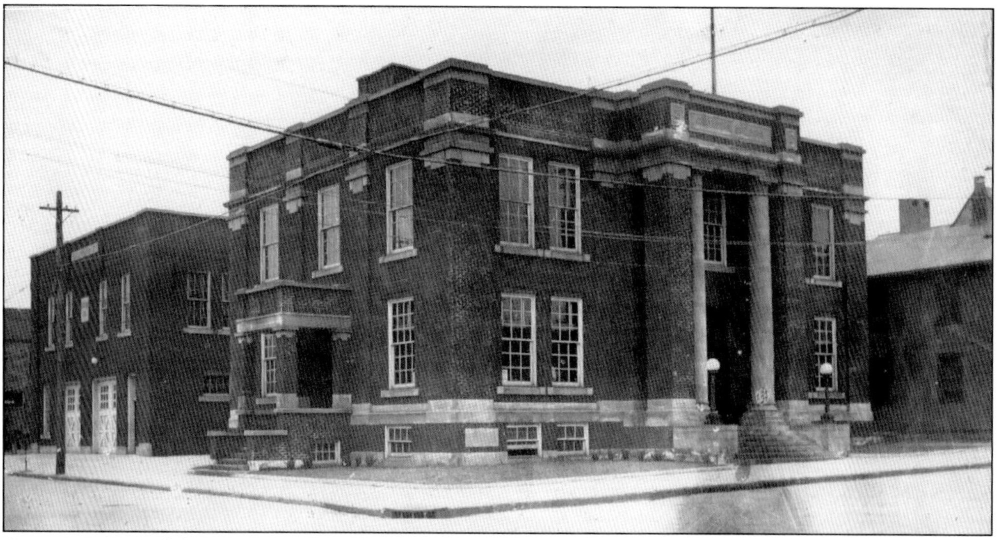

Construction of the new municipal building started in 1919, and it was built of Corry rose craft brick and finished with Ohio grey sandstone. At the main entrance on the left were the offices of the mayor and city clerk. To the right was a large meeting room of the city commission. On the second floor were two rooms for the board of commerce and two large assembly rooms. The police station was in the basement, with its entrance facing east South Street.

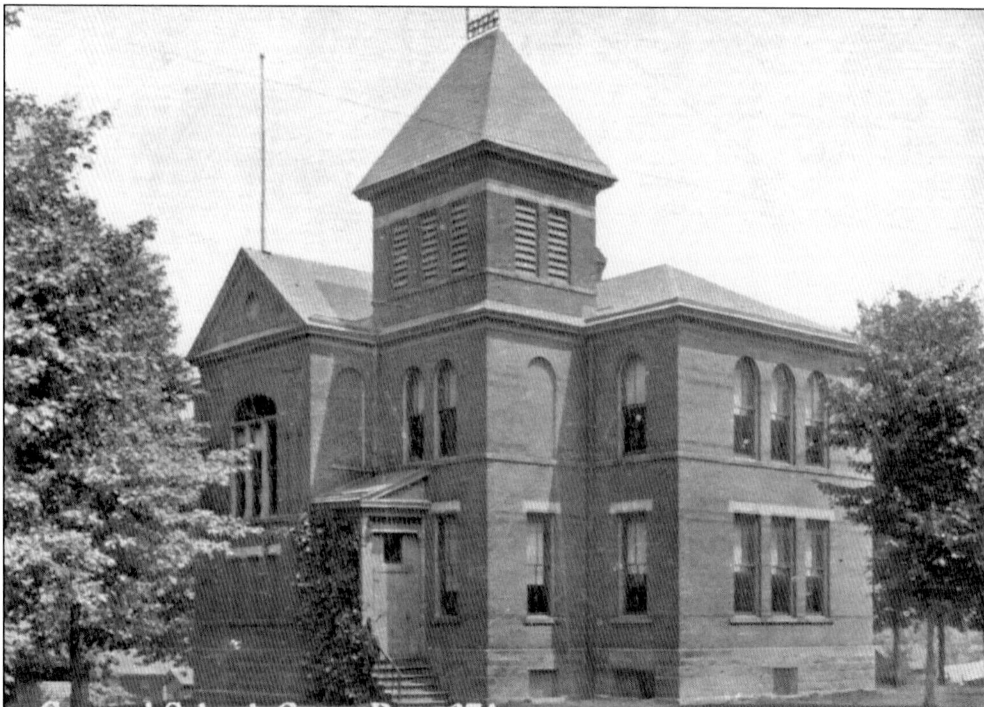

The educational showcase and the root of the Corry school system, the Concord School, was built in 1886 to replace the wooden structure that was built in 1863, when the population of Corry was 1,600 and the Civil War was one year old. The building was replaced in 1964 and used until 2007. The students were then sent to the new Corry Elementary School on Wayne Street.

Methodists have been active in the area since 1830. Around 1864, a wood-framed church was built on the corner of Concord and East South Street. It served the congregation until 1903, when the new beautiful church, designed by Mount, was built on the corner of South Center and East Pleasant Streets. The new church could seat 300 to 500 people. In 1913, a new Estey pipe organ was installed.

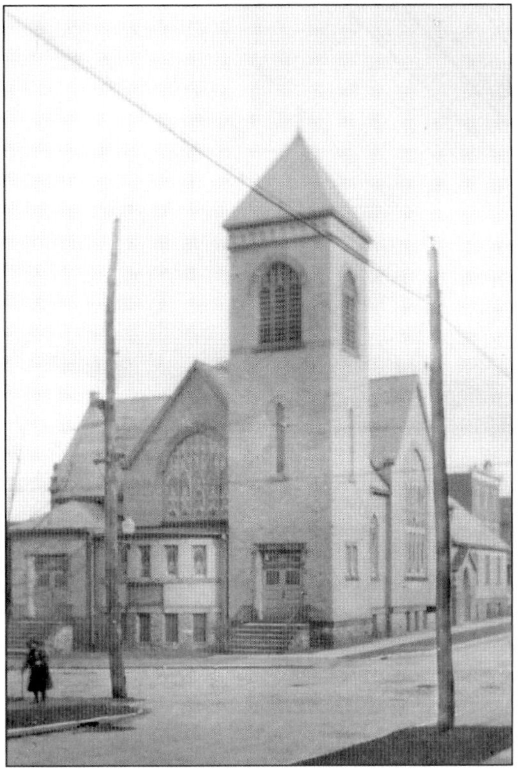

First Baptist Church was organized on October 18, 1863, with seven members. The meetings were held in a hall on the second floor of the building on Washington and West Wayne Streets (now Mead Avenue). In 1864, a church was built on the southwest corner of Second Avenue and West South Street. In 1895, a new church was built of light-colored brick on the site of the first building.

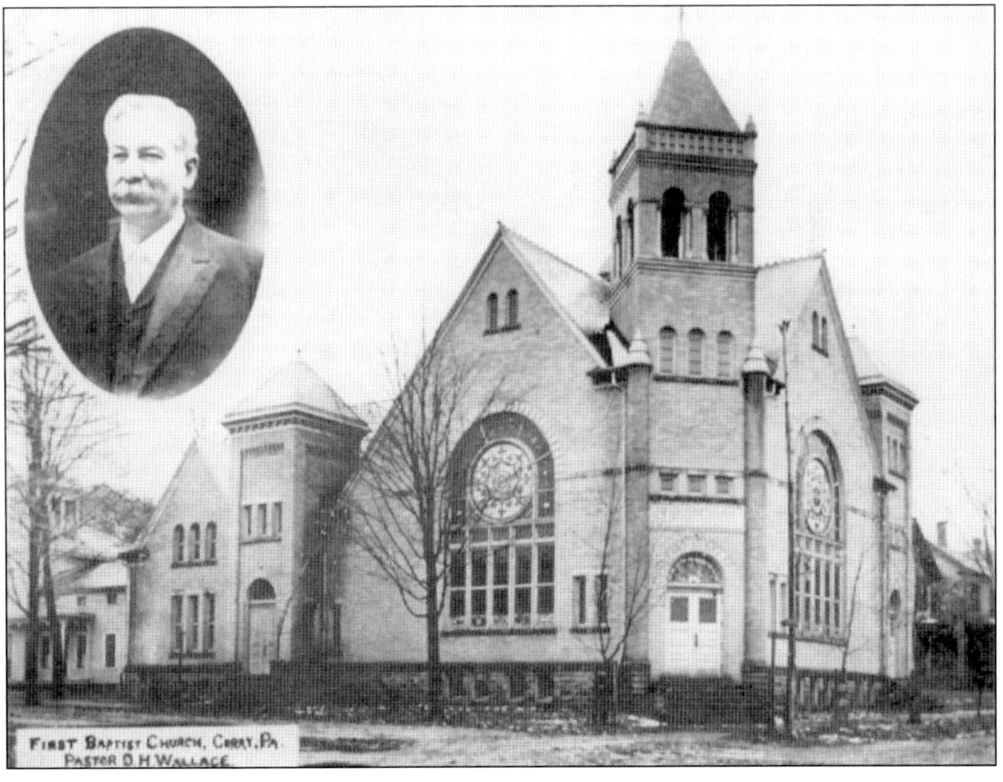

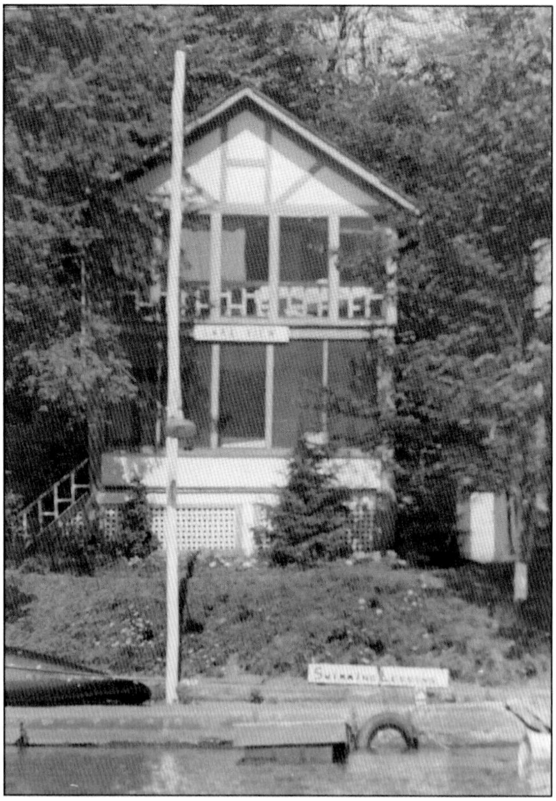

Mount also designed many cottages at Findley Lake, New York. Federal Eliphalet Whittlesey, president of Raymonds Manufacturing; Asa Howard of The Howard Broom Company; and trolley conductor Oscar Fritz are among some of the Corry residents who hired him to design their cottages in the early 1900s. There were so many people from Corry who had cottages at the lake that one area was nicknamed "Little Corry."

In 1919, the construction of the fire department building on Pleasant Street commenced. The Stanford hose company's new quarters, located on the second story of the fire department building, was complete with a pool room, card room, and meeting room. The first floor housed two trucks, bunkrooms, the alarm system, and storerooms. There is one department on each side of the tracks, since trains stopped traffic as they waited at the depots.

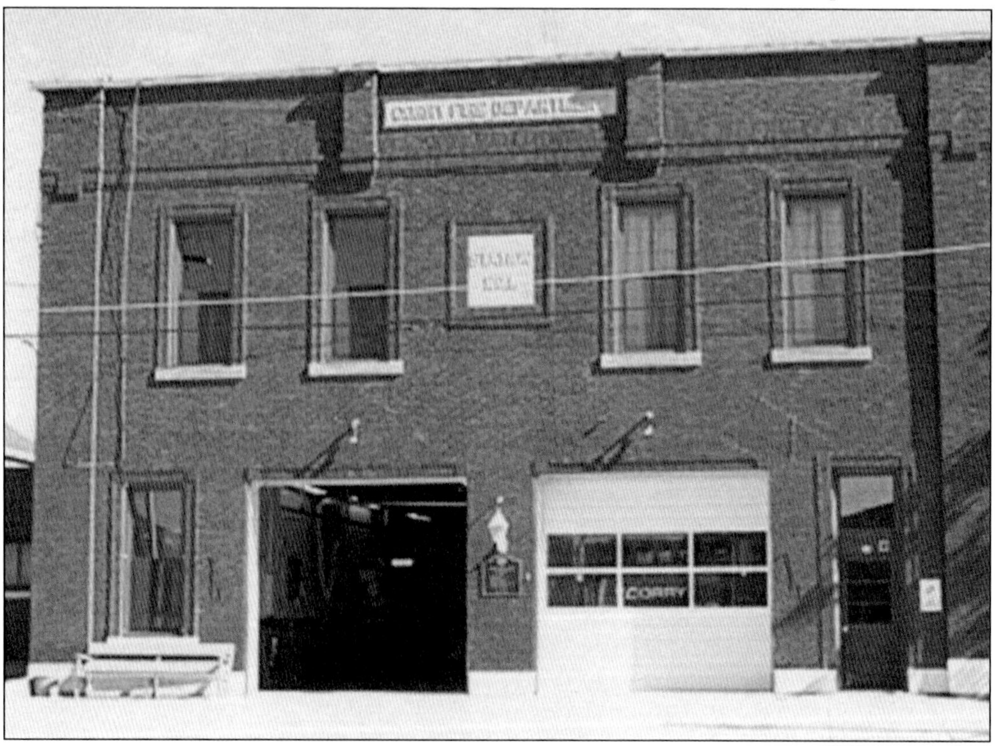

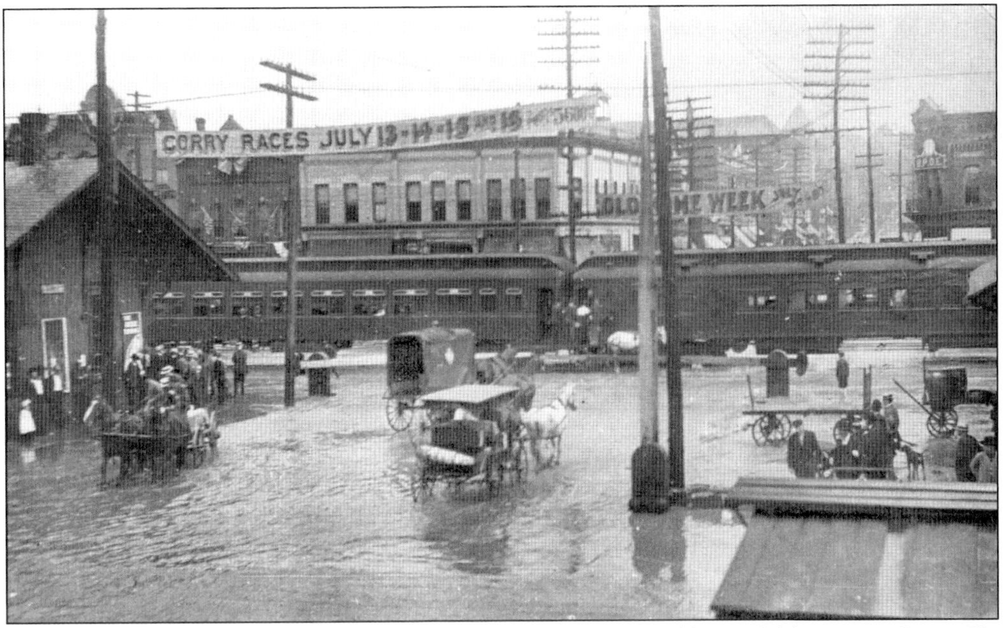

A.P. Mount designed many of the most important buildings and beautiful homes in Corry. He designed both Barlow blocks on the opposite corners of South Center and Main Streets. He designed the Whittlesey house on West Church Street in 1902, and in 1916 he designed the J.J. Desmond house. He also designed his own home on West Church Street. The ones listed are still standing as of 2011.

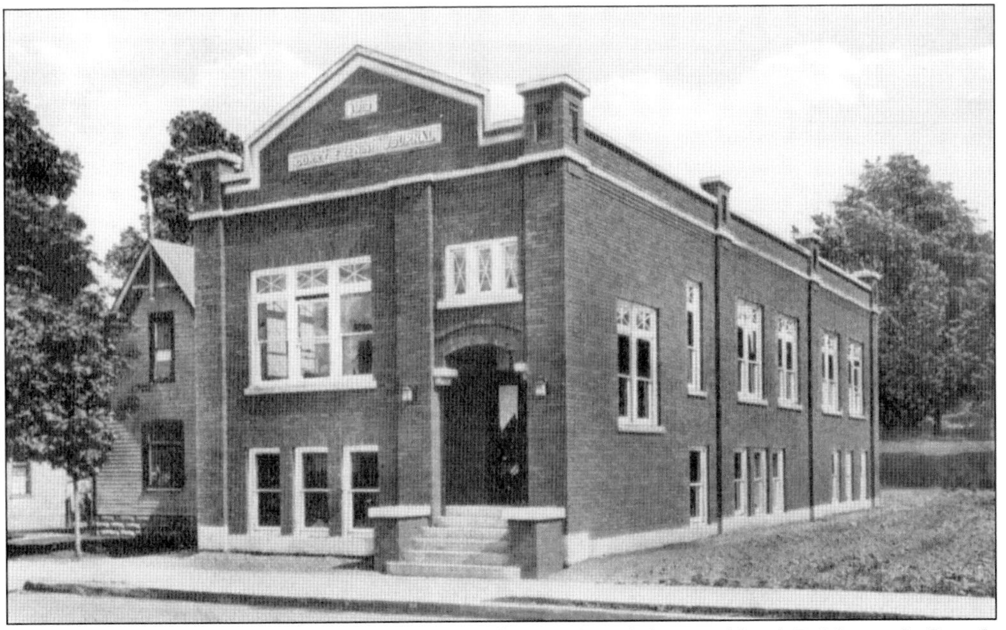

The *Corry Evening Journal* building was erected in 1913 and designed by A.P. Mount & Son. It provided accommodations for the business office, editorial rooms, stock rooms, and commercial printing department. The exterior is constructed of Turkestan brick and trimmed with grey Ohio sandstone. The floors are three-inch thick southern pine overlaid with a seven-eighths-inch select hard maple top floor. The walls are oak and yellow pine.

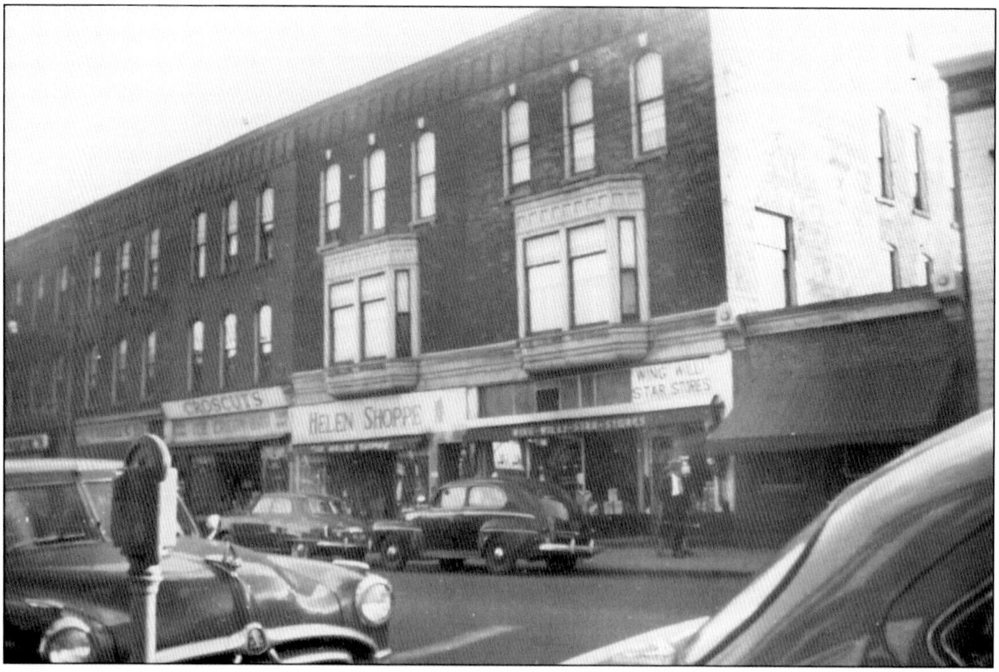

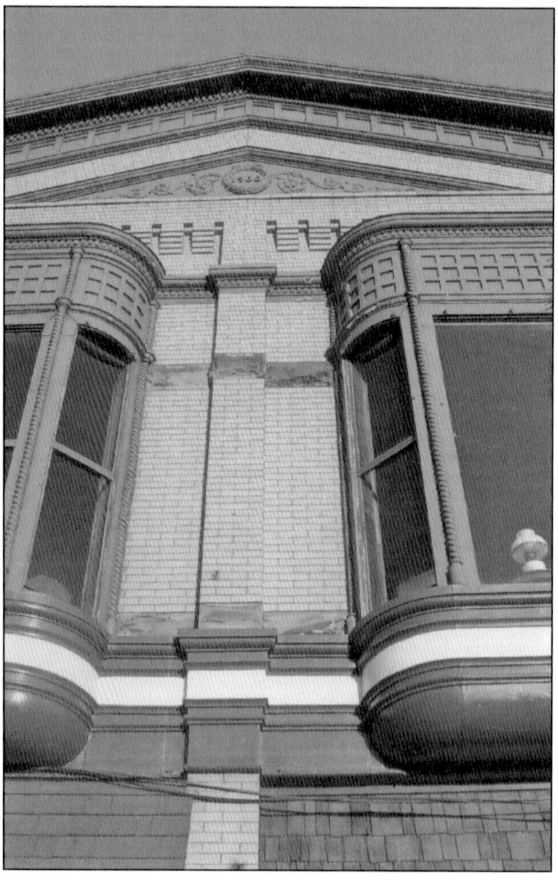

Over the past 100 years, memories have faded, original drawings burned or lost, and many remain in an unknown attic. The buildings in this chapter have seen many businesses constantly moving in and out of their shelter, but over 10 decades later, they are still in use in the 21st century. (Courtesy of Bob May.)

A.P. Mount was born in 1851. His career as an architect spanned four decades, starting in his younger years, when he was a builder. This provided him with a thorough understanding of what he was drawing. As part of a 1902 fundraising pamphlet of favorite quotations of the Corry people, his wife entered the following quote: "Every noble life leaves the fiber of it interwoven forever in the work of the world" (Ruskin). Mount died in 1928. (Author's collection.)

Five

Built in Corry

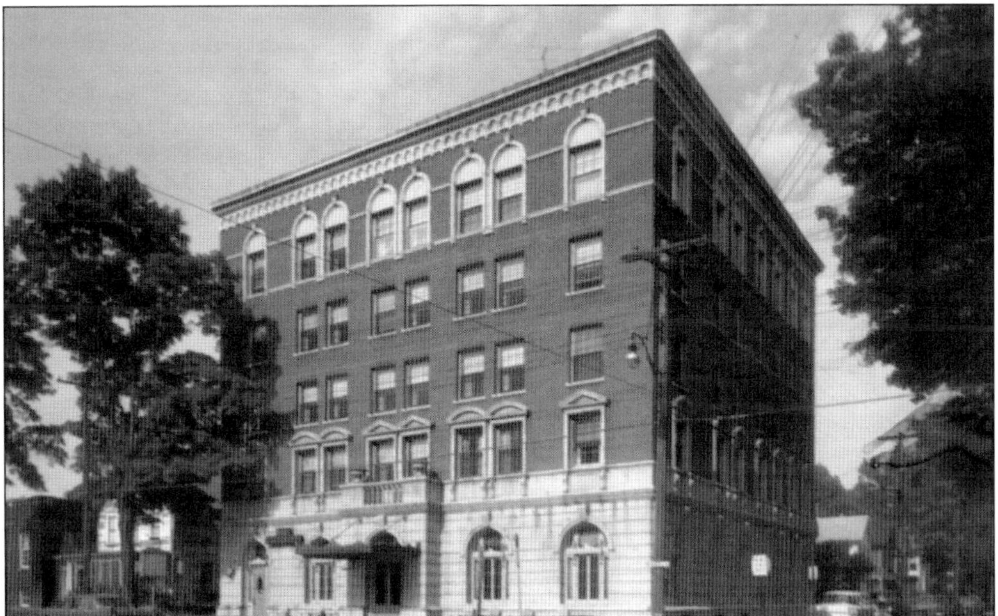

As soon as the town started to develop economically and a source of income or trading agreement had been established, people began to gather into groups of their shared religion and other common interests. They met wherever they could, many times using the same large rooms over the stores on Main Street on different days. As soon as possible, they built their own meeting rooms and churches for each faith.

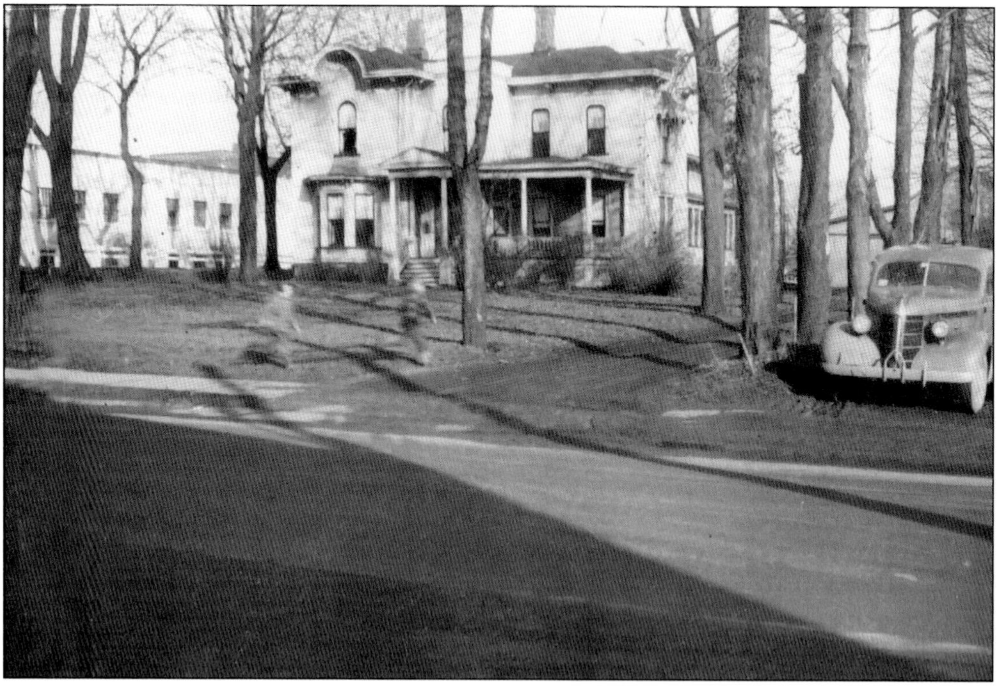

Great changes have been made in 150 years on every corner. One example is just off Center Street, where Hiram Cory's home was in the West Washington Street area prior to 1861. As Corry developed into a thriving town, big Victorian homes were built. The flow of time, however, turned these big homes into Rich's Cancer Hospital and the VFW headquarters. Again, time changed the area into the A&P store and the new VFW headquarters, with a full-sized plane displayed on the front lawn and parking lots. The VFW became the Salvation Army Church, and the grocery store gave way to the new library in 1996. (Below, author's collection.)

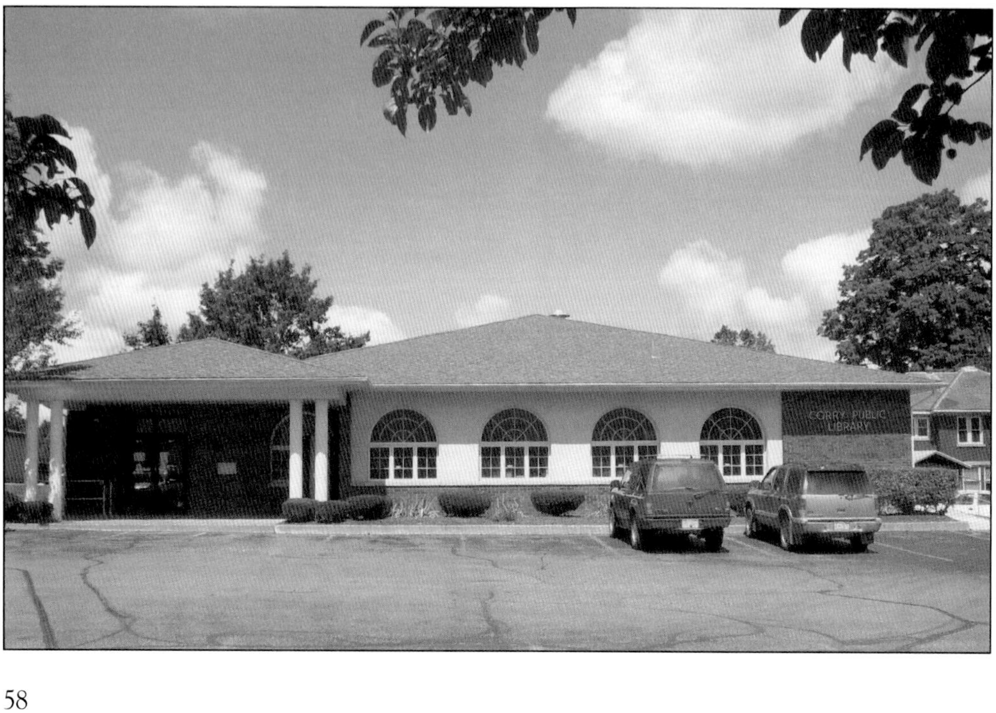

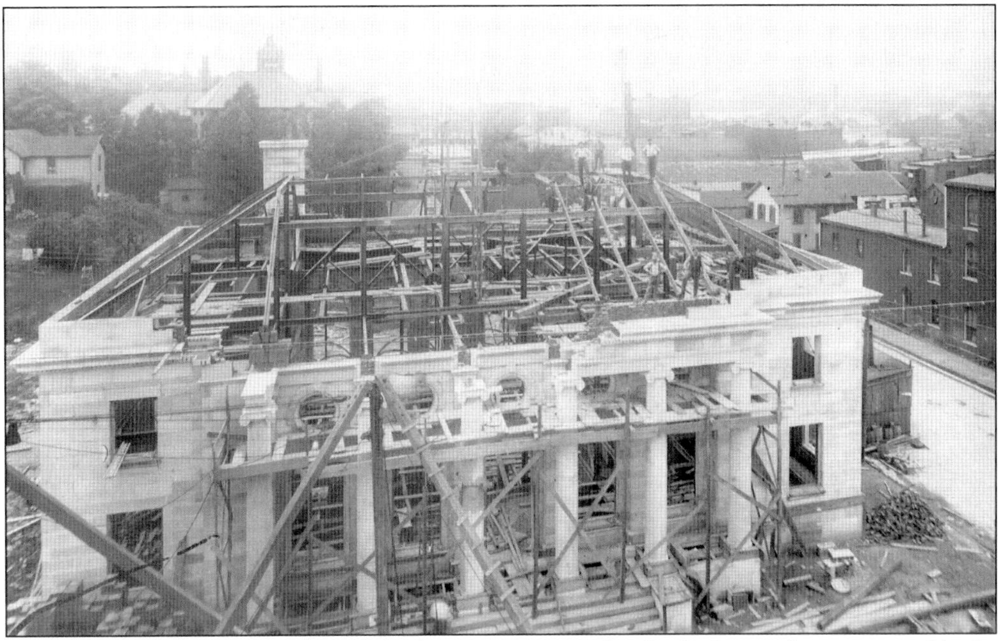

The new, Colonial-style post office, built in 1914, was 88 feet by 58 feet in dimension and had a two-story Mezzanine. Built with limestone from Indiana with steps made of granite from South Carolina, it was one of the most expensive post offices built at that time. One of the most interesting things constructed in this building is the "lookout" system, so an inspector could "spy" on the clerks and other employees. This system relied on secret passageways with openings that had louver-slat windows looked out into the rooms, through which the inspector could observe anyone and not be seen. These passageways connected with each other, so an employee could be followed throughout the entire building.

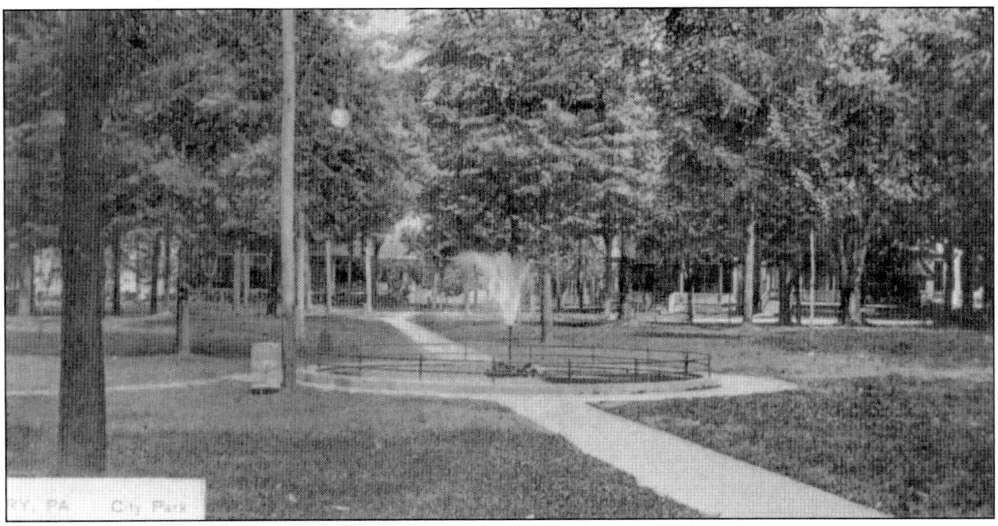

William Henry Leland Smith (for whom Smith Street was named) was sent to Corry by Samuel Downer to buy land for the Downer Oil Company and eventually became Corry's first mayor. Smith donated five acres of land to be used as a park, and the Grand Army of the Republic veterans erected the Civil War monument, dedicating it in June 1901. Planted with trees, it became a prime location for new houses.

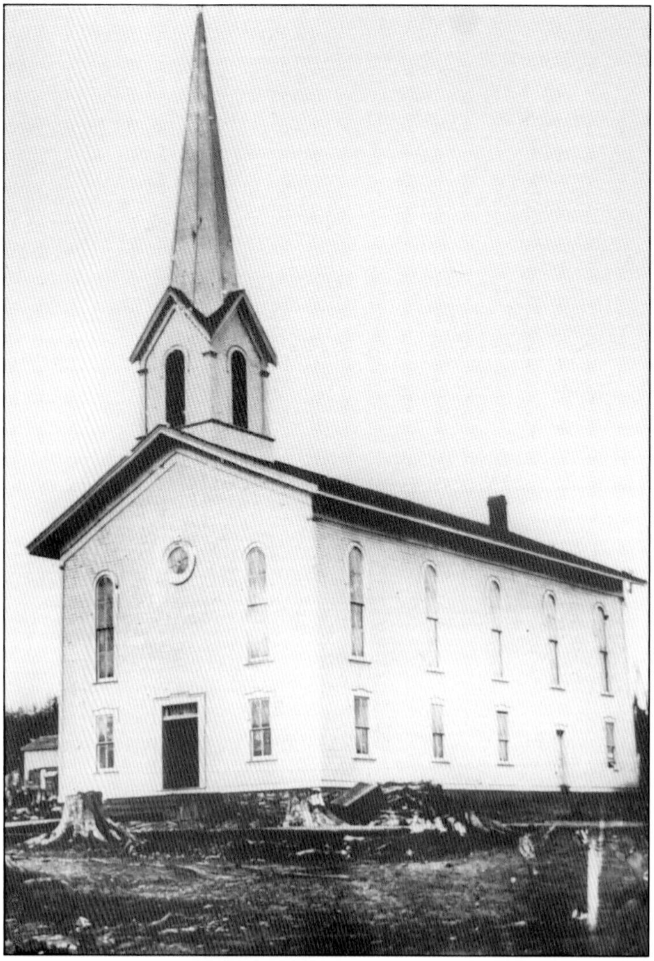

The first Methodist church opened in the summer of 1862 in a shanty on Concord Street near South Street. In 1863, a Sunday school class was held in the second story of a new unfinished building at the corner of West Washington and Mead. By 1864, the membership was large enough to build a church on the corner of Concord and East Pleasant Streets. It served the congregation until 1903.

Kurtz Brass Bed Company remodeled the old Methodist church on the corner of Concord and East Pleasant Streets in 1903. The company produced 40 beds daily for eight years. In 1911, a huge plant was built that measured 300 by 100 feet on the east end near the Erie Railroad, and turned out more than 200 beds daily. Kurtz became one of the largest brass bed factories in the country.

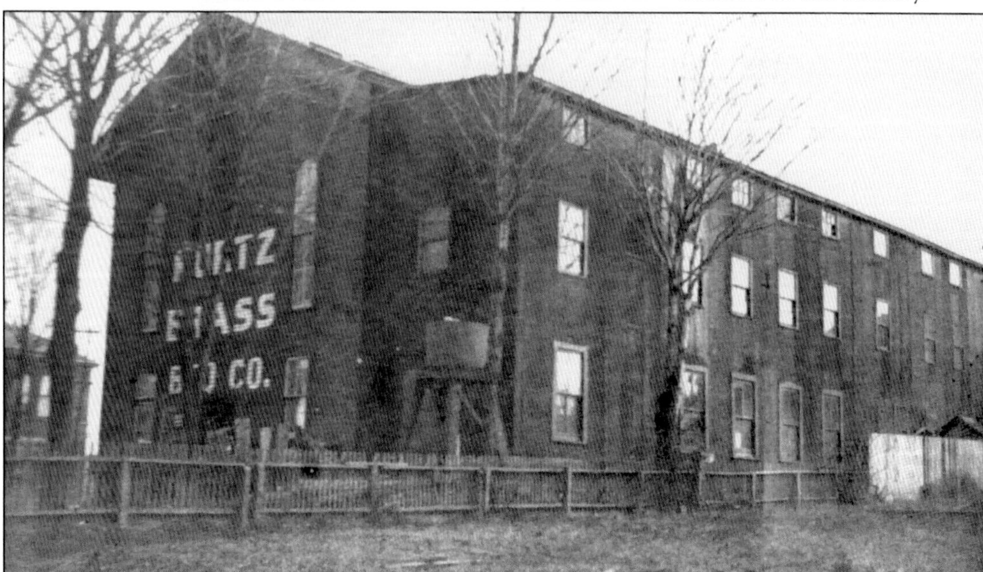

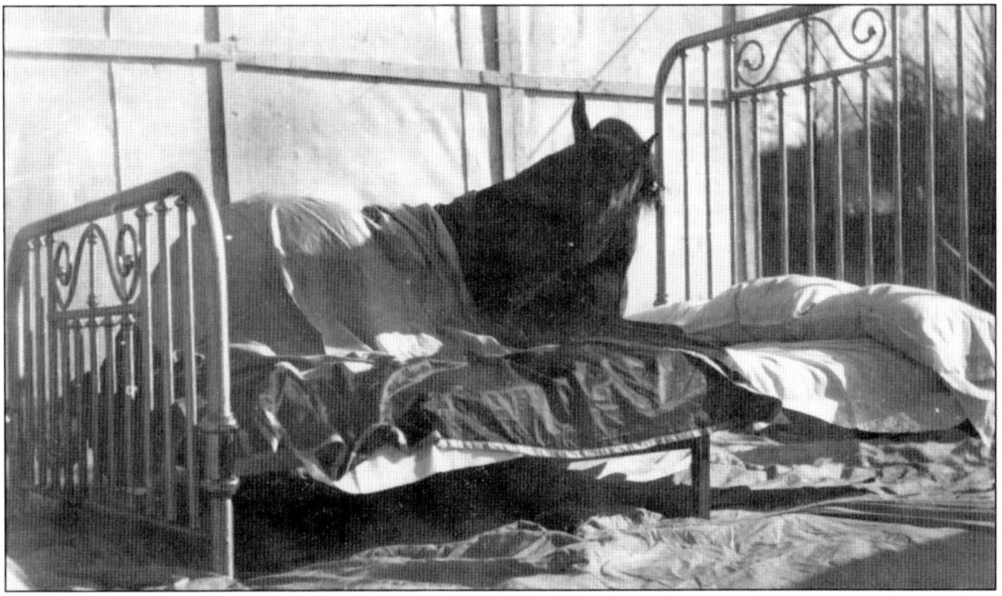

Otis and Nettie Houghtaling, of 458 East Main Street, used a brass bed exclusively built by the Kurtz Brass Bed Company that would be big and strong enough for their celebrated and trained horse, Colonel Fred, to sleep in for their act. In 1912, the manager of one of the biggest circuses in the country contacted the company to have a similar bed constructed that would be sturdy enough for an elephant.

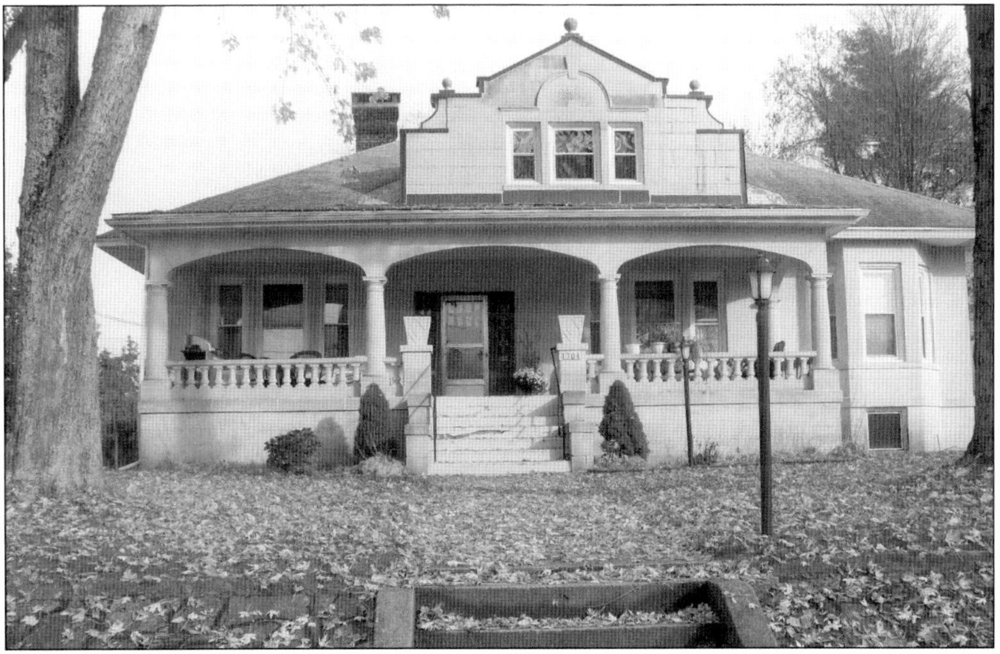

On the same corner of Concord and East South Streets, a private home was built with the excess granite and other materials from the construction of the Corry Post Office in 1914. After being used as a private home for decades, the house and a trust fund to remodel and maintain it was willed by Sila Foster in 1959 to the Methodist Church to be used for the parsonage. (Author's collection.)

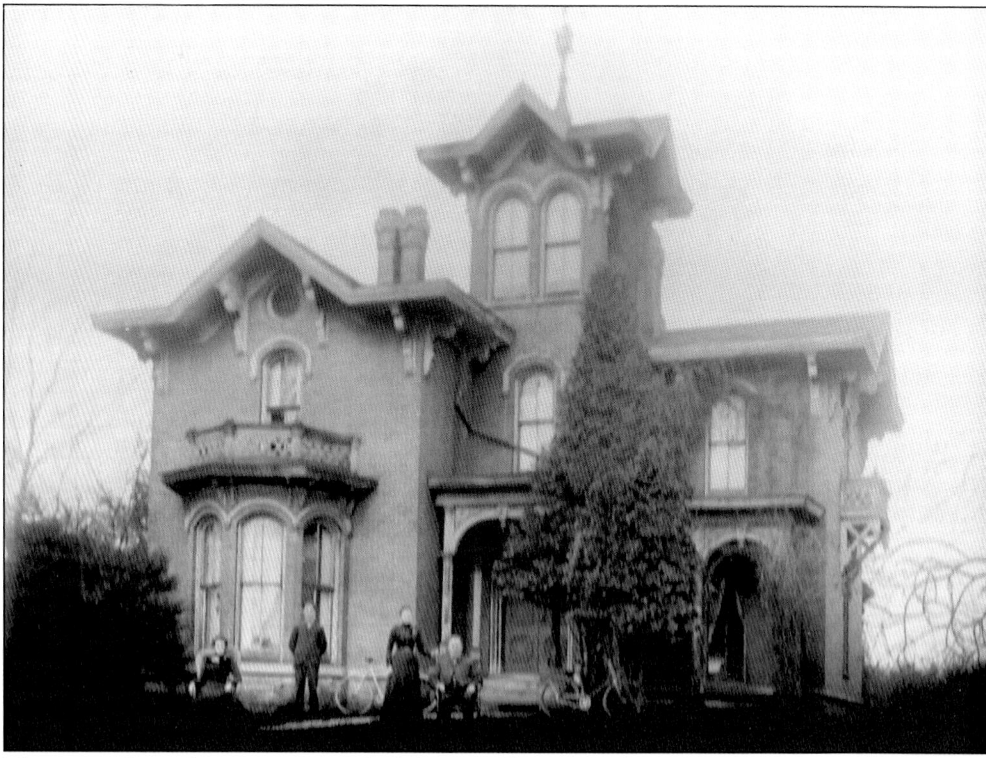

This magnificent house was typical of dozens of houses built in the 1860s and 1870s. This one was on the north side of Washington between Mott Street and First Avenue. Pictured in 1875 from left to right are Ella Coyle, Mark (son), Clara (daughter), and Lawrence Coyle. This house later became the VFW meeting place, torn down to be replaced by their new headquarters. The Salvation Army offices replaced the VFW in 1984.

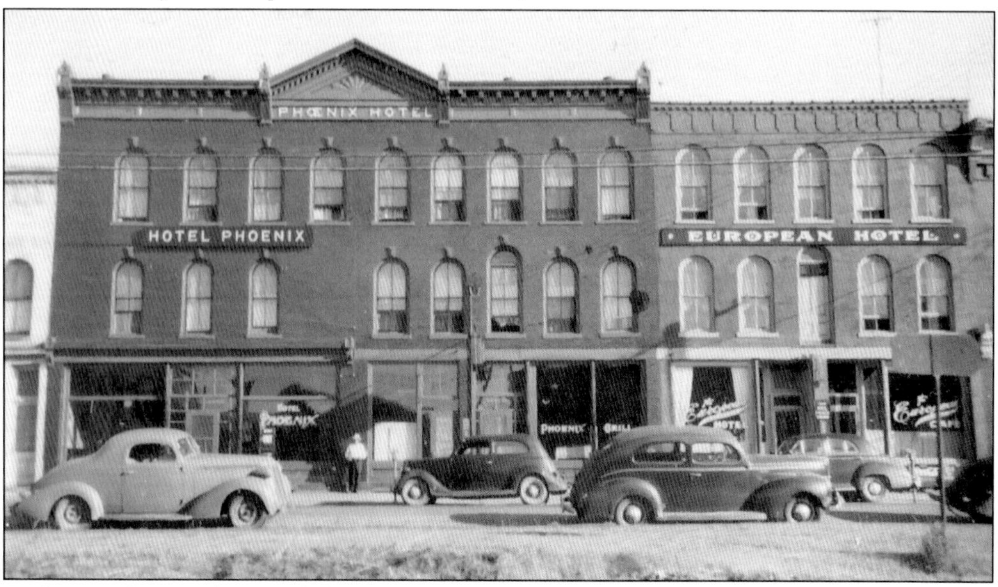

Right next-door to the Hotel Phoenix, or Phoenix Hotel (pictured earlier on page 45), was the European Hotel. The vehicles date this image to around the 1930s.

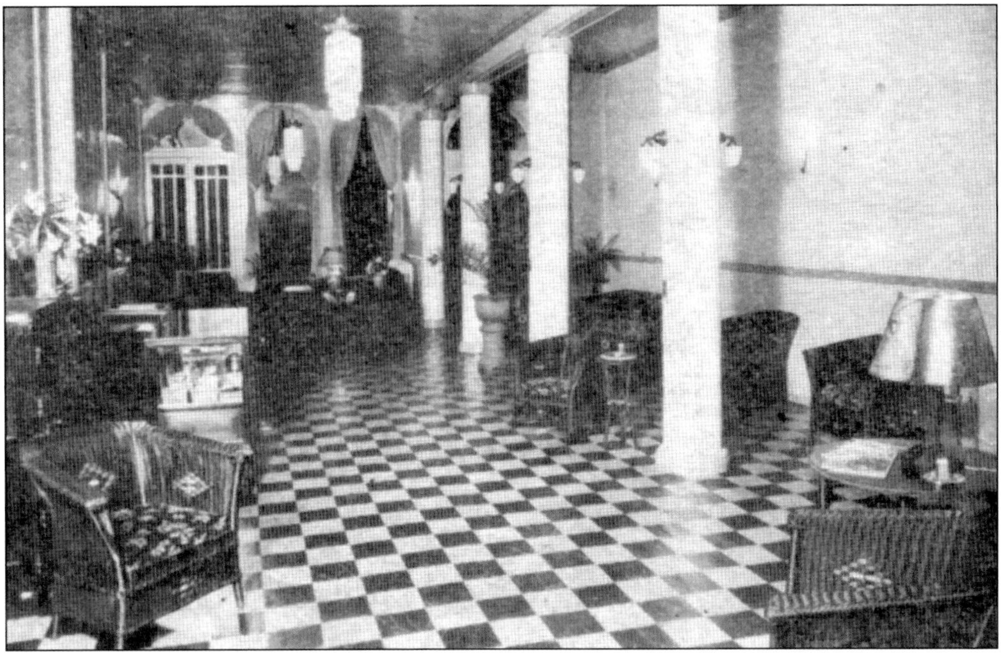

The Hotel Corry opened for business in 1925, and for 66 years it served as a hotel and restaurant. In the early days, chairs were placed out front for overnight guests and passersby to sit, visit, and watch the traffic go by. By the 1970s, it was known as the Corry Motor Inn, and then as the Corrian. In 1991, it became the Corry Higher Education building.

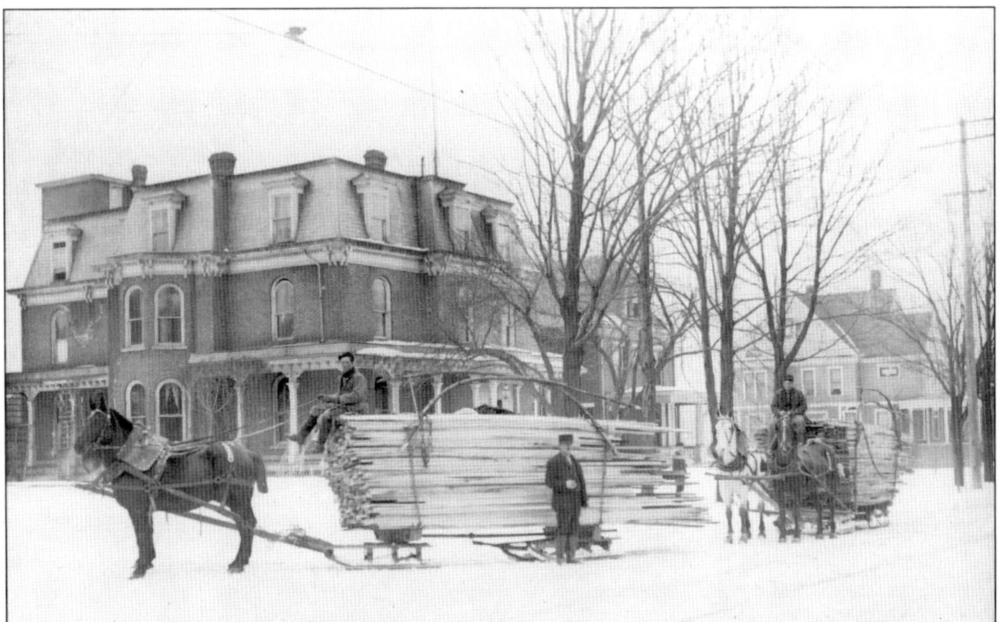

In 1896, the Corry Hospital and Training School for Nurses was built on the corner of Center and Smith Streets. It was so successful that, in 1909, a third floor was added that had a capacity of 60 beds, many times filled to the limit. Around 1912, an operating room was added. In 1904, a very fine nurse's cottage was built next to the hospital.

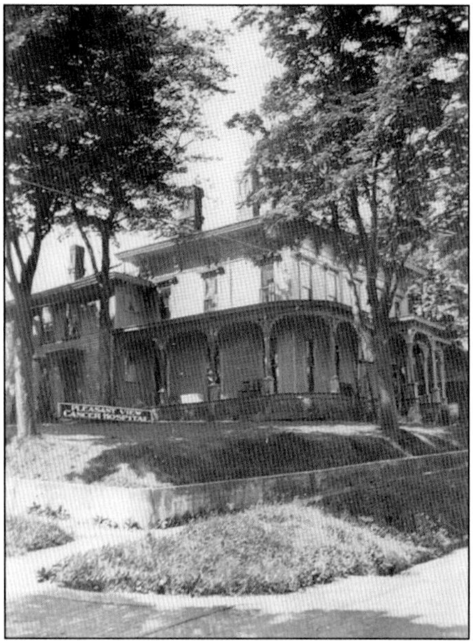

Dr. J.W. Irwin managed the Pleasant View Cancer Hospital on West Pleasant Street. Born in Canada and educated at the University of Michigan, he practiced medicine in various places before moving to Corry in 1921. Bernice Lindsey is pictured here at the cancer hospital just after graduating from the nursing school, which was located next to the old hospital on the corner of Center and Smith Streets.

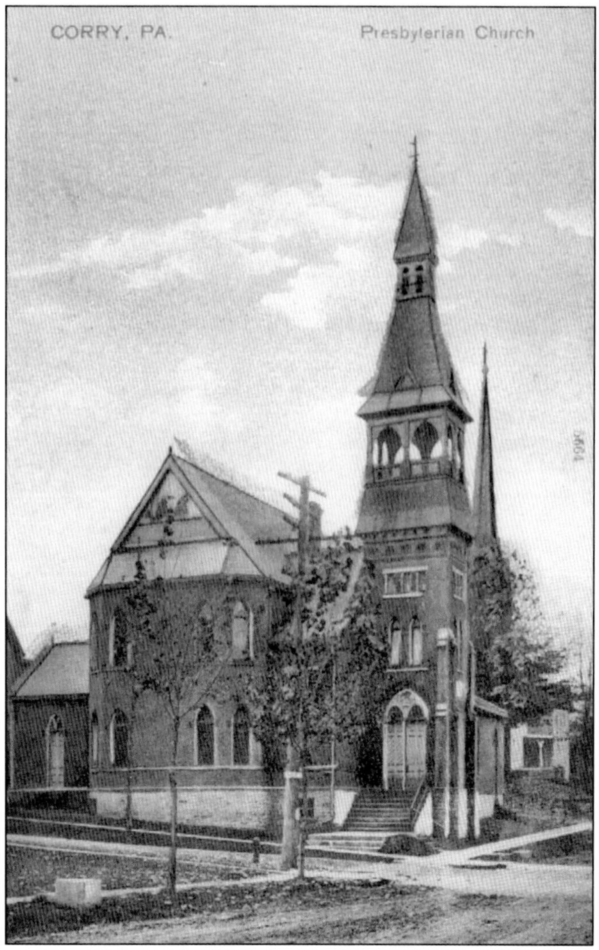

The first Presbyterian Church was organized on January 18, 1864, in the Concord Street schoolhouse. In its first year, there were 21 members. The first services were held at the schoolhouse on alternate Sabbaths. They shared with the Methodist Episcopal Church the McKenzie's Hall on Main Street and the Continental Hall on the corner of Second and Pleasant Streets. In 1866, a new church was built on the South Center.

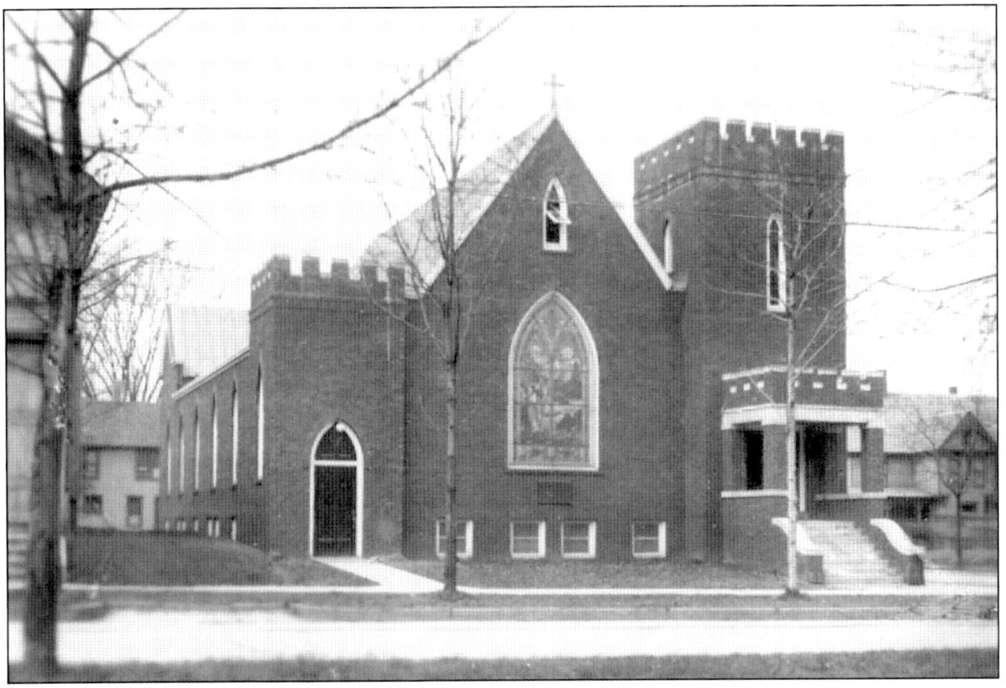

In 1861, there was no one settled where Corry would be; however, in 1864, there were 7,000 people living in Corry. The first services of the Episcopal Church were held in that year in McKenzie Hall. In 1865, the parish was organized, and they bought land on the corner of Center and West Smith Streets and started building a church. In 1913, the congregation numbered 182 members and the church school taught 60 students.

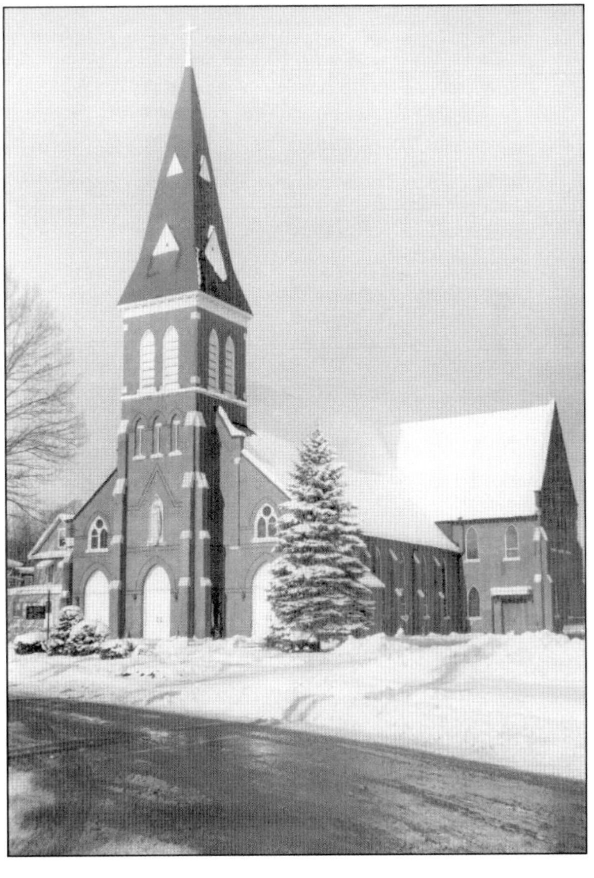

St. Thomas Roman Catholic Church was build in 1862 and dedicated by Bishop Younge, with Rev. Thomas Lonergan having the duties of being the first priest. It is located on Washington Street at the end of First Avenue.

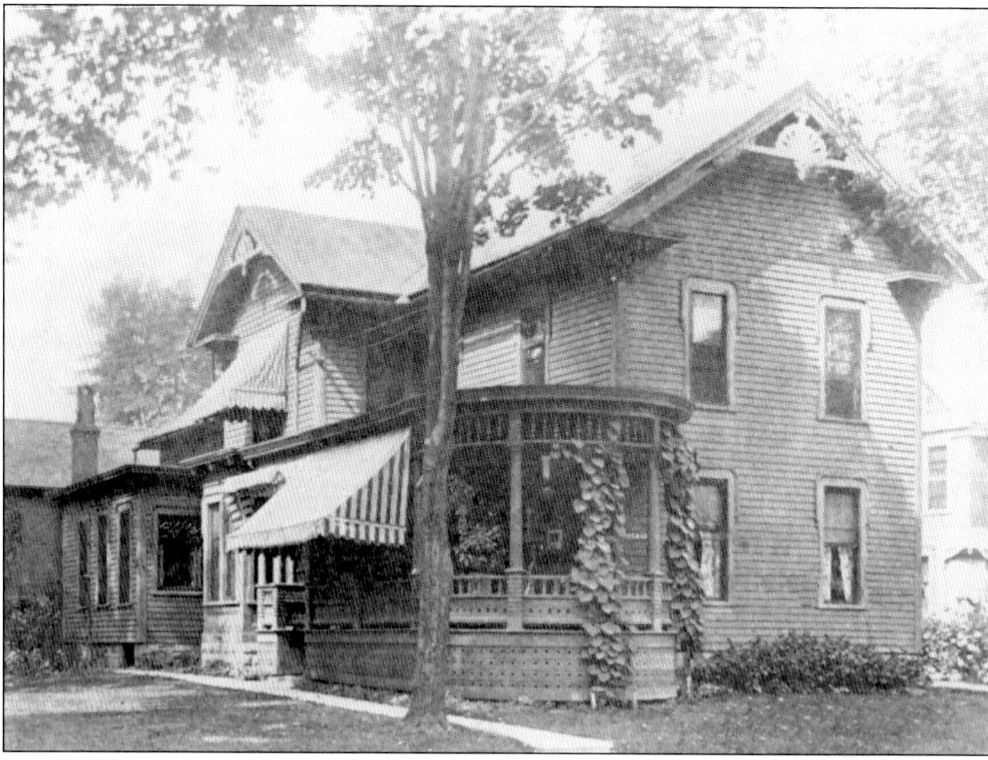

The Kibler house was built in 1867 on the corner of West Park Place and North Center Street. Mary Ann Gentilman became a nurse in 1930 and married Dr. John Kibler, who owned the house. After he passed away, she decided to become a doctor. Because of her age, she was unable to go to school in the states, so she learned how to speak Spanish and was accepted into medical school in Mexico. Afterwards, she became a well-known doctor in Corry. She later won the election for mayor and still holds the distinction of being the city's only female mayor. The house was brick-veneered in the early 1970s.

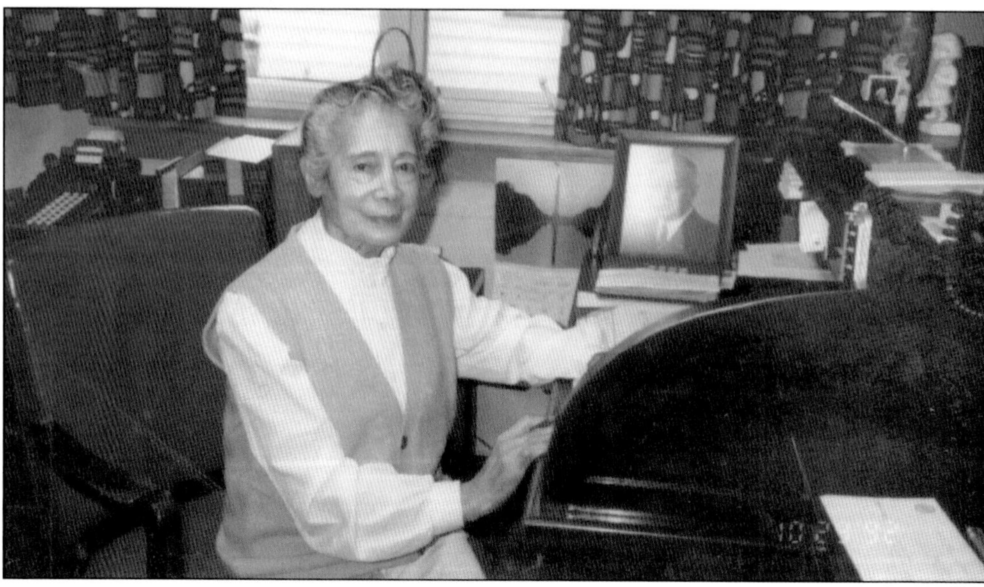

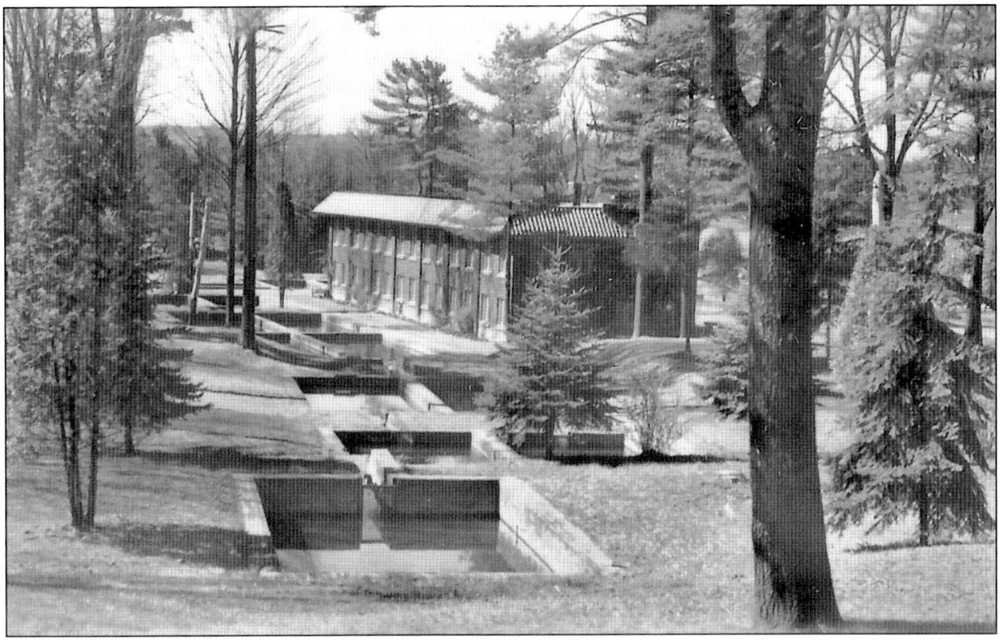

The Corry Fish Hatchery was established in 1876 by the Pennsylvania Fish Commission. It is the longest continuously operated hatchery this side of the Mississippi. It is supplied by the abundant springs of uniform flow and temperature. For years people viewed it as a park and would walk around the property and enjoy the trees and fountains and feed the huge carp and observe the tiny newly hatched fish.

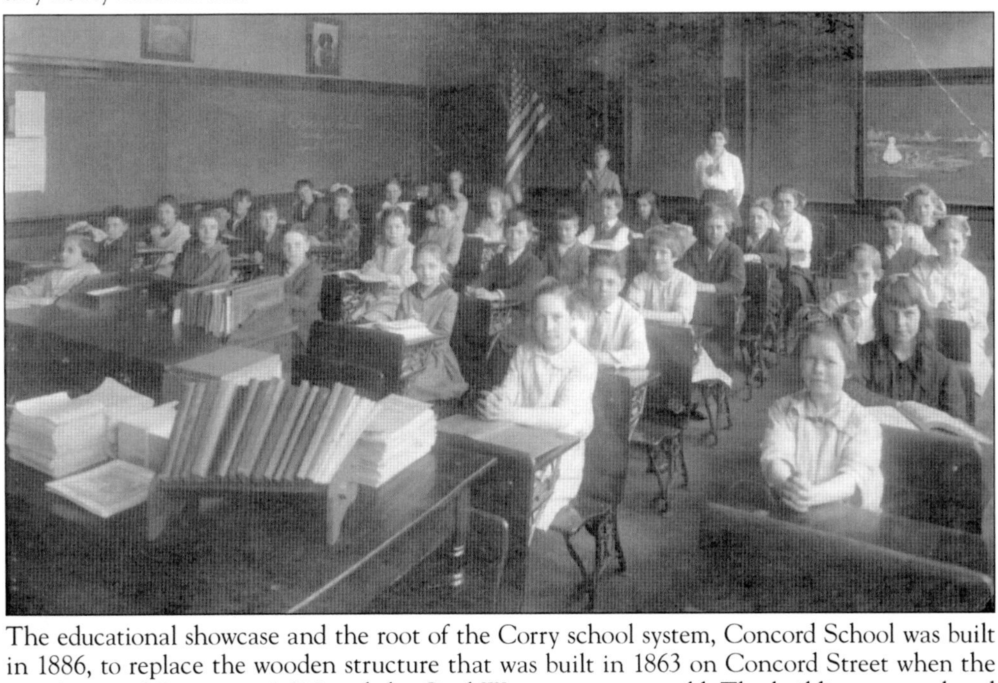

The educational showcase and the root of the Corry school system, Concord School was built in 1886, to replace the wooden structure that was built in 1863 on Concord Street when the population of Corry was 1,600 and the Civil War was one year old. The building was replaced in 1964 and used until 2007; the students were then sent to the new Corry Elementary School on Wayne Street.

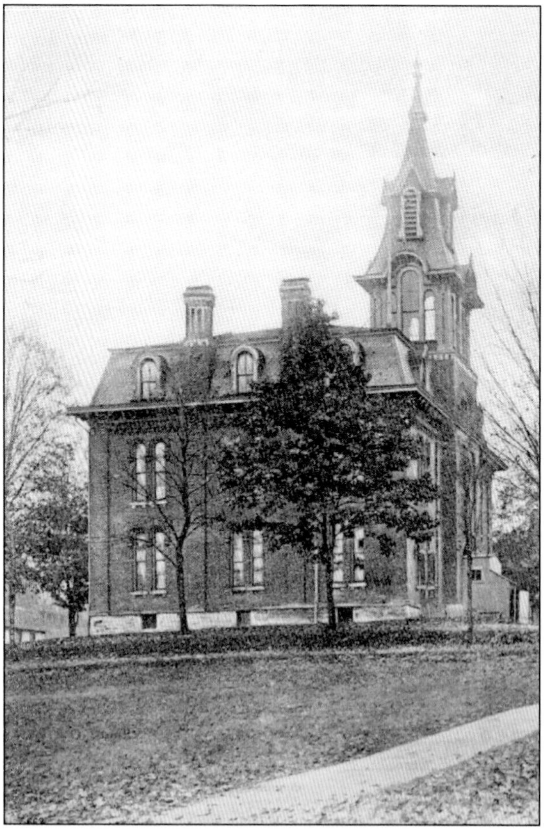

Fairview School was built in 1909. The contract for the construction was given to Henry Drake for a bid of $14,580. This building, which occupied a commanding site on the corner of Second Avenue and Fairview Street, was a three-story brick building of pretentious architectural style that was adapted to the requirements of a grade school.

In 1870, in order to provide for the rapidly increasing school population, the school board began construction of a large brick building on Congress and Wright Streets known as the Hatch School, named after John L. Hatch, who taught at the first school in Corry. This building was afforded accommodations for the high school from 1871 to 1899 and maintained a high rank among the educational institutions in the state of Pennsylvania.

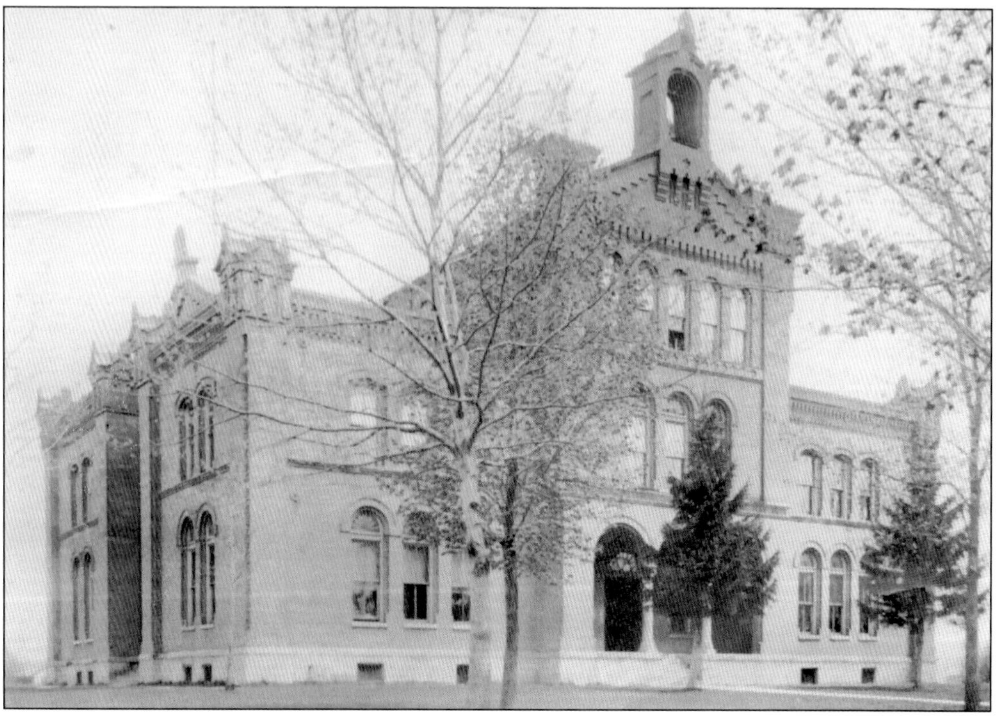

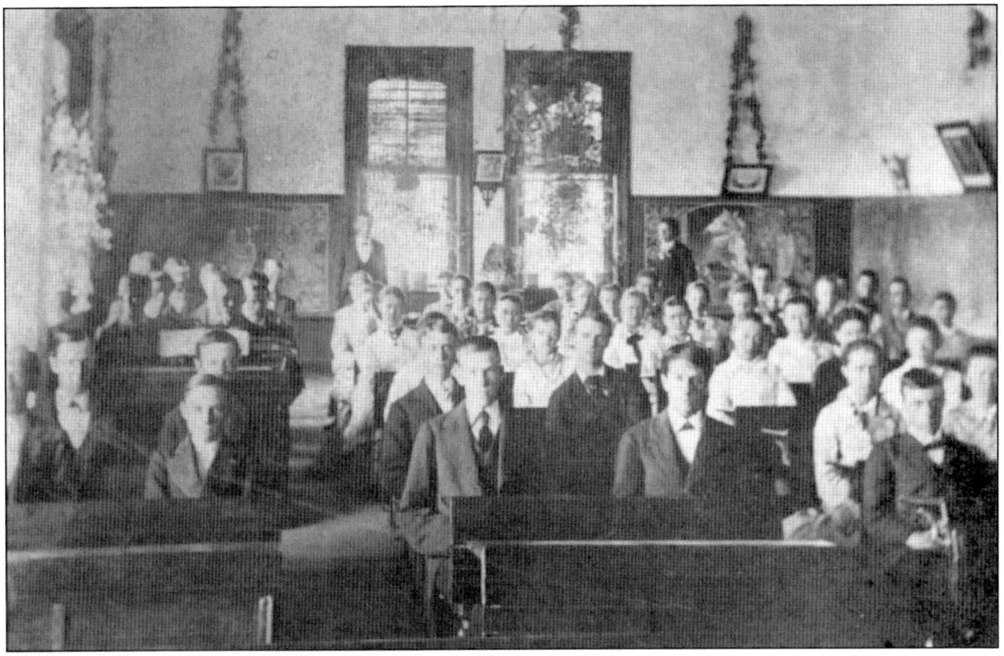

A good school building constitutes no small factor in educational work, and its influence on the community cannot be overestimated. The elegant and commodious school building, imposing in its style of architecture and complete in its equipment, does much to refine and ennoble the character of the children who attended the school and the character to a city to stimulate civic pride. The new Hatch School building was bigger than any school built in the city up to 1871. It offered the high school students a convenient means for widening their scope of instruction. It provided classes and new equipment that were unavailable in smaller schools. Science, business, cooking, and sewing were just a few of the new classes that were offered.

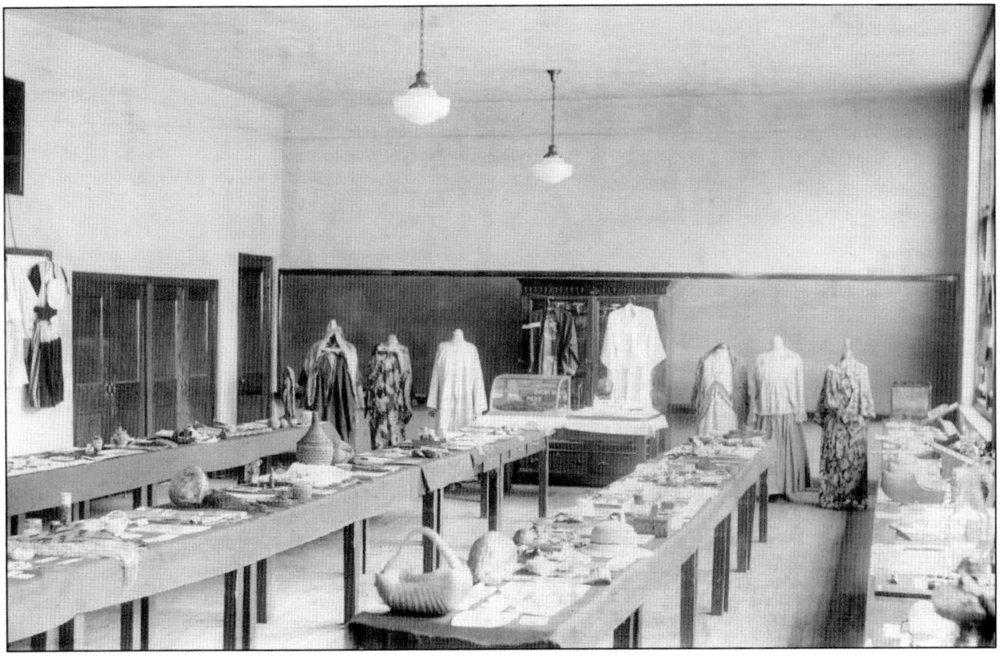

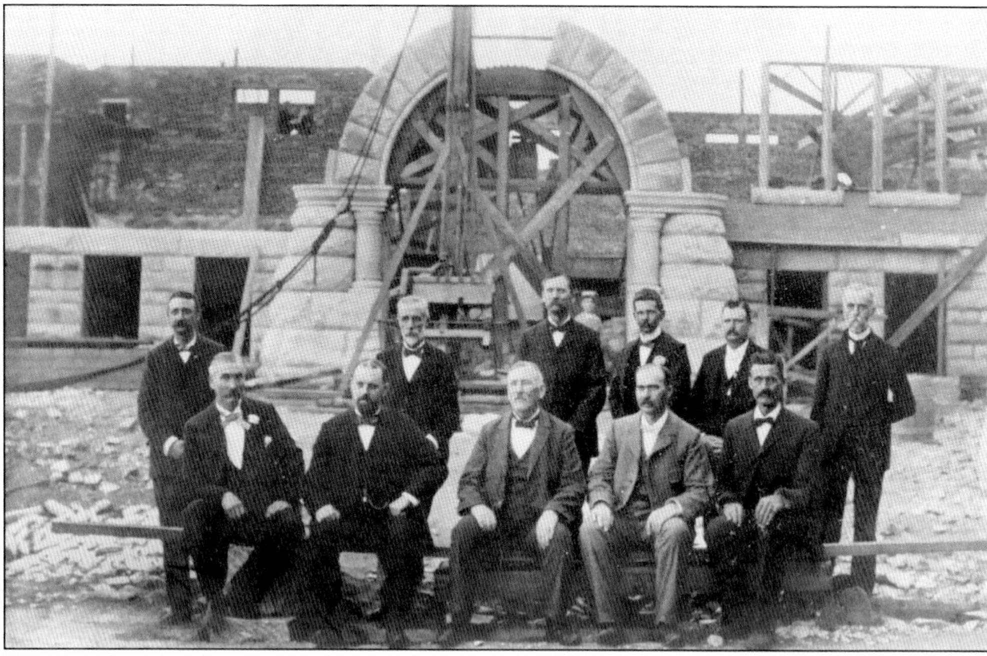

Thoroughly imbued with the idea that large beautiful buildings were a symbol of city pride and student success, the board of education realized that they were building for the future. The board of 1898–1899 showed rare wisdom and forethought and conferred an inestimable boon on the city of Corry when, in 1900, they planned and erected the magnificent high school building on South and Pleasant Streets. It was the pride of every public-spirited citizen and the admiration of all who saw it, standing as a proud monument to the enlightened public sentiment of the people of Corry. This noble building had a spacious auditorium that had the seating capacity of 600 and a large study hall that could accommodate 200 students. It was abandoned in 1954 and eventually torn down.

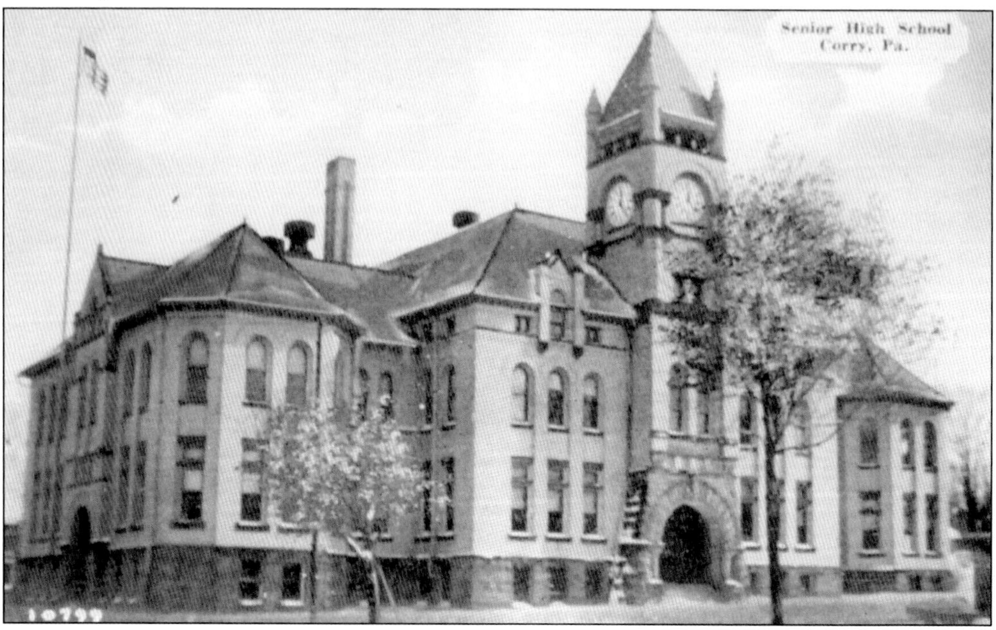

Six

Lived in Corry

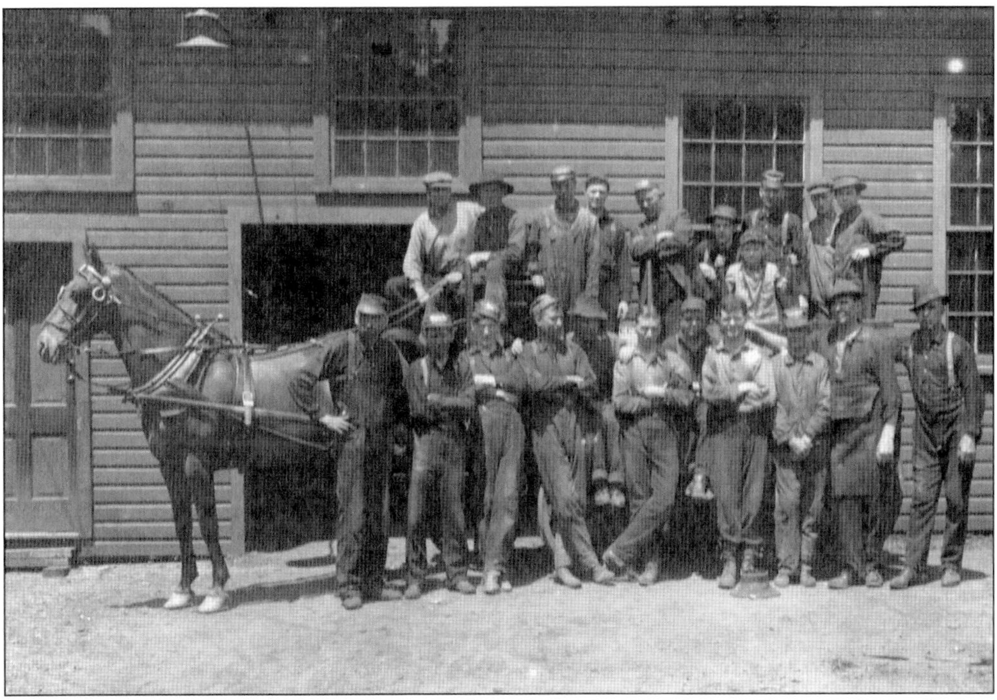

It takes a village to make a successful city. As oil was being discovered in northwestern Pennsylvania, money started to pour into the area. Methods of transporting the valuable liquid were being developed, and people from all over the world were moving here to begin new businesses and new lives. The influx of oil money meant that every type of business was needed, from grocery stores, to hotels, to wagon makers, and undertakers. Hundreds of people worked to build the railroad, cut trees, build houses, make bricks, start furniture factories, establish banks, and develop a dependable water supply. A vibrant, successful city evolved from a heavily forested swampy valley in a very short time. This is an early photograph of McInnes Steel.

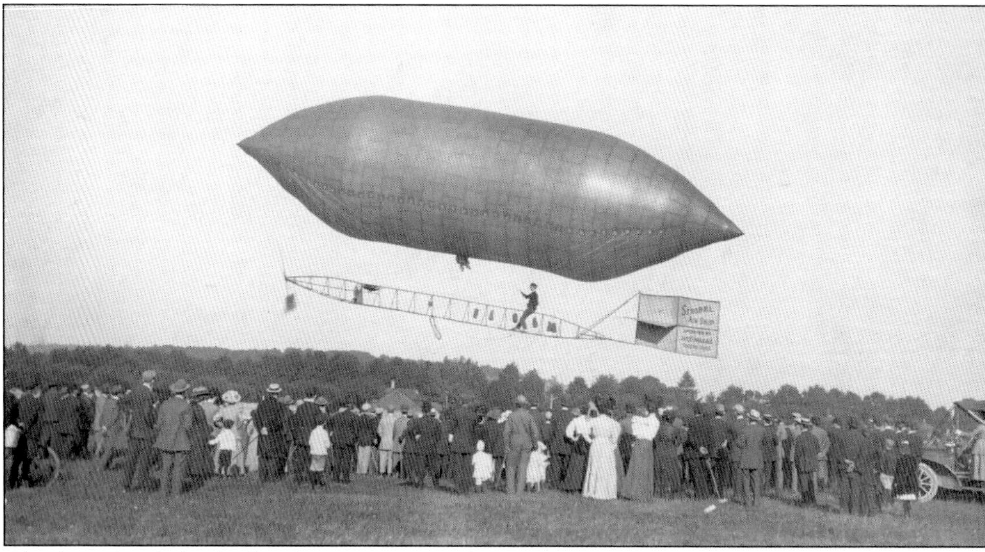

Charles F. Ritchel, who lived in Corry around 1878, was best known for his airship experiments, for which he was awarded US patent no. 201.200 for an "improvement of flying machines." The barrel-shaped gasbag, which was made of rubberized fabric 25 feet long and 13 feet in diameter, weighed 66 pounds. It was flown by hydrogen produced by the standard method of adding sulfuric acid to metal shavings.

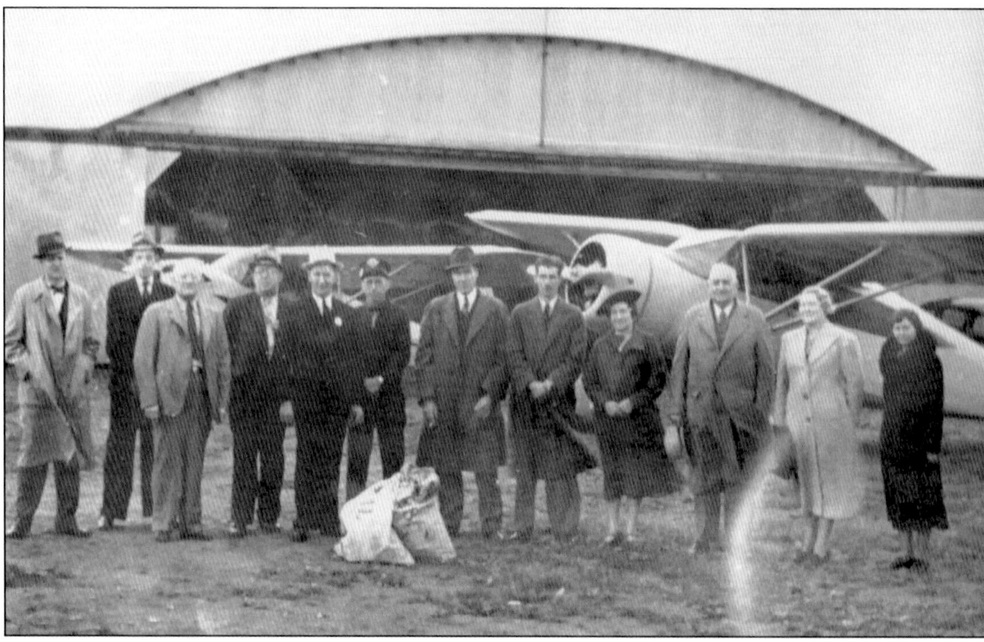

This photograph was taken on May 19, 1938, at the Corry Airport when Lawrence Thomas flew the first airmail out of Corry. Thomas was granted a one-day commission to fly the US mail. He picked up the mail from Corry, Union City, Waterford, and Wattsburg. None of these towns had an airport, so Thomas landed his plane in designated farmers' fields. He then flew the mail to Erie Airport. Pictured from left to right are Ralph Sperry, Harold Shannon, Reubins Randall, Clyde Hall, Perry Nichols, postmaster James Sullivan, Myra Thomas, Mayor and Mrs. Franklin Hepler, and Bertha Nichols.

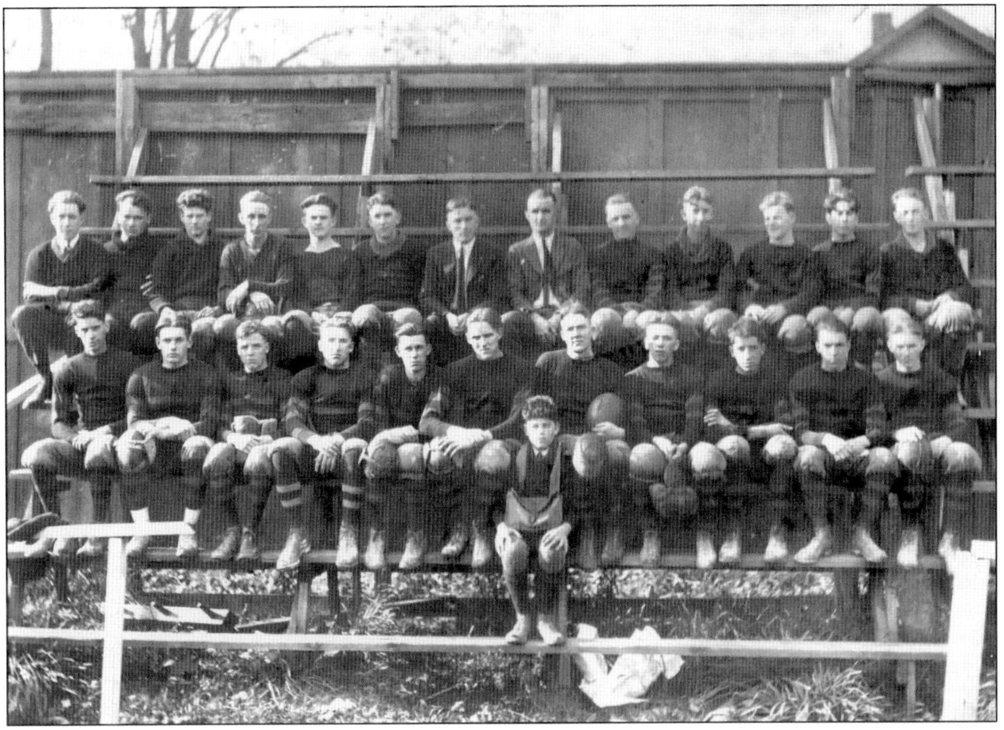

Ferdinand Johnson (pictured in the top row, second from the left) graduated from Corry High School in 1923. He became a cartoonist at the *Chicago Tribune*, where he became acquainted with cartoonist Frank Willard and his creation, *Moon Mullins*. Johnson spent 35 years working with Willard and his comic strip, which appeared in some 200 newspapers across the United States. In 1957, he completely concentrated on *Moon Mullins*.

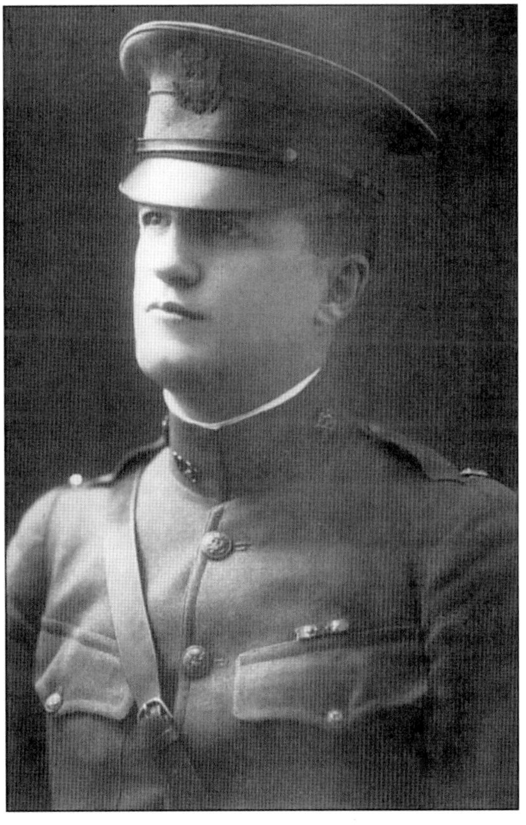

Charles Peter Keating was born in Corry in 1879, and at the age of 38, he enlisted in the US Army to fight in France during World War I. He had recently graduated from embalming school and was assigned to quartermaster corps. After the war, in 1921, as a civilian employee of the government he was involved in selecting the "Unknown Soldier."

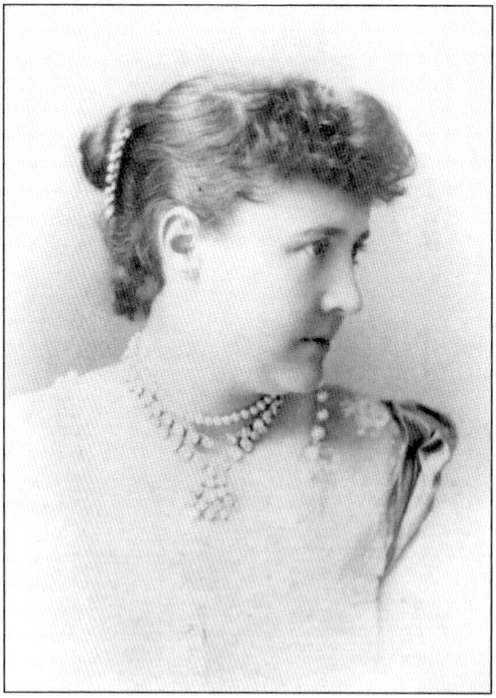

Inez Mecusker (1855–1941) was a world-famous soprano with a range of three octaves. She sang with the Gilmore Band and the John Philip Sousa Band, then went on her own in 1894 and achieved world fame. Inez performed for the Emperor of France, Napoleon III, and Empress Eugene and was given a reception and a diamond necklace by Queen Victoria of England. Between concerts, she sang in vaudeville, wrote and produced her own shows, had her own troupe of performers, taught voice, and composed music. She was born just outside of Corry and spent her free time at her cottage on Findley Lake, New York, and at her home on Fairview Street across from the Fairview School. On nice days, when the windows were open, the students could hear her singing.

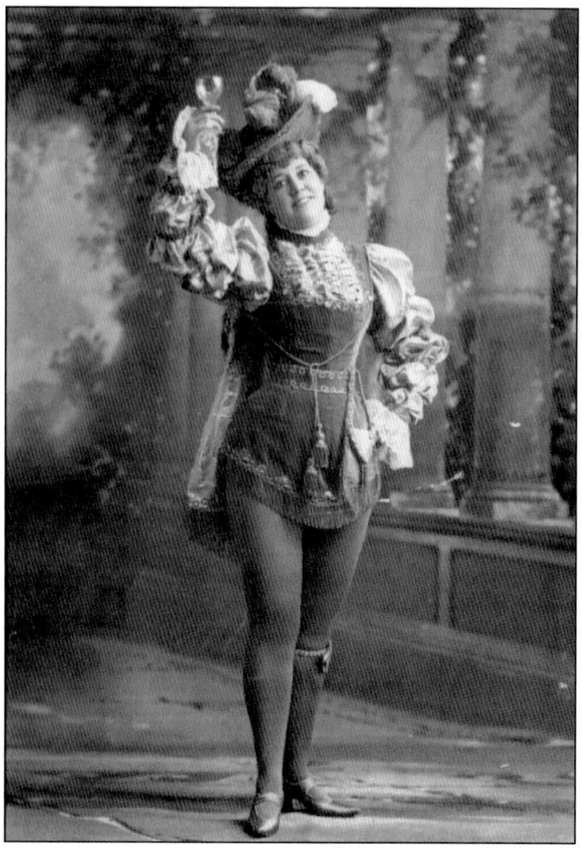

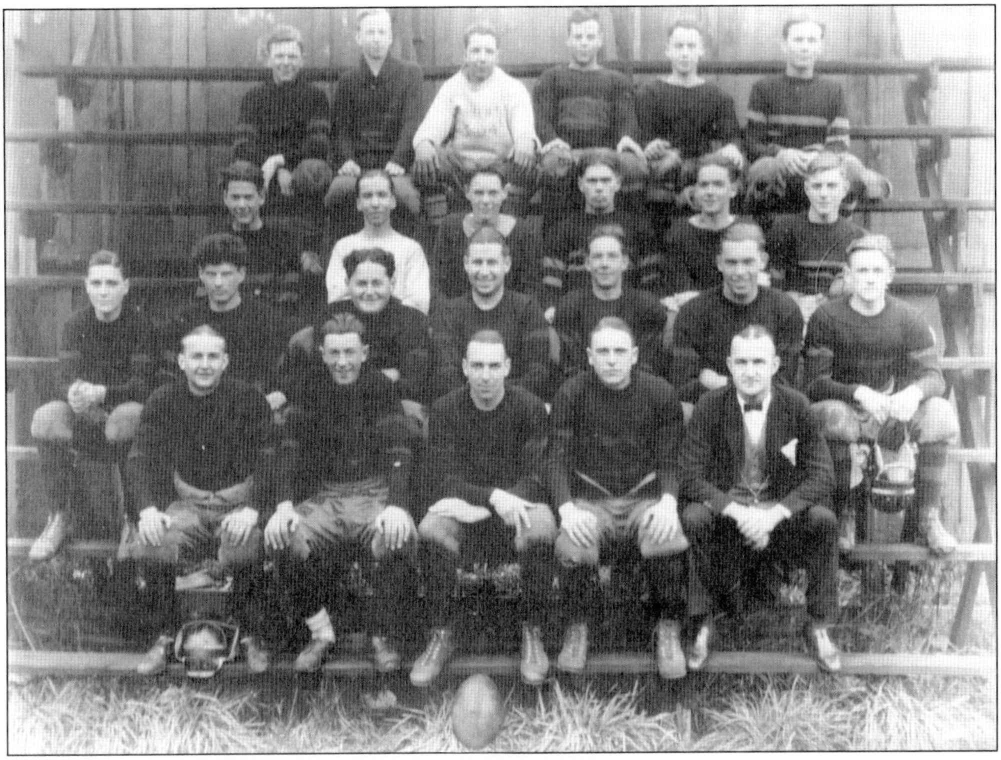

Maj. Gen. Clarence "Shoopy" Shoop (pictured in the front row, second from the left) graduated from Corry High School in 1925. He was a reconnaissance pilot during World War II, and in 1945 he became base commander at Muroc Army Field, now known as Edwards Air Force Base. Shoop was vice president and head of flight-testing at Hughes Aircraft Company. In 1957, he became commander in chief of the Air National Guard.

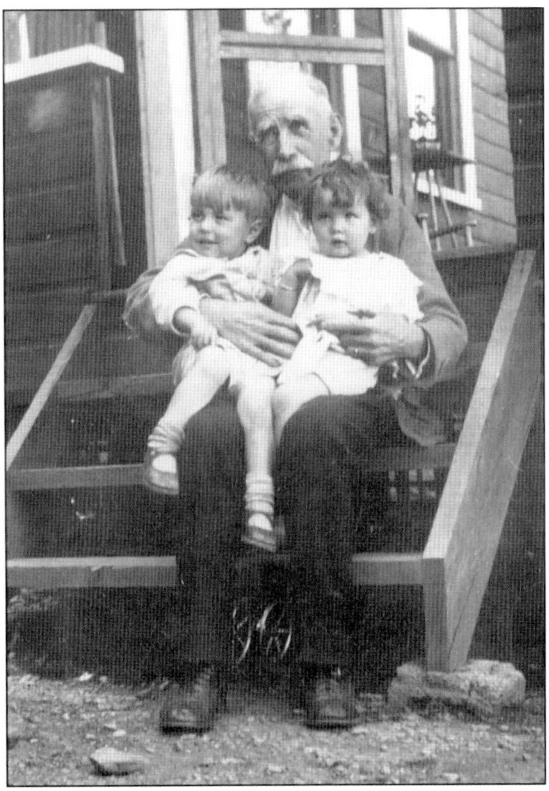

Asa Howard was born in 1848. He established the Howard Broom Company, which he operated for many years. Around the turn of the century, he became a road agent for Climax Manufacturing, delivering locomotives to California, Oregon, Washington, and British Columbia. From 1906 to 1924, he traveled across the continent 104 times, the distance of about 24 times around the world. (Courtesy of Audrey Young.)

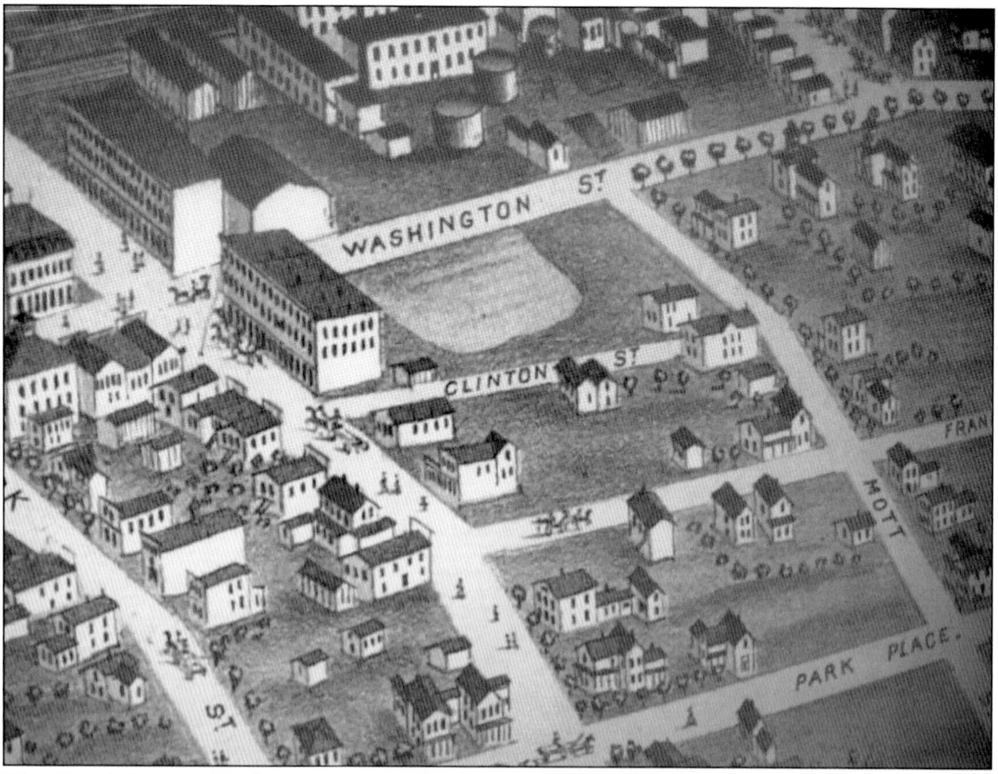

Thaddeus Mortimer Fowler was a mapmaker for more than 50 years, from the Civil War to World War I. The panoramic maps are sometimes referred to as bird's-eye-view maps, because they are drawn as if viewed from above. During World War I, Fowler began adding airplanes and dirigibles circling the city as part of his trademark. This gave the impression that the information was actually gleaned from an aerial trip; however, this was not the case. Fowler was once accused of being a German spy and jailed. He was eventually released, suffering injury only to his pride.

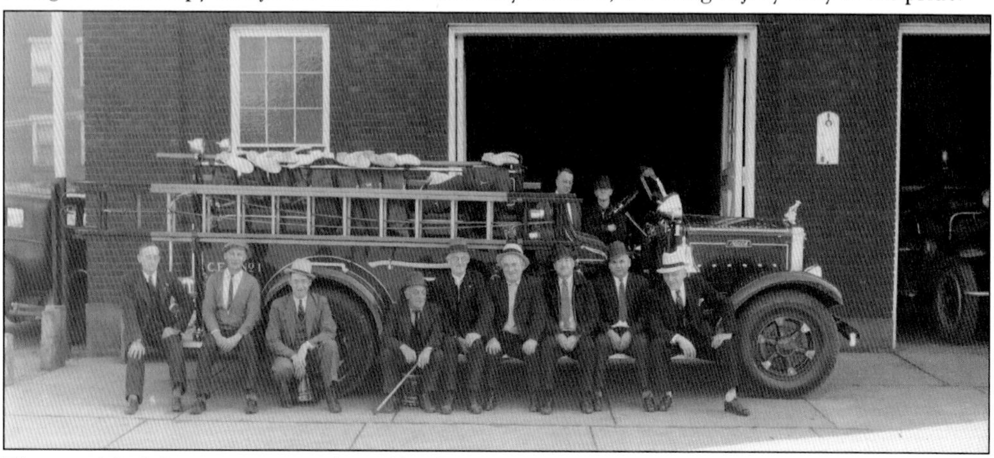

The new Mack Pumper was purchased by the Corry Fireman's Relief Association and donated to the City of Corry in 1936. Pictured are (sitting) Tom Garrity, Frank Kinley (driver), James Sullivan, Charles Pain, Charles Kinley, Tom Green, Charles Craker (assistant chief), Andy Paulson (chief), and Fred Weaver (councilman); (standing) Mr. White (Mack dealer), and Tom Cournean. The fire truck is on display at the Corry Museum.

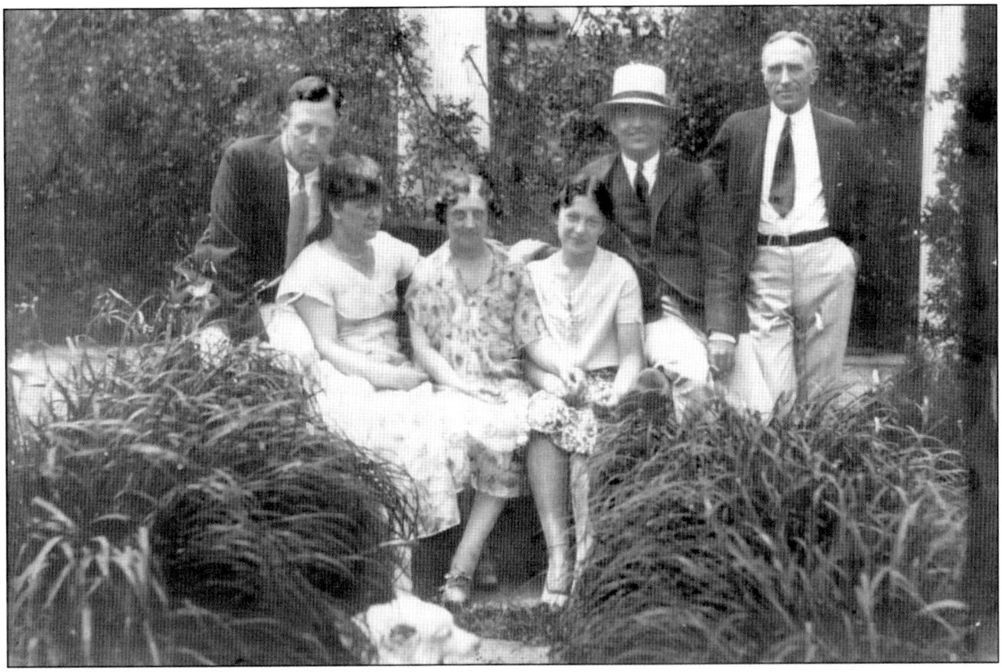

Joseph Jessie—better known as J.J. Desmond—was an important part of Corry history, but little is known of him today. He was president of the Citizens National Bank, Howard Tannery, NuBone Corset Company, and Corry Fair and Driving Park. He owned Dromana Farms, a poultry farm that sold tens of thousands of chickens and eggs. He was an important part of having the post office and trolley established in Corry.

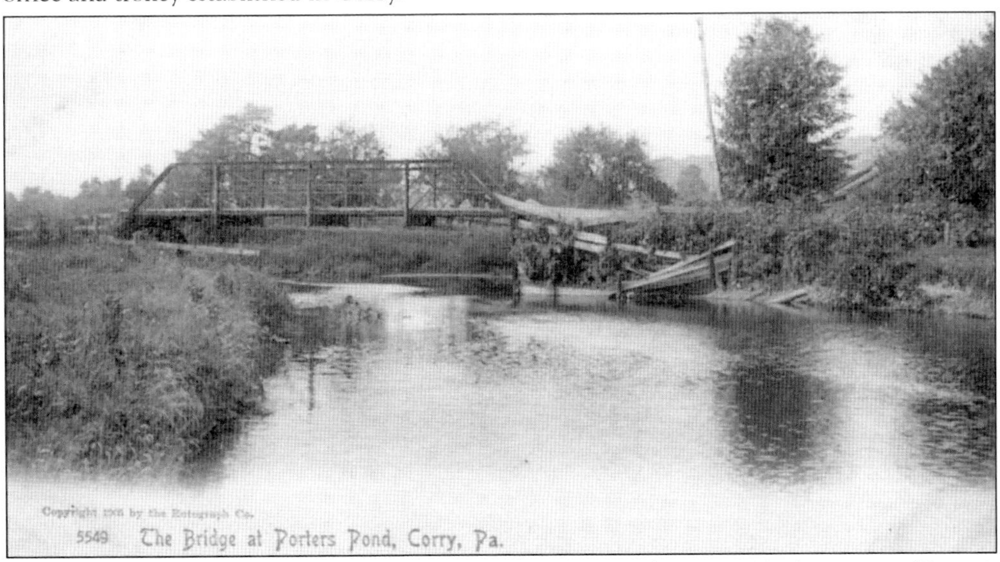

After Benjamin Harrison defeated Grover Cleveland for president in 1888, the owner of Porter's Pond, Charles Porter—known as the "Ice Man"—surprised the town by coming out Center Street and up Main to First Avenue with a span of horses hitched to a flat-bottom boat, gliding through the soft mud at 15 knots. He was flying political banners and flags advocating for the "SALT RIVER PACKET," a political issue of the day. He was cheered on as he picked up local Democratic businessmen.

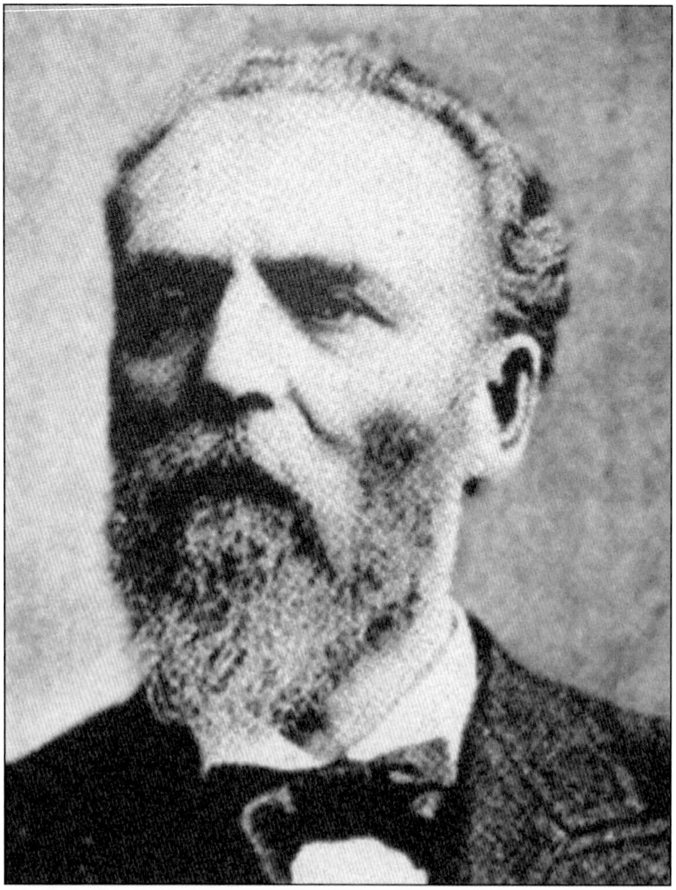

George Washington Newton Yost invented the Caligraph typewriter in Corry in 1883. The Caligraph was the first typewriter to have both small and capital letters on one machine. The American Writing Machine Company of Corry manufactured this rugged and dependable typewriter, employing 150 men who turned out 84 machines per week.

Yost was the leading shipper of oil from Titusville during Corry's early oil days. With his own money, he also built a congregational church on Pleasant Street, which was big and beautiful. He later fell into spiritualism, and in his later years tried to invent a machine to talk with the dead. Spiritualists settled Spirit Hill north of Corry, thus the name, "Spirit Hill."

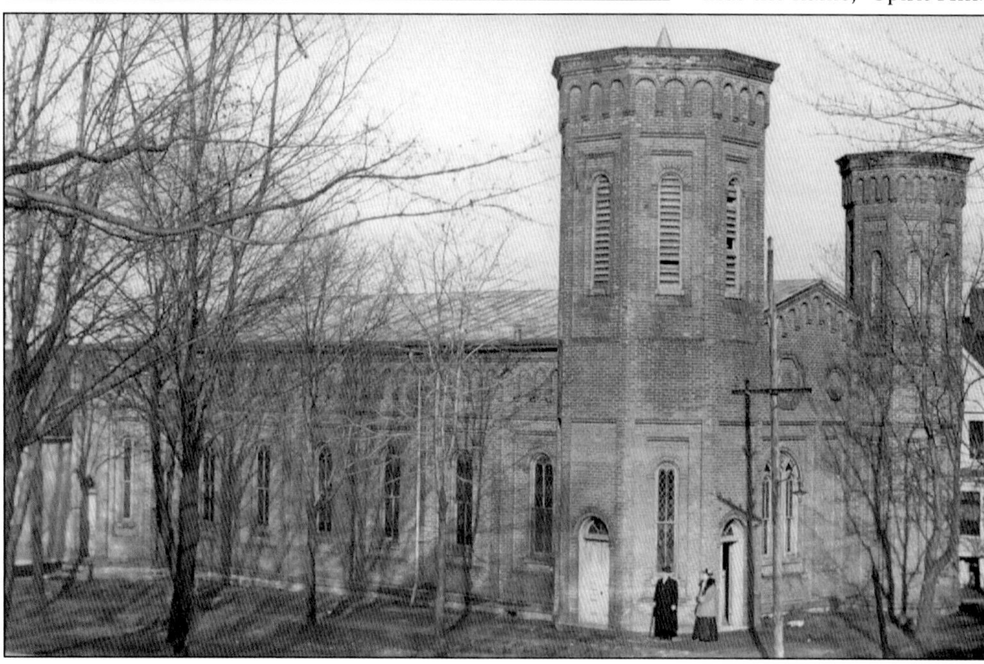

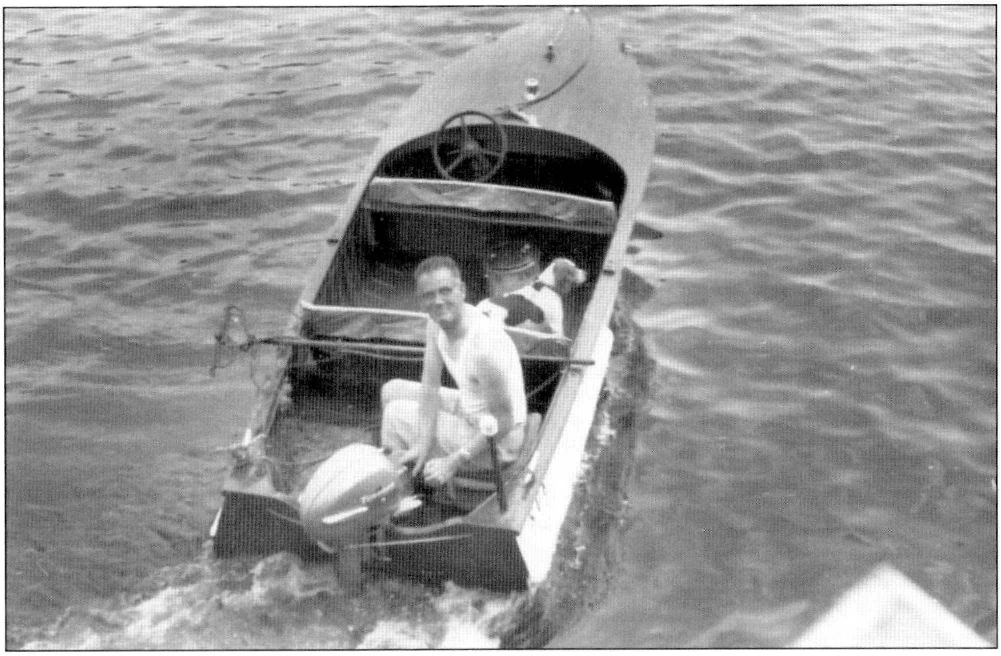

Fred Kinley was the trolley conductor during the trolley's last trip, when it was hit by lightning at the corner of East Columbus Avenue and Wayne Street in 1923. Kinley was mayor of Corry from 1949 until 1961. He is pictured in front of his cottage on Findley Lake, which he bought from fellow trolley conductor Oscar Fritz. (Courtesy of Al Young.)

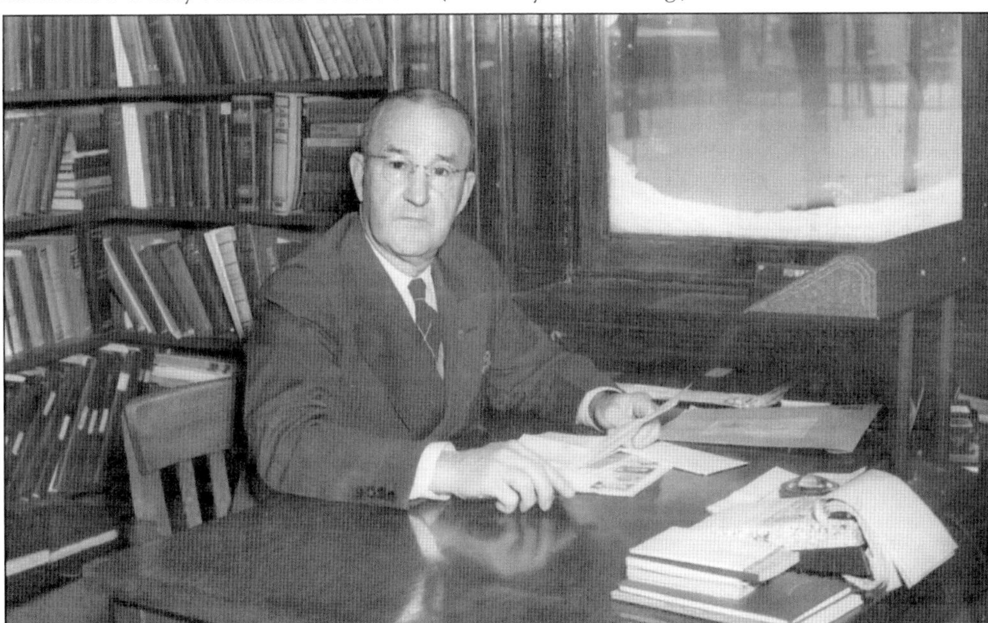

Howard J. Sheen served the Corry School District from 1919 to 1960 as a science teacher, coach, athletic director, and vice principal. He was the high school principal for 34 years. The high school football field was dedicated to him by the class of 1960. "Pop" Sheen was said to be Corry's number-one sports fan, a gentleman, a friend, and a person who cared greatly about Corry.

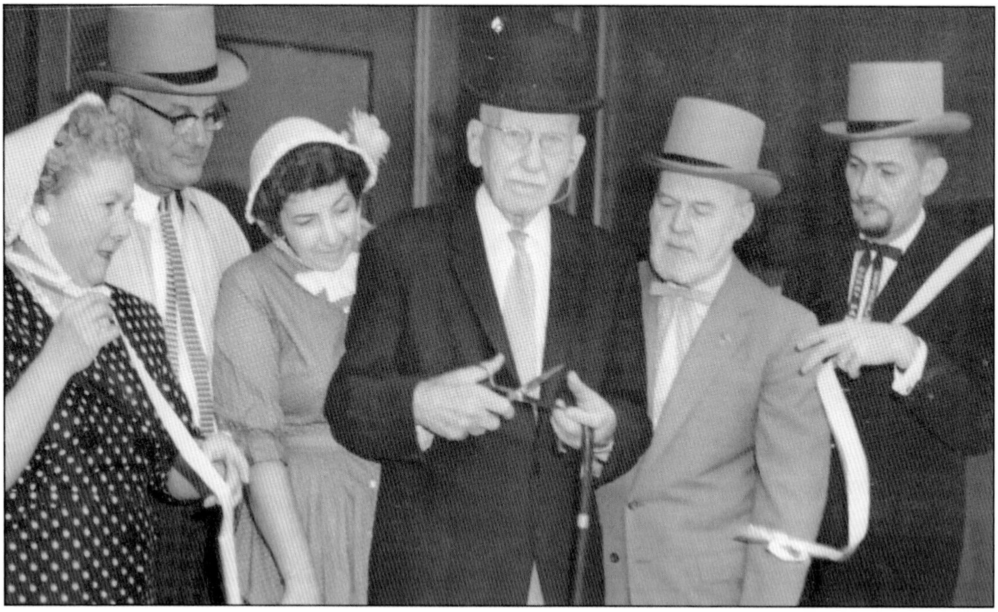

F.E. Wittlesey started a valve cup factory with his family that made leather cups for oil wells. They bought Raymond's Manufacturing in 1893, which made springs all types, including springs for the Wright brothers' plane. They eventually progressed into television and spacecraft. He was president of McInnes Steel from 1914 until 1937. He is pictured here cutting the ribbon in the opening ceremony for Corry's centennial in 1961. (Courtesy of Bob and Ruth Ann Grice.)

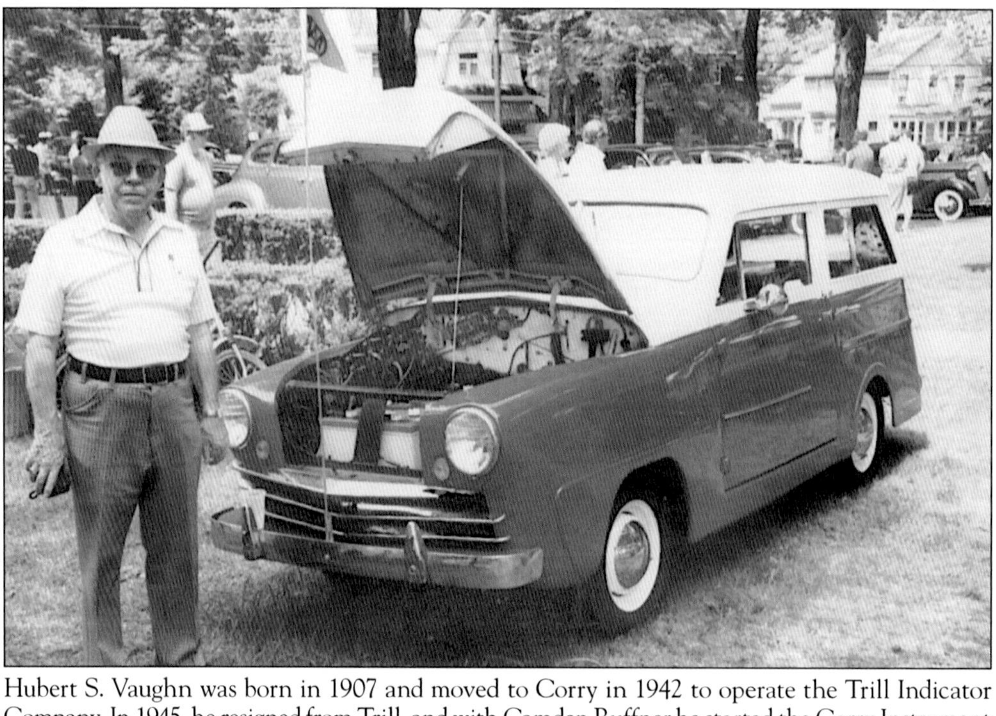

Hubert S. Vaughn was born in 1907 and moved to Corry in 1942 to operate the Trill Indicator Company. In 1945, he resigned from Trill, and with Camden Ruffner he started the Corry Instrument Company, later known as Corry Manufacturing. He was an industrialist and active pilot into his 80s, but he is best remembered for driving around town in his 1952 Crosley electric car.

Seven

The Corry Fair and Driving Park

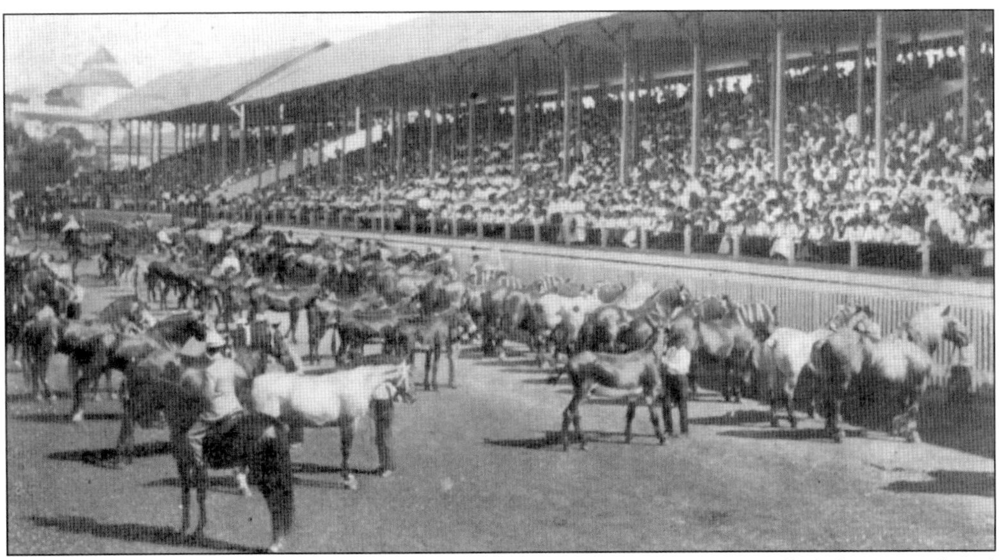

The first Corry fair took place in 1871, in a field north of Corry. It was called the Agricultural Society North Western Annual Fair. Farmers got together to show off their livestock, vegetables, grain crops, plow horses, canned goods, and fretwork projects. They also had a nice picnic on a quiet afternoon. A few years later in the same abandoned field, the huge fair and horseracing track was organized.

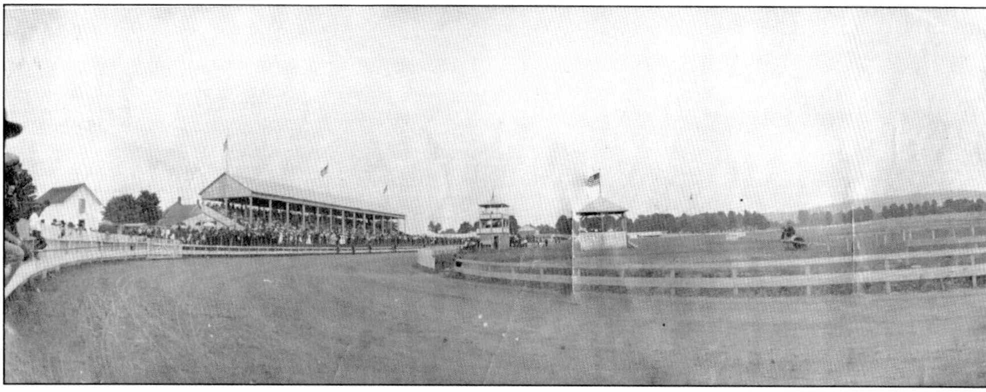

In 1905, a group of businessmen and stockholders from Corry organized a new Corry Fair with the intention of creating the biggest and most popular fair in the state. They purchased additional land and planned improvements. Additionally, they needed to make it a financial success, so the Corry Fair and Driving Park Association was formed.

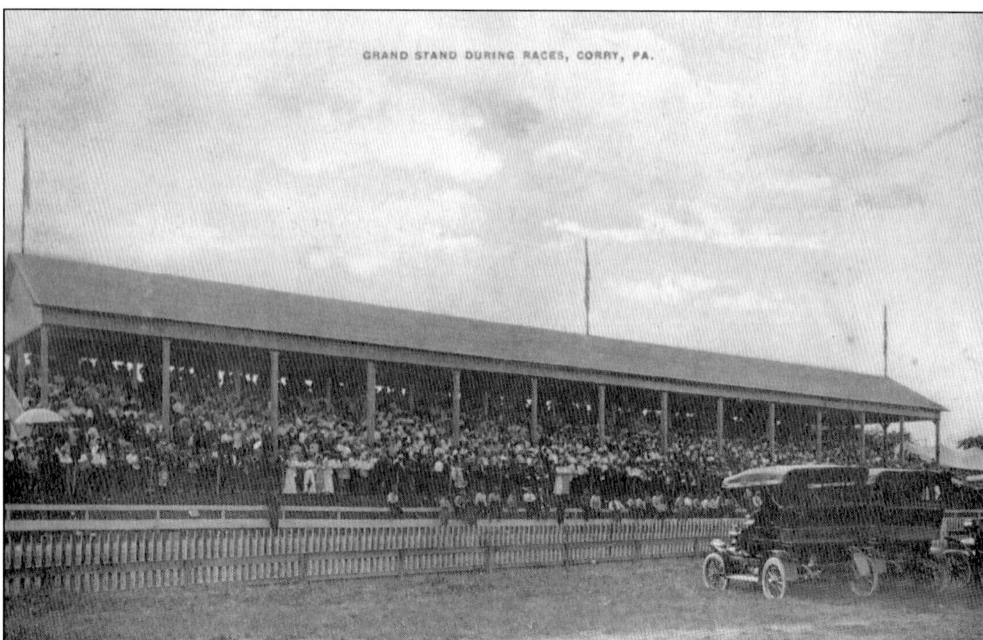

J.J. Desmond was president of the Corry Fair and Driving Park Association when the Corry Fair was revived in 1904. He announced at the first meeting plans of improving the land and the racetrack. He claimed that accommodations needed for a large fair and harness racing track included grandstands that are 200 feet long 28 deep, which could seat 2,500 people.

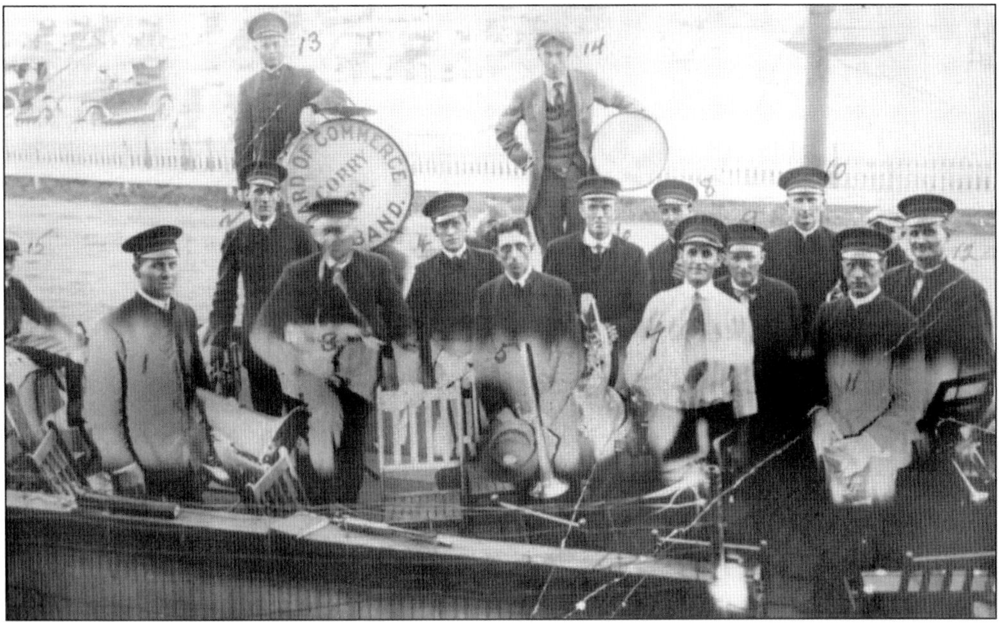

The plan was to arrange for interesting attractions, comfortable and convenient buildings, and the racetrack, which needed to be perfect in accordance with the regulations. The first year was advertised extensively and boasted Corry's railroad advantages, hotels, and restaurants. Nothing stood in the way of making the Corry Fair and races among the greatest in the state.

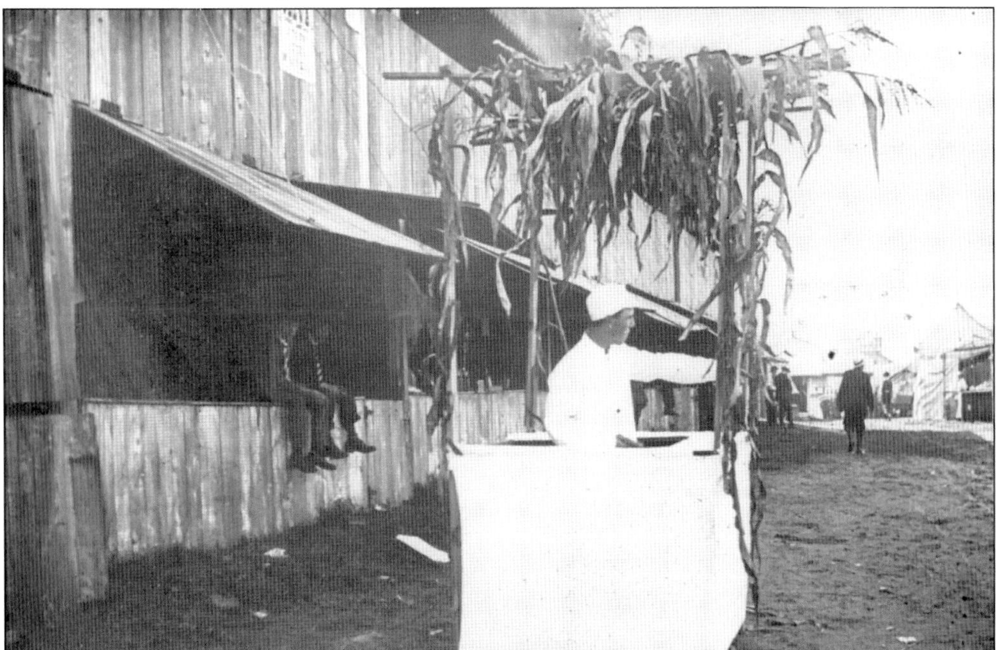

Every year, improvements were made, entertainment was added, and the crowds were in awe of the fair displays of farm machinery, new products, and the latest inventions. Everything was bigger, better, and faster. Everyone in the crowd saw airships, airplanes, and motorcycles for the first time. A whole new world opened up to people who spent most of their days working on their farm.

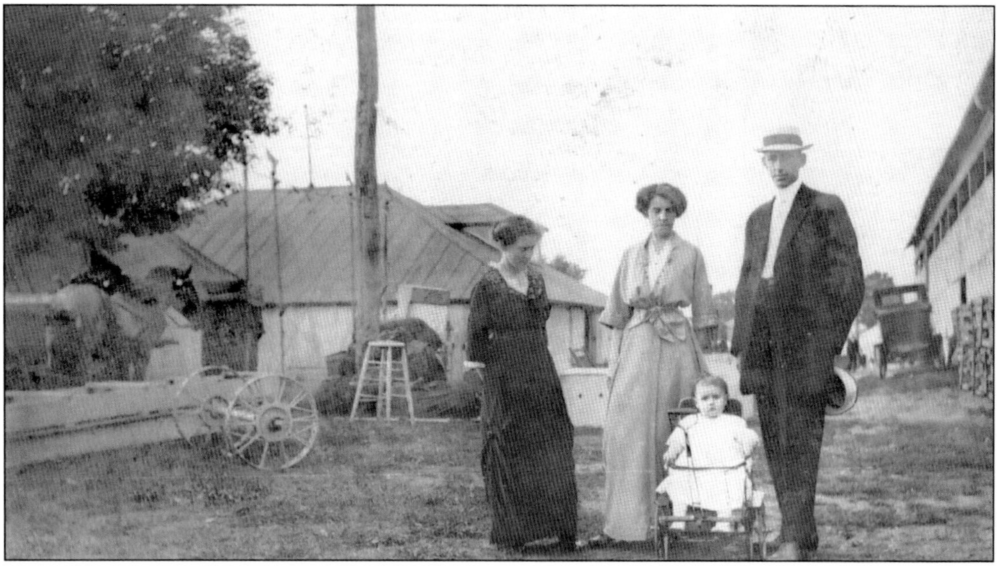

George A. Olmstead wrote the following in his diary on September 20, 1877: "We went to the fair again today. The attendance was larger than I had expected to see. There was quite an addition to the cattle and some that was first rate. The poultry show was not first rate. There was a good many wagons and farm implements but one thing appeared to attract people while it lasted and that was the baby show. There was one set of triplets. When the tent door was opened for the inspection of the children there was a great rush, all appeared eager to see the babies. I saw them but failed to see any better looking children than I had often seen before."

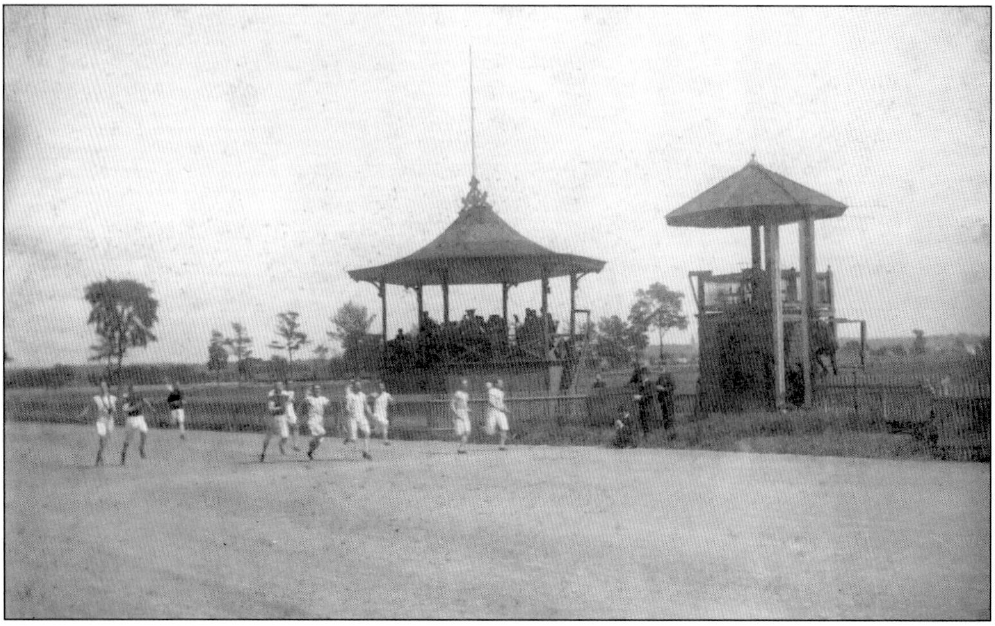

The Century Athletic Club hosted an athletic meet at the fairgrounds on Labor Day 1911. It may have been one of the largest of its kind. Warren, Jamestown, Kane, Erie, and Union City had athletes registered for the five-mile race, 125-yard hurdle, and various other events. A relay race was arranged for Corry shop teams and fraternal organization teams. The weather was good, and a huge crowd attended.

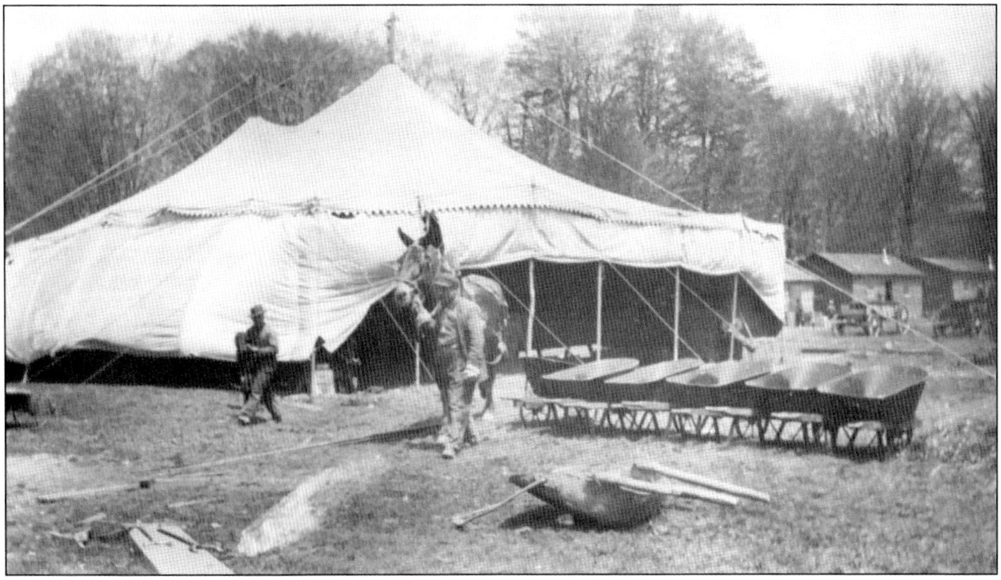

In May 1909, the grand Cole Brothers' Circus came to Corry in three long trains with 700 employees and performers. Hundreds of animals, such as black tigers, a herd of elephants, several hundred horses, ostriches, zebras, camels, and hundreds of wild birds were in attendance. A live hippo and rhinoceros were also traveling with the circus. They brought their own waterproof tents, which could seat 10,000 people. When the circus was set up, it covered seven acres of the fairgrounds. The performers brought all the possessions they owned, and the cooks provided three meals a day for the entire troupe. Everything was well planned and went smoothly.

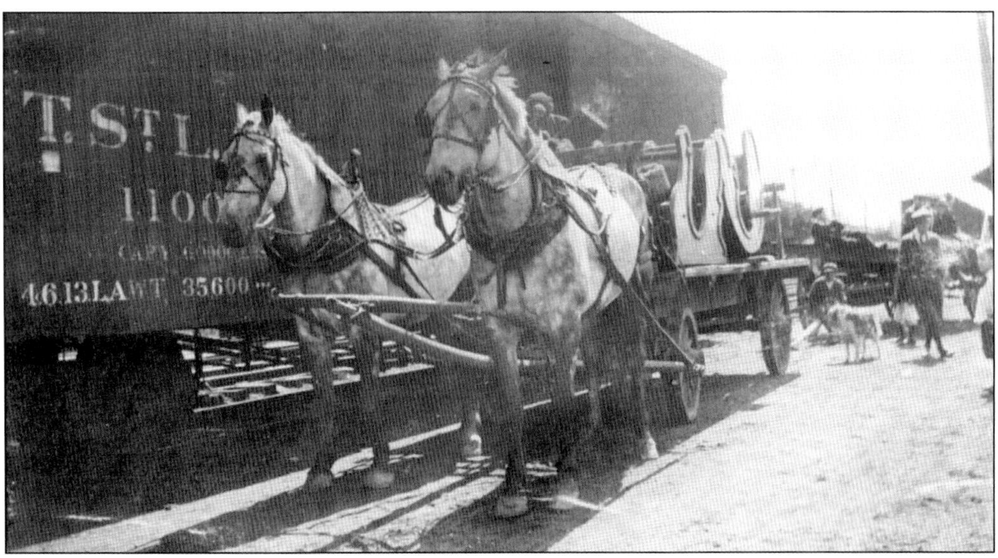

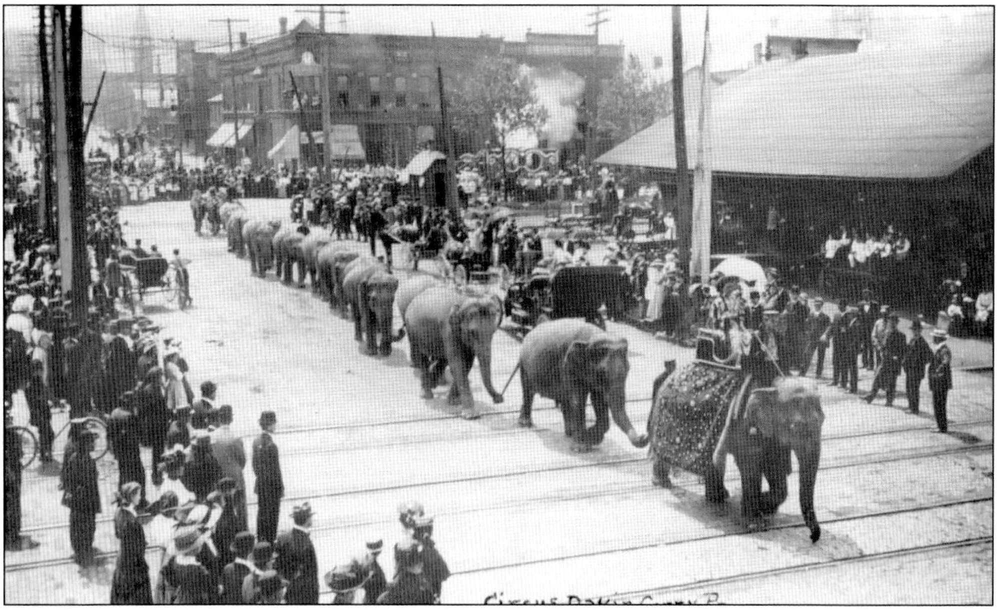

Circus advertising boasted their parade as being the "grandest eye feast ever perfected in the overpowering gorgeous street parade." Leaving the fairgrounds at 10 o'clock, the parade was over a mile of the bewildering, imposing, inspiring and spectacular. The parade included over 1,000 richly robed riders and elegantly caparisoned animals. Five bands, steam pianos, floats, dozens of clowns, open dens of animals, and a congress of strange people paraded through the streets of Corry and then back to the fairgrounds.

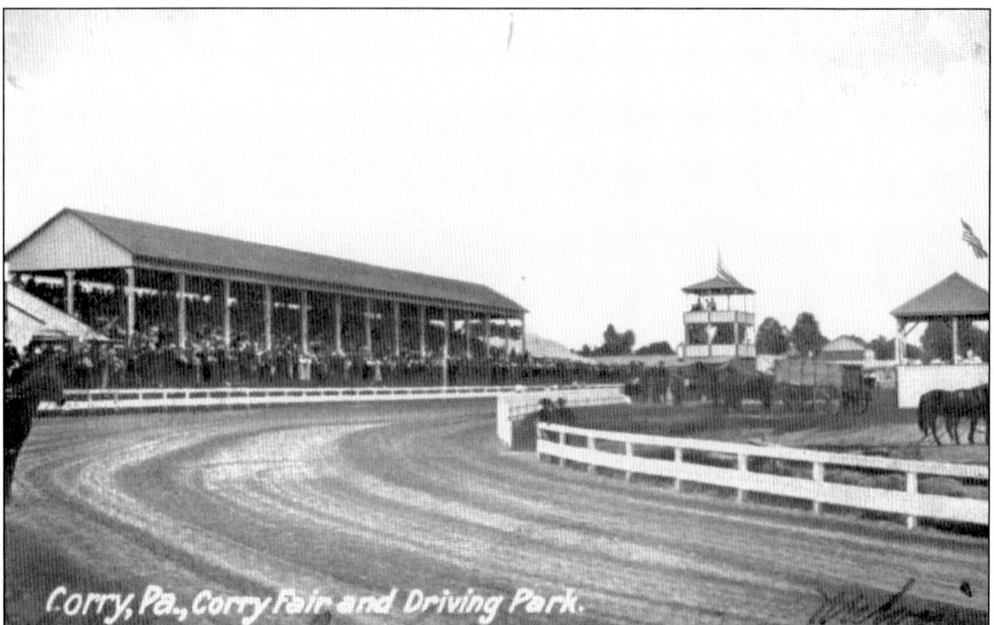

A fast race was planned for Saturday, October 18, 1916. A friendly rivalry was planned between Dr. G.E. Bennett and Messrs. Van Tassel and Miller concerning the merits of their fast horses, White Sox and Rebel Pledge. Both owners said it would be a good-natured affair, but it would be a real race.

During the fair in September 1909, the balloon ascension was the chief attraction among the amusement features and took place each day. The crowds followed the bandwagon to the fairgrounds. The weather was ideal, and with 25 acres of exhibits and attractions, the crowd was a record breaker.

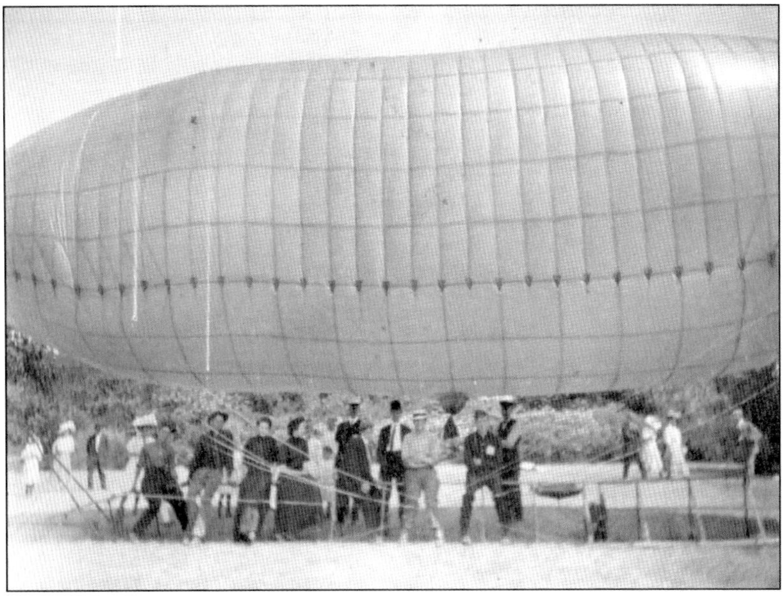

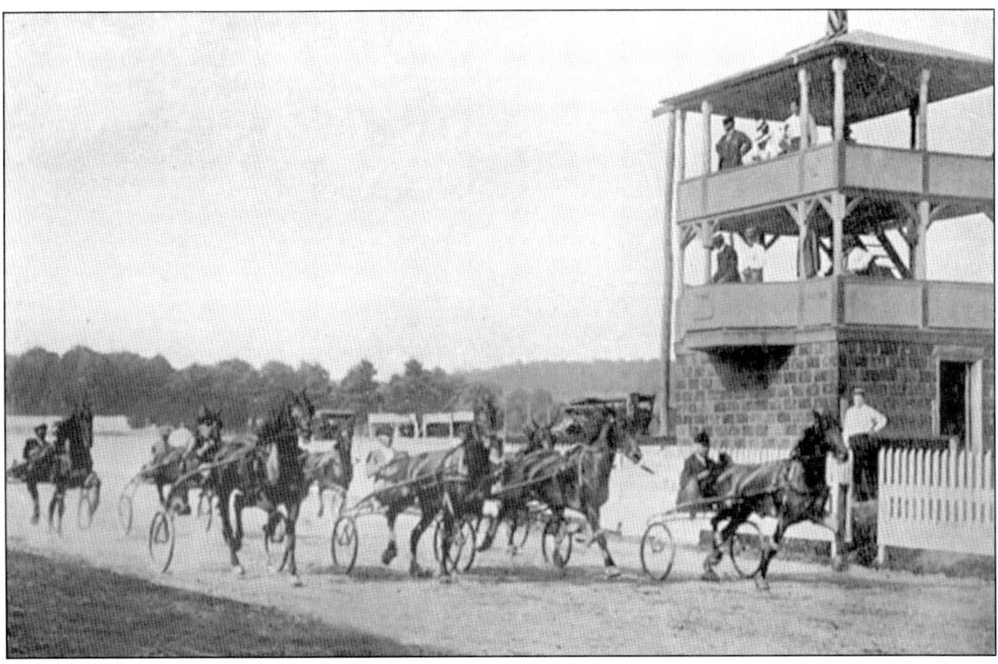

The *Evening Journal* noted the following: "August 12, 1905—The Corry Fair and Race Track will close tomorrow. Yesterday 3,000 people attended the races. Erie sports backed Minnie Florence because the mare won at the Erie Track last week. The horse and riders are now walking home to Erie. A telephone message at noon said that the boys were as far as Waterford. (Must be they lost in Corry and couldn't afford the train ride home)."

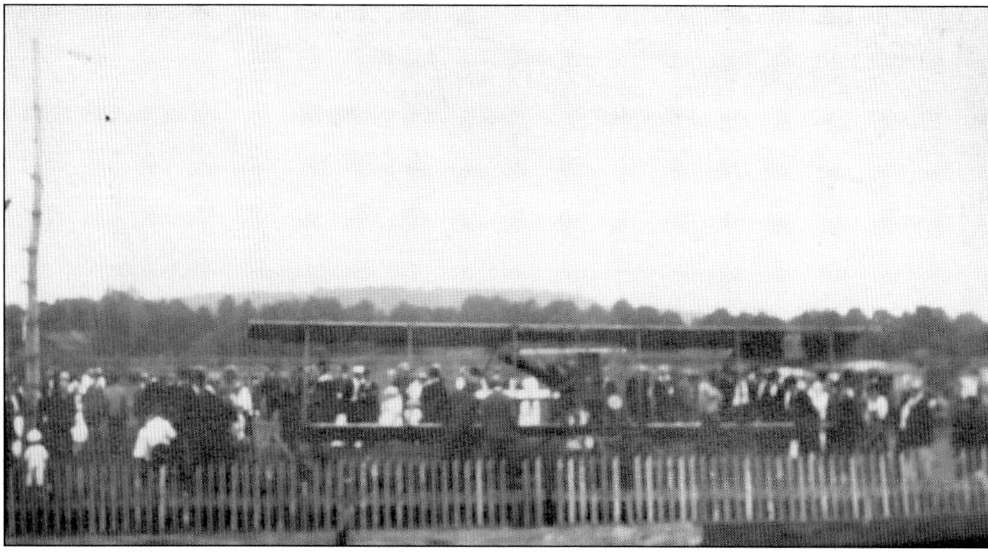

Merrill Riddick, a super pilot of the Aerial Mail Service and Adams Transportation Company, landed at the fairgrounds in October 1919. Passengers were provided air rides for $10 for 12 minutes. Several local manufacturing plants provided plane rides for their employees to witness the fairgrounds from the air. A race between the fastest car and the plane around the track was also an exciting performance.

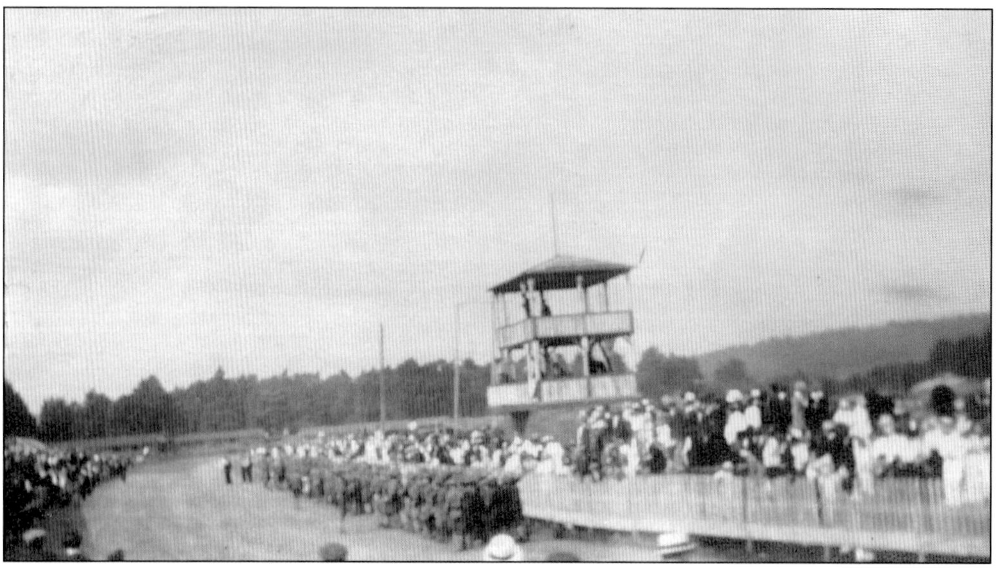

On Wednesday, September 19, 1877, George A. Olmstead wrote the following: "Have concluded to go to the fair today instead of tomorrow. Took Ettie and went to the fair. Had a fair show of horses and hogs and sheep, but the cattle department was not so good. But the vegetable department I consider first rate, also the domestic department was good. There was a fair attendance. The last performance before I left was the race two steers and a bull with a rider on their back each one doing their best to win the race. The bull was too young to carry such a burden so far, his rider got off drove him but one of the steers won the race, there was a great amount of cheering."

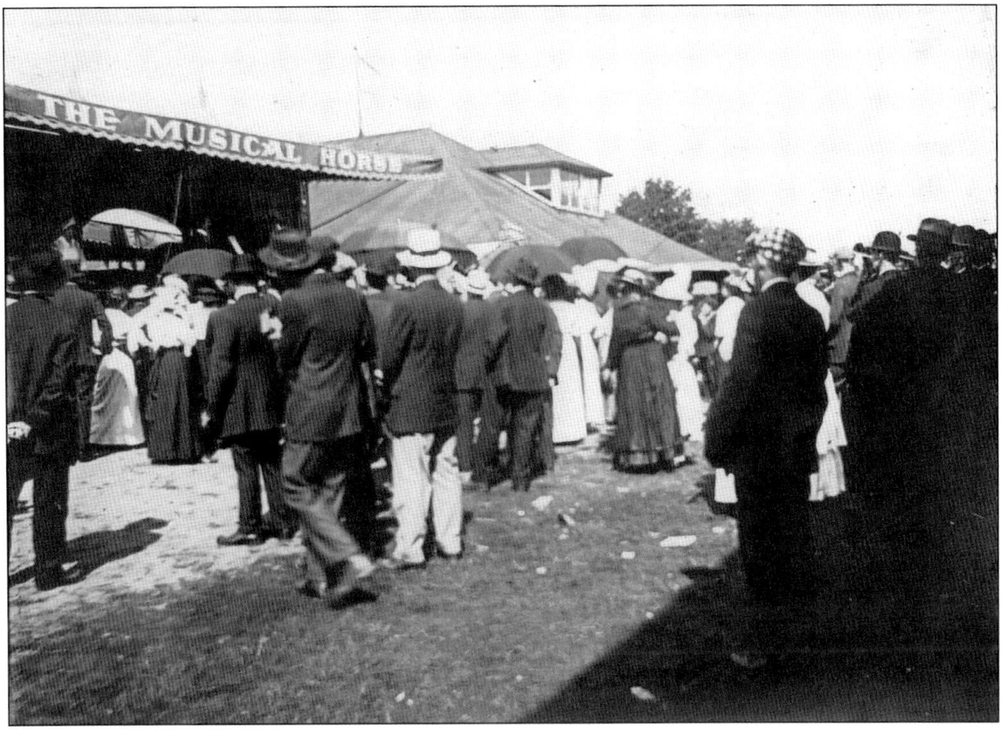

The "Big Corry Fair" was an incredibly exhilarating event in its time. Most of the population rarely left the farms and factories. To see all the displays, try food they never heard of before, and see things such as an ostrich racing a horse around the track was thrilling. They were in awe of all the music, colorful costumes, and trained animals they would never forget.

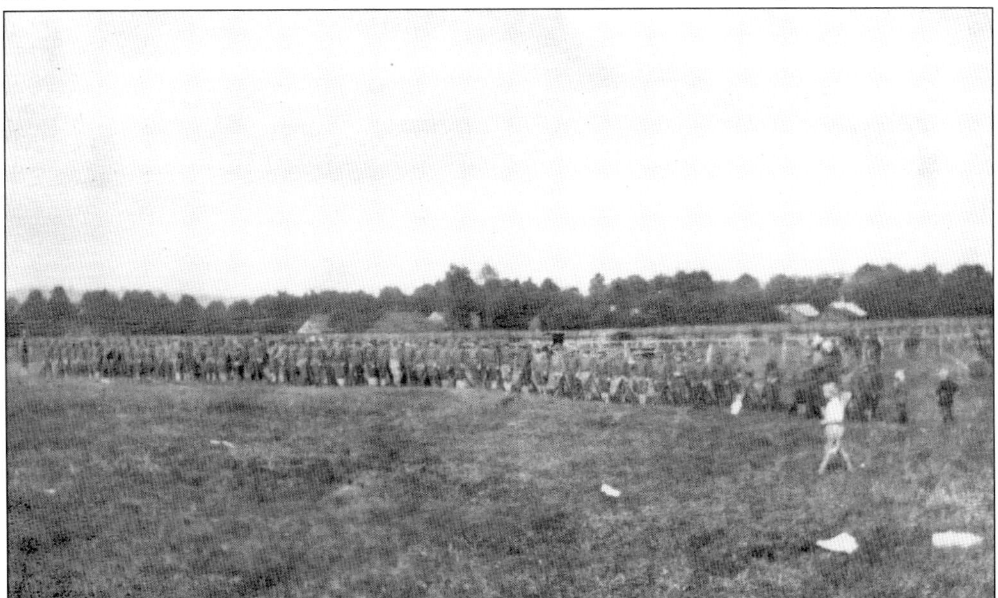
Company A marched from the armory on Washington Street to the fairgrounds a few weeks before they left to serve in World War I. They proudly displayed their finely coordinated drills for the crowds in the stands. The crowd cheered loudly for their hometown heroes.

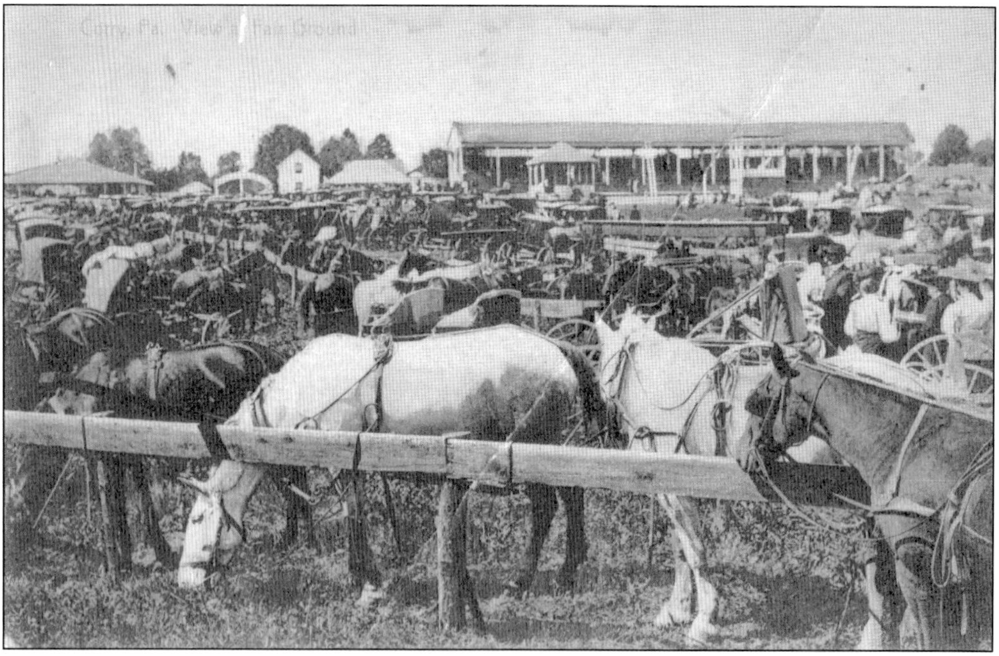

In 1914, a record number of visitors descended on Corry for the fair. The Philadelphia and Erie Division of the Pennsylvania Railroad brought a vast throng of people in incredible numbers. All of the feed stables in the city did a record amount of business, and it was believed that more than 400 carriages were driven into the city on the morning of September 3. The streets were lined with carriages and buggies. Local people reported one of the biggest days of the fair in its history. All hotels, restaurants, and stables were filled to their limits. The fair brought thousands of dollars into Corry's economy.

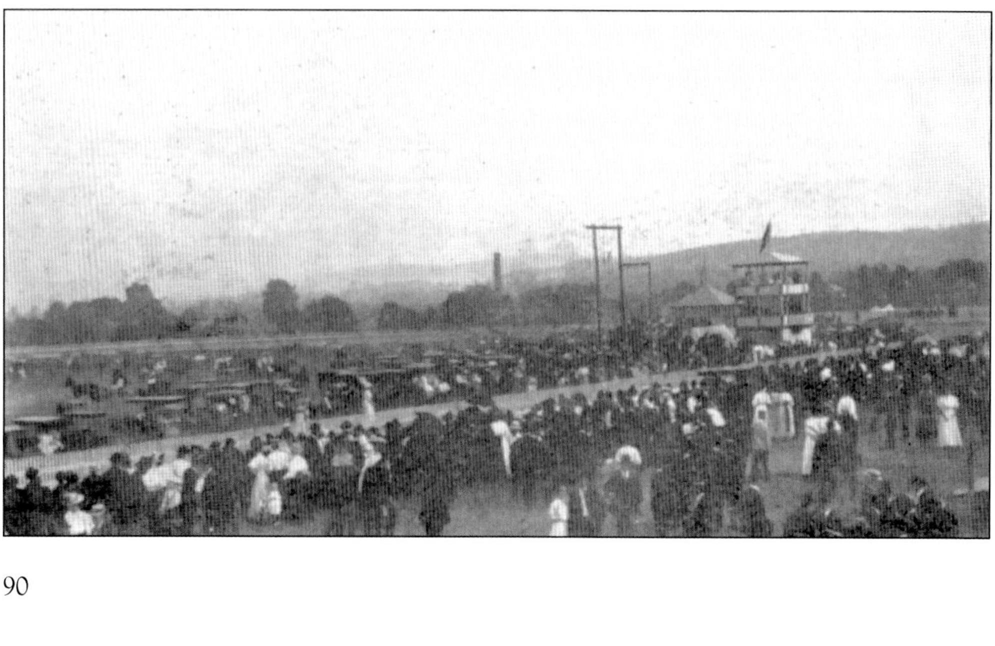

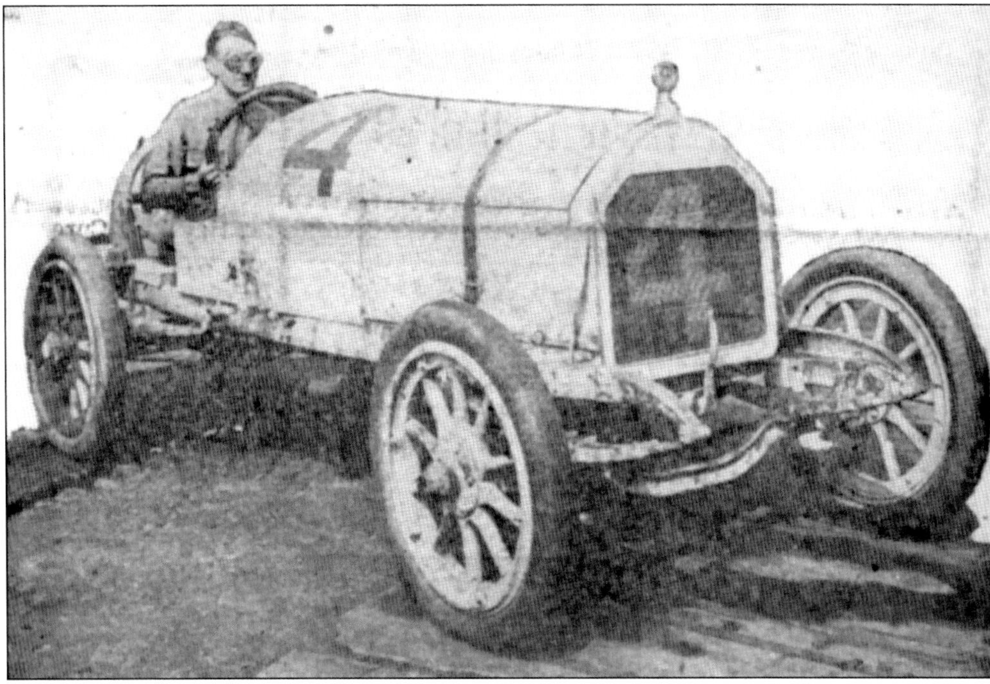

By 1919, interest in car and motorcycle racing was becoming popular, and the fairgrounds were the ideal place for them to be held. Michigan Special, Packard, Disbrow, and Stutz were some of the cars that raced. On September 18, 1919, the last race of the night, R.M. Franklin (in the Packard) went over the eastern bank and turned turtle, but the driver was uninjured. The Corry band furnished music throughout the program.

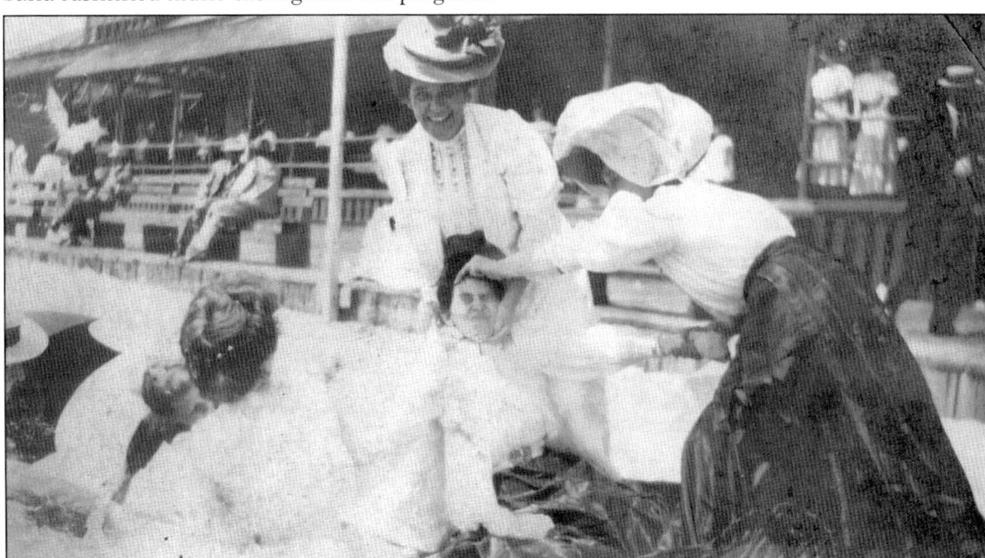

During a sermon at a local church in 1915, the reverend made a public notice on the officials of the Corry Fair and Driving Park Association. He warned that if gambling or other immoral shows were permitted on the grounds during the coming year, the true facts in the case would be formally carried to the governor—if it became necessary to proceed that far in order to stop the alleged illegal practices.

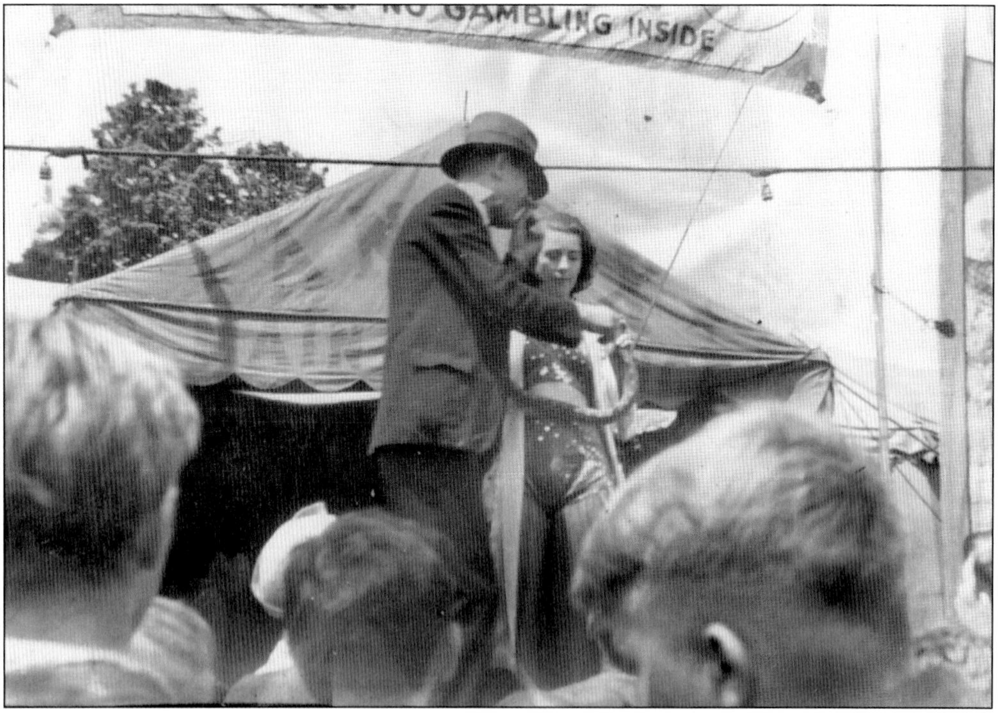

As the fair became more popular and crowds became bigger, problems also increased. Con men were drawn in from great distances to cash in on the great amounts of money the fair brought into town. Sneaking in without paying, pickpockets, sucker games, drinking, robbery, and excessive gambling were rampant. Local churches waged a fight against the sinful behavior and eventually forced the fair and racetrack to close.

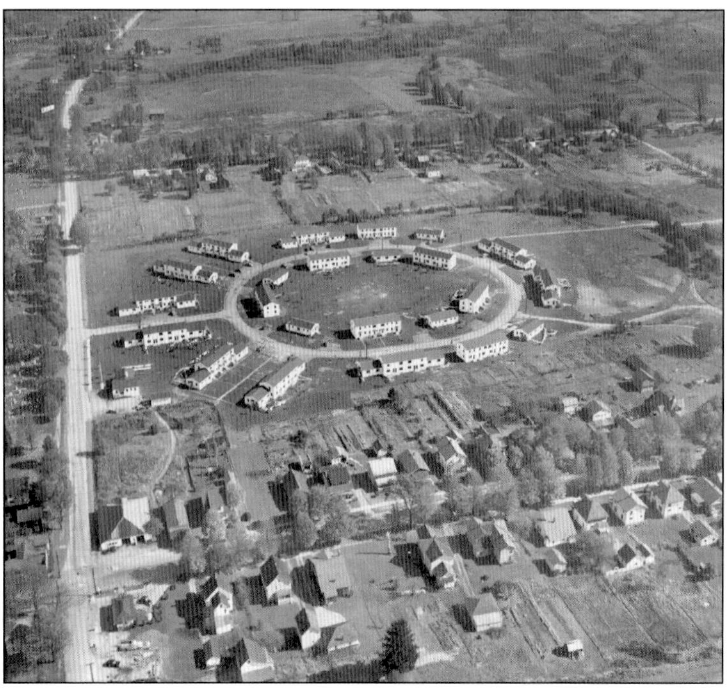

A disagreement arose between James Wright and the Corry School District about the ownership of the fairgrounds property as well as 20 years of unpaid taxes. This discrepancy was brought to the attention of the federal government, who bought the site for a housing development called Fairhaven. The development provided housing for World War II soldiers coming home after the war and their families. It is now know as Snyder's Circle.

Eight

Corry to Columbus Street Railway

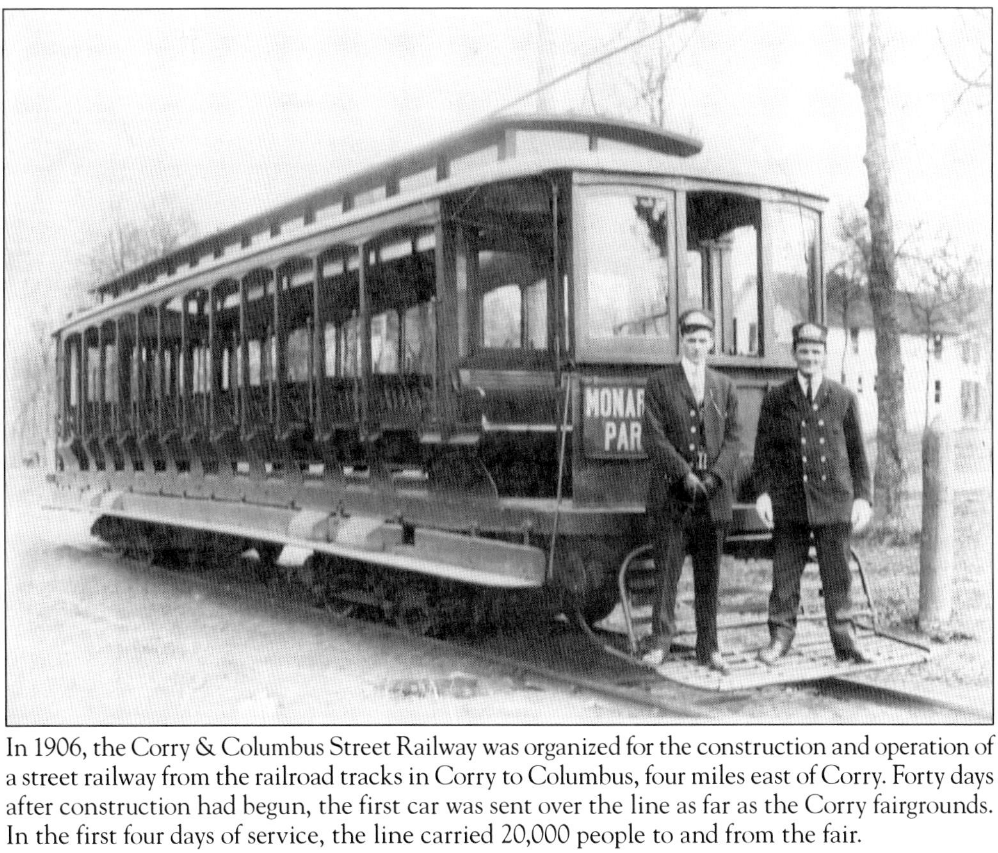

In 1906, the Corry & Columbus Street Railway was organized for the construction and operation of a street railway from the railroad tracks in Corry to Columbus, four miles east of Corry. Forty days after construction had begun, the first car was sent over the line as far as the Corry fairgrounds. In the first four days of service, the line carried 20,000 people to and from the fair.

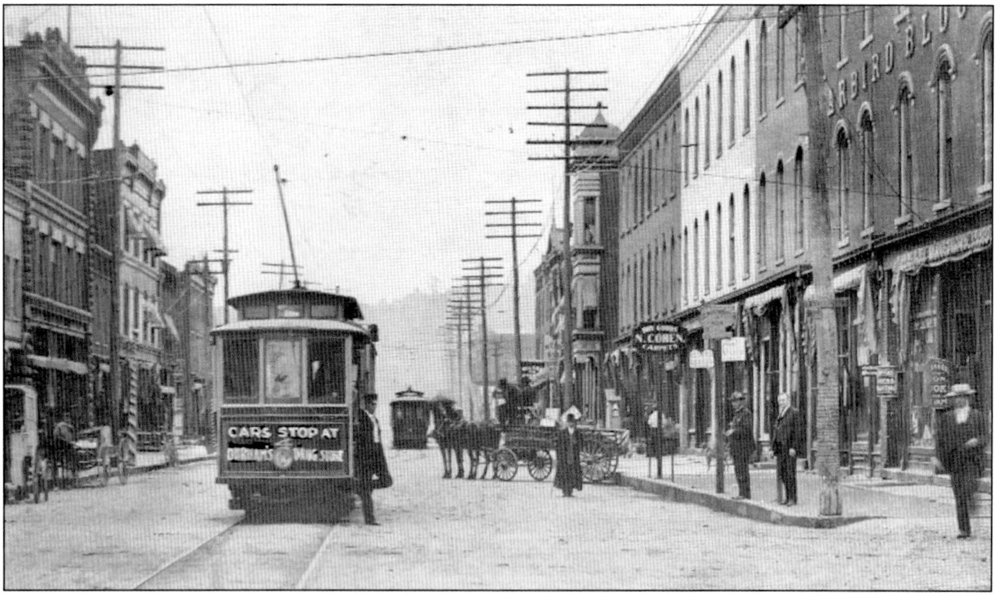

On September 27, 1906, a Citizen's Banquet was held in honor of the Corry & Columbus Street Railway. The menu included oyster cocktail, saltines, olives, and celery for appetizers; sirloin of beef, brown gravy, mashed potatoes, bread, hot brown bread, tomato salad, sliced ham, and cold tongue for the entrée; and current jelly, catsup, and salted nuts served on the side. Ice cream, assorted cake, coffee, bonbons, and cigars were served for dessert.

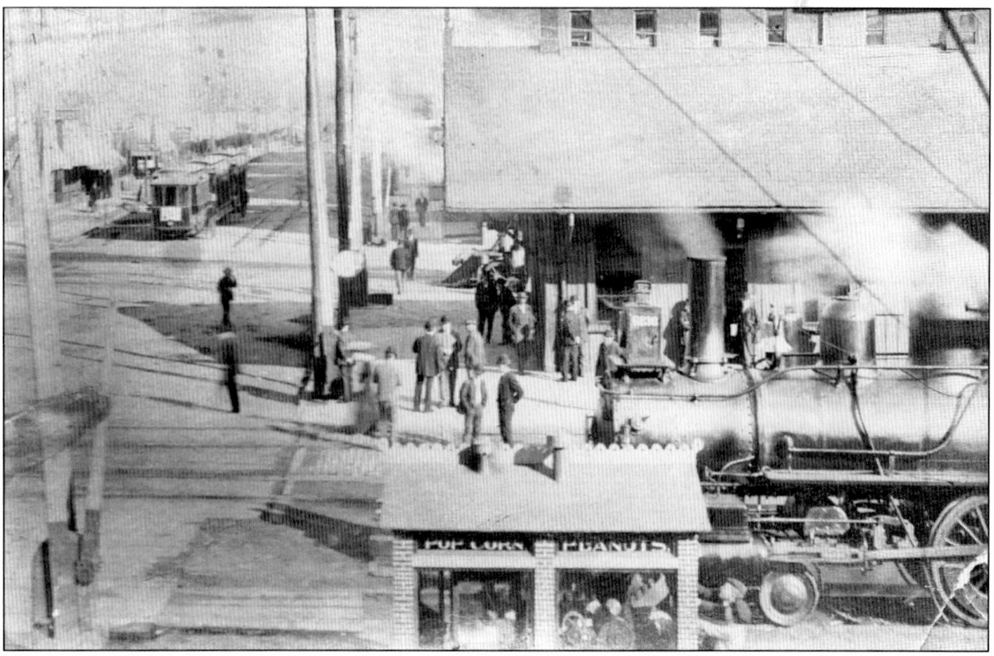

This photograph shows the trolley stopping in front of the Traction Building, which was known as the Gaston Building before it was remodeled into a beautiful waiting room with a restaurant, arcade, and souvenir shop. It was conveniently located within steps of the depot for both train and trolley passengers to wait to transfer from one to the other, thus the name "Traction" Building. Clough's peanut stand in the foreground was famous for a quick snack.

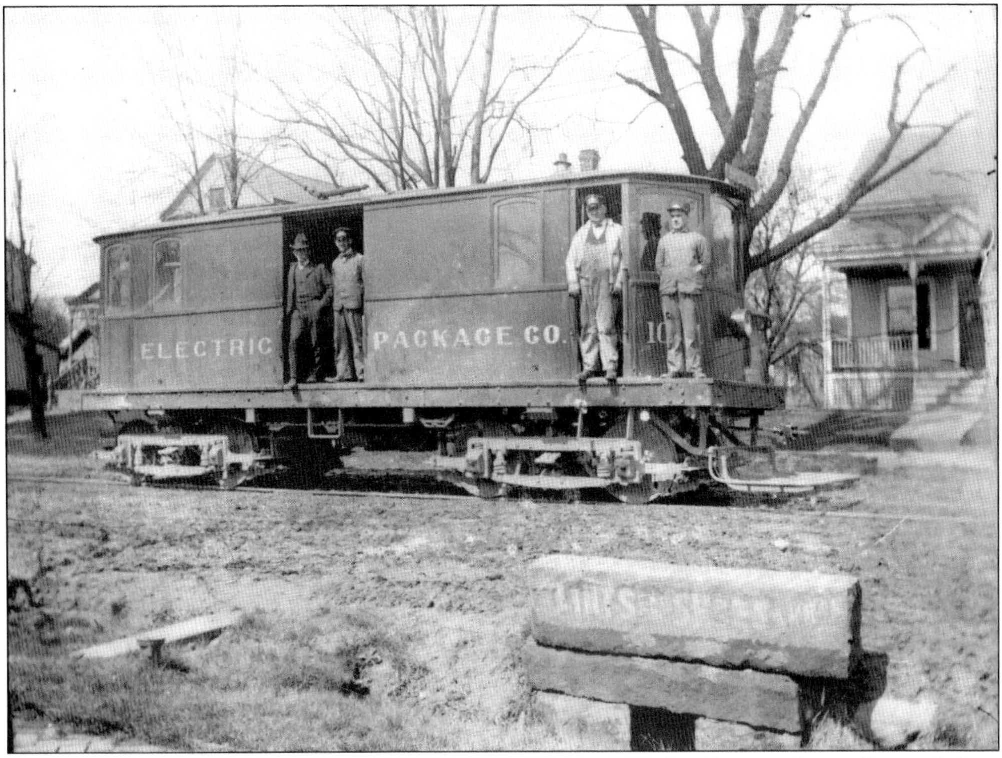

Wooden butter tubs that were made in Corry were sent to Columbus on the trolley and then filled at the Columbus Creamery, located on the west side of Brokenstraw Creek. Tons of butter was shipped on the train to Erie, Buffalo, and Pittsburgh. The cream and butter were loaded into specially designed refrigerated cars and then hooked to the trolley for its regular trip back to Corry.

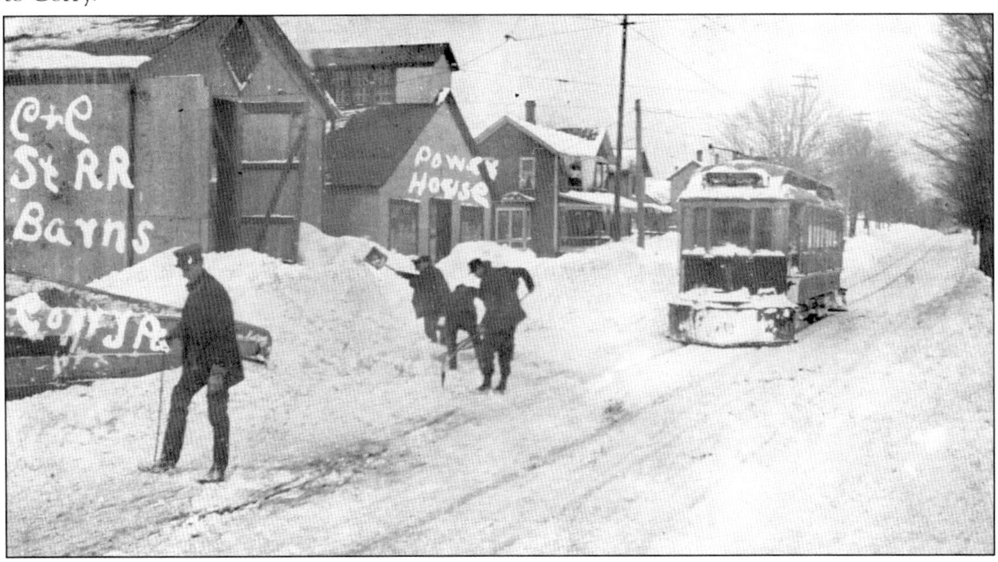

In 1906, two buildings were constructed on the west side of Center Street on both sides of Bear Creek. The powerhouse was built on the north side of the creek, and the car barns were on the south side. There was a catwalk across the creek to get from one to the other.

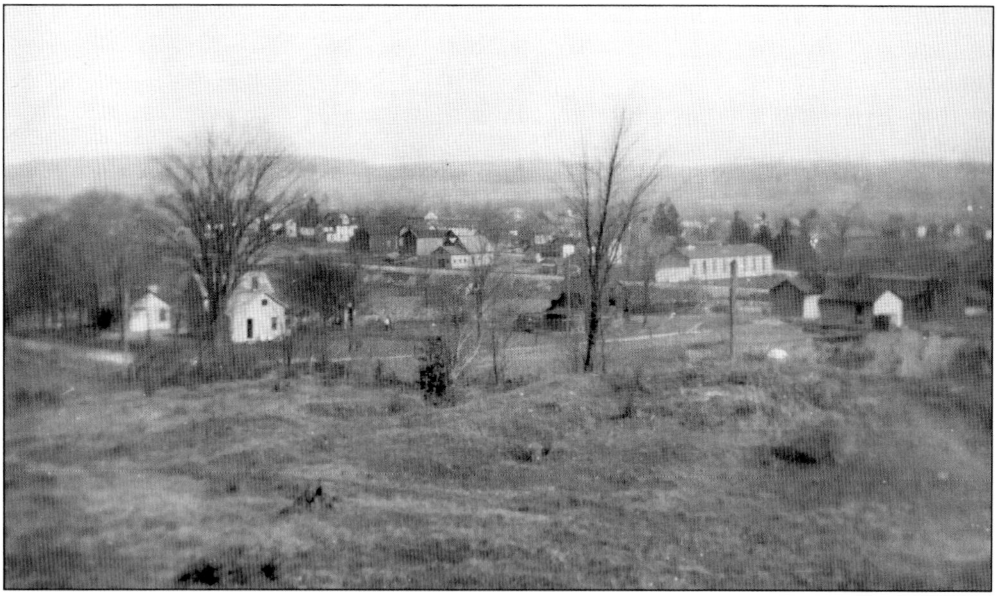

The trolley pole extended above the roof to a grooved pulley wheel that made contact with a "hot wire." The current came down the pole and was wired to the motor. The smaller cars had one motor on each end, and the larger no. 24 had two motors on each end. The trolley ran on electricity, partly from the city electric company and partly produced from a generator at the powerhouse (near the trolley barn seen in the distance in this photograph). A 110-horsepower, twin-cylinder Struthers Wells engine, running on gas and weighing 30,000 pounds, powered this generator. The direct current went through a transformer, which adapted the power to the 550 volts necessary to operate the streetcar.

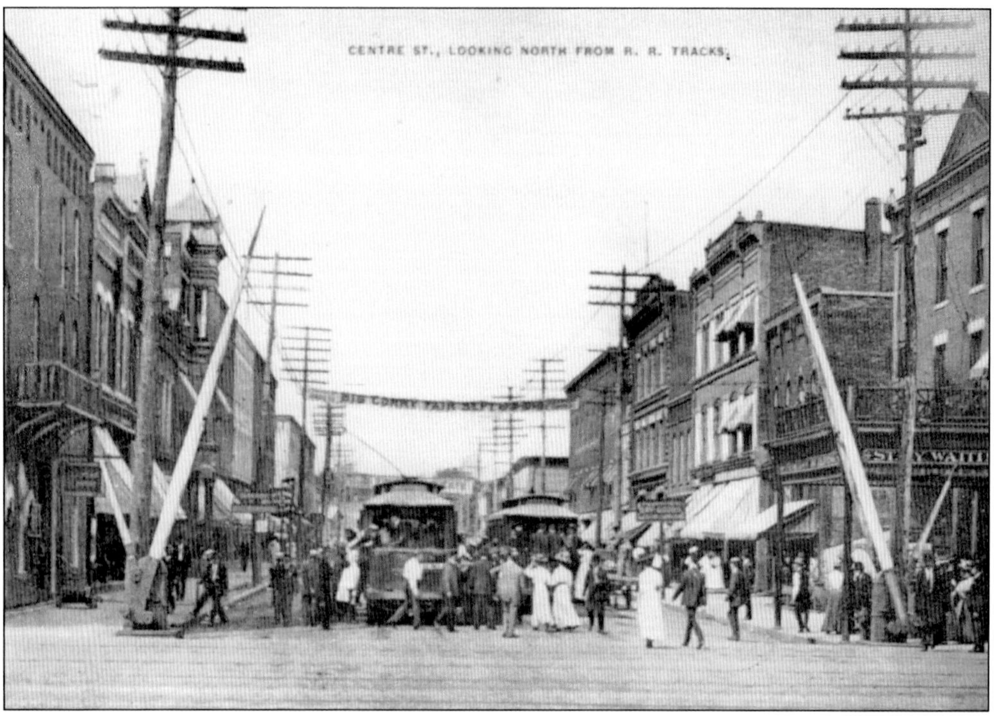

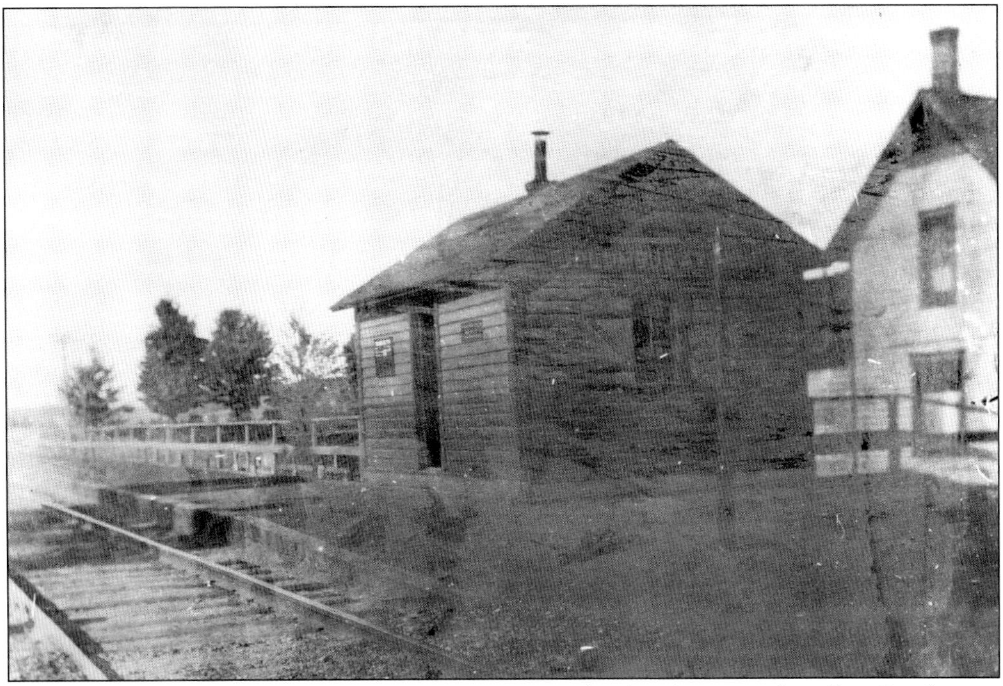

North Corry depot was two miles north of Corry on Columbus Avenue, where Ritz Candy store is now. In 1916, the Buffalo to Pittsburgh train stopped at Columbus Avenue every day. It was faster to get off the train here and take trolley into town then it was to stay on the train, go past town, wait for another train to leave, then back up to the depot to disembark.

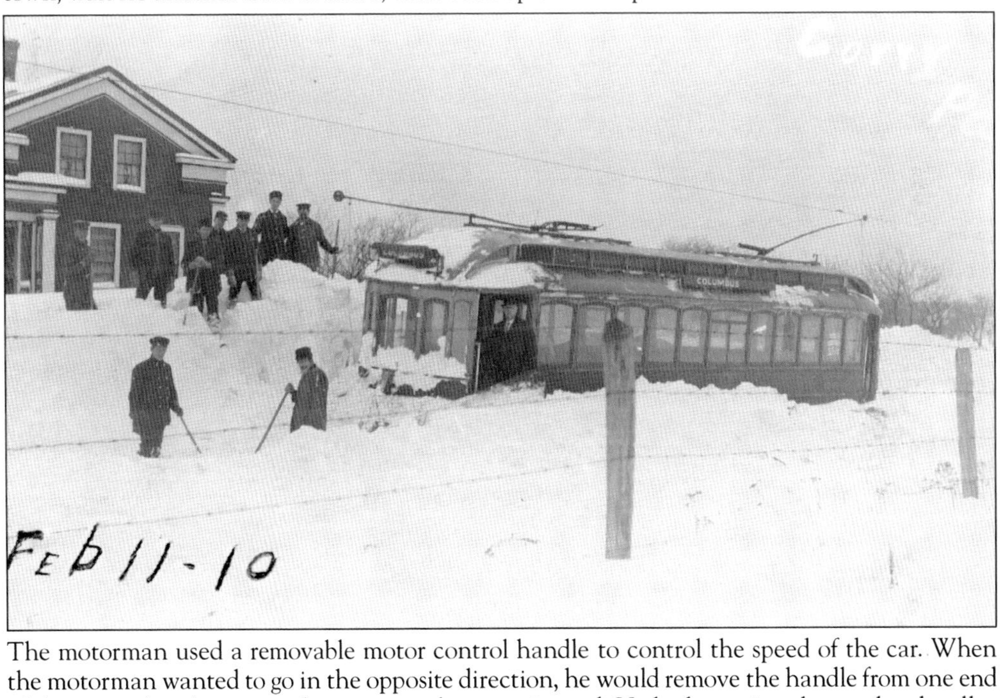

The motorman used a removable motor control handle to control the speed of the car. When the motorman wanted to go in the opposite direction, he would remove the handle from one end of the car and replace it on the motor at the opposite end. He had to swing the overhead trolley pole so it would make contact to the opposite motor; then he was ready to go.

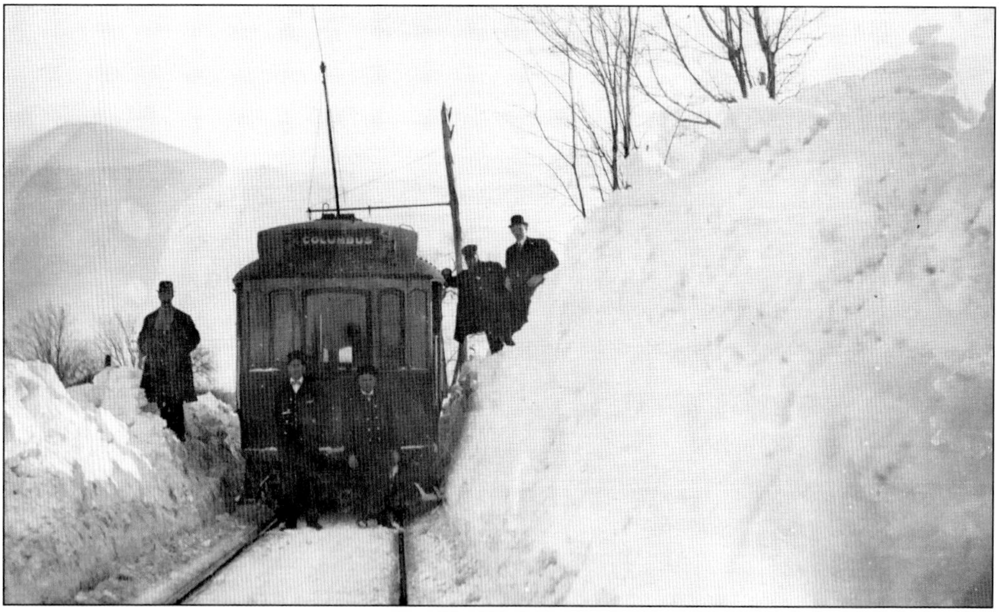

The summer cars had open sides and outside running boards along the sides. Car No. 24 was the largest and the pride of the fleet. It was enclosed, double-trucked, had red Wilton velvet plush seats, air brakes, and electric heat. It was used the most during the winter, as it was heavier, more comfortable, and carried the snowplows. The streetcar was the main way of plowing Center Street, and the city became dependent on the big plow to keep traffic moving in deep snow. A large "V" plow was used first to clear the center of the street, and then a wing plow was mounted on the side to clear first the left then the right side of the street.

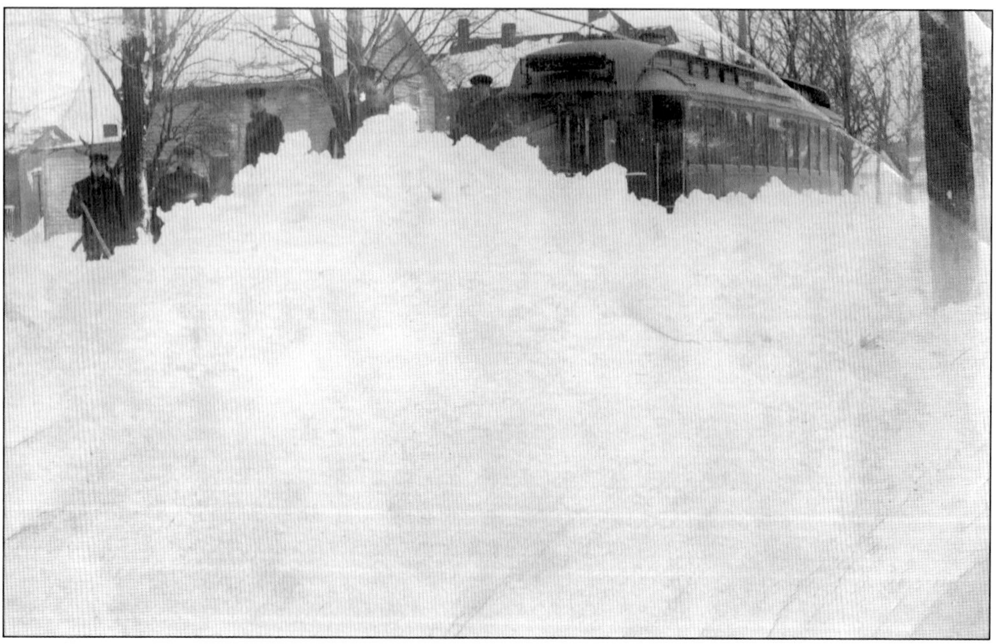

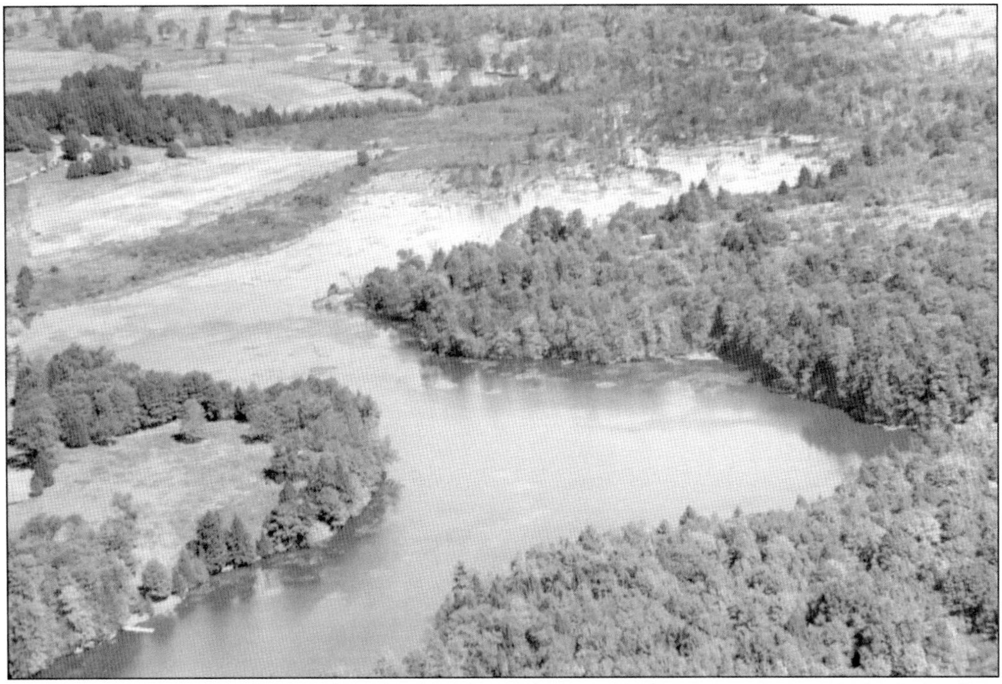

As well as transporting thousands to the fair, the trolley provided transportation to Lake Columbus. A dam was built in the Brokenstraw Creek in Columbus, Pennsylvania, creating a seven-mile lake stretching almost to Clymer, New York. A paddle wheel steamer capable of seating 80 passengers and a smaller gasoline launch carried crowds to Brokenstraw Park at the north end of the lake. The east side of the lake was a popular area to build cottages and spend the summer. Here, the weekender could fish, picnic, watch a ball game, eat at the restaurant, or dance to a local orchestra and then ride the trolley back to Corry.

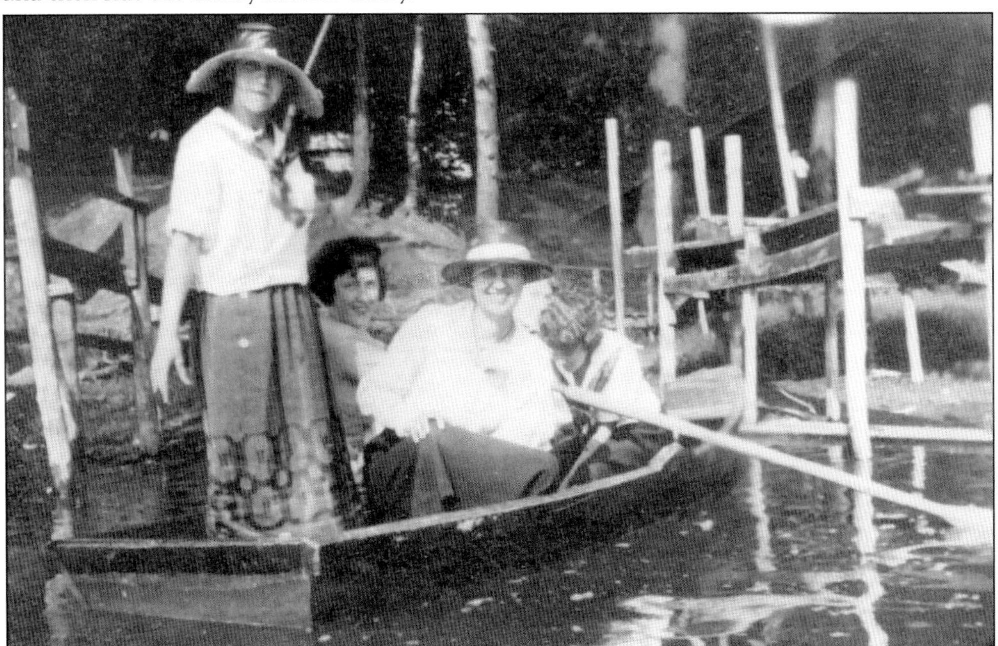

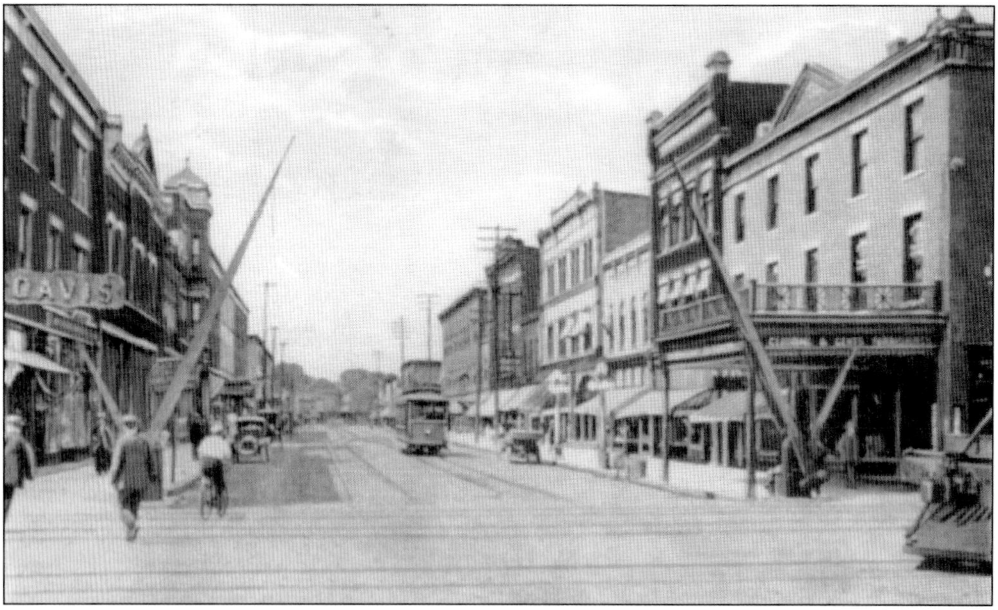

The four earliest small cars had a seating capacity of 30 passengers. When business was brisk, aisles were also jammed full. The car bodies were wood and steel, and the interiors were wood trimmed with mahogany. The summer cars had slat-type seats made of cherry and mahogany. The original five cars were closed and suitable for year-round use with seat coverings made of woven straw fiber.

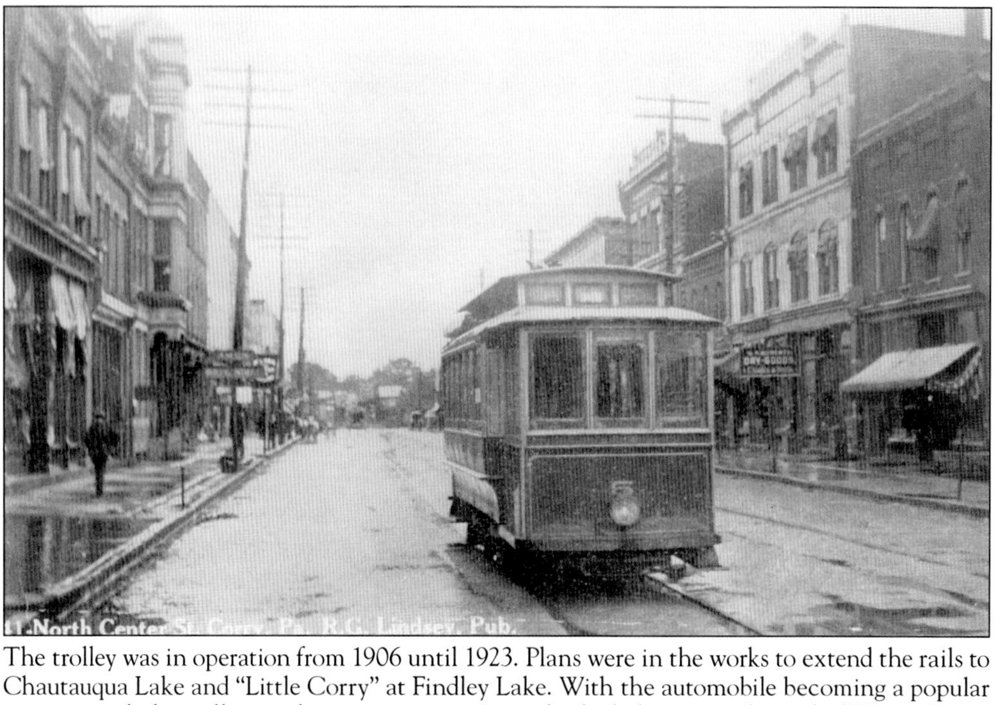

The trolley was in operation from 1906 until 1923. Plans were in the works to extend the rails to Chautauqua Lake and "Little Corry" at Findley Lake. With the automobile becoming a popular way to travel, the trolley was losing customers. It was hit by lightning at the end of Wayne Street on August 22, 1923. Fred Kinley was the motorman on this last run, and he later became mayor of Corry.

Nine

People to See and Places to Go

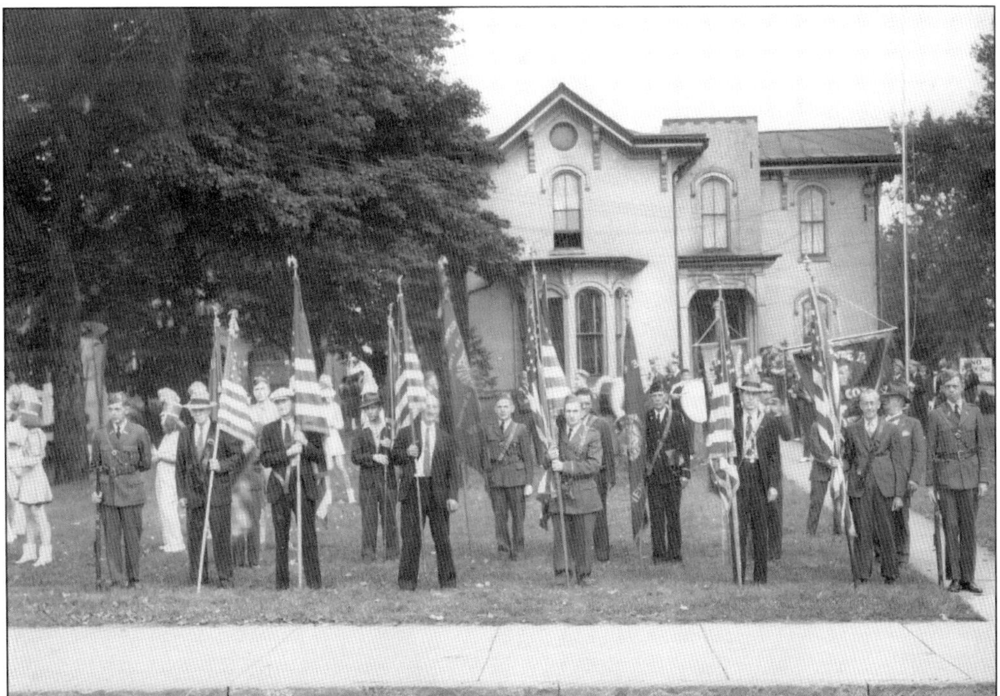

The Veterans of Foreign Wars is only one of many organizations that have been in the Corry area since people started to gather in the city. They started groups that had a common interest, such as groups to play games, make quilts, or accomplish a particular goal. Some groups collected dues as insurance against some tragedy striking one of the members.

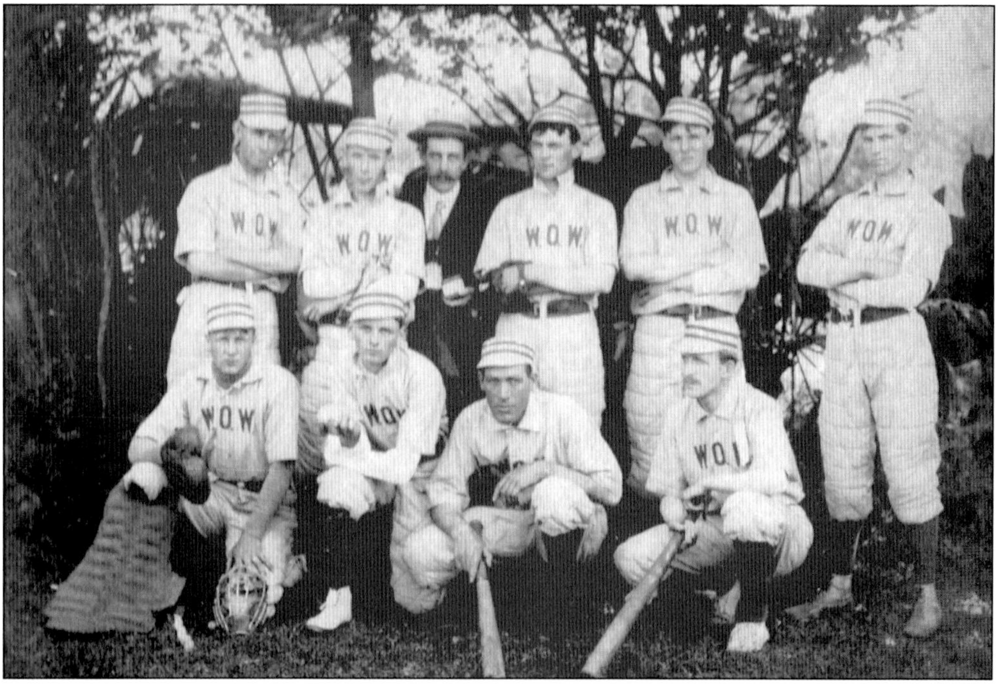

Woodmen of the World, camp no. 15, is a fraternal organization organized in 1892. The first meetings were held at what was then the Starbird Block at the corner of Center and Washington Streets. In 1913, they moved to the elegant, commodious, and convenient quarters occupying the upper story of the Traction Building, with clubrooms, billiard and pool tables, and lodge room.

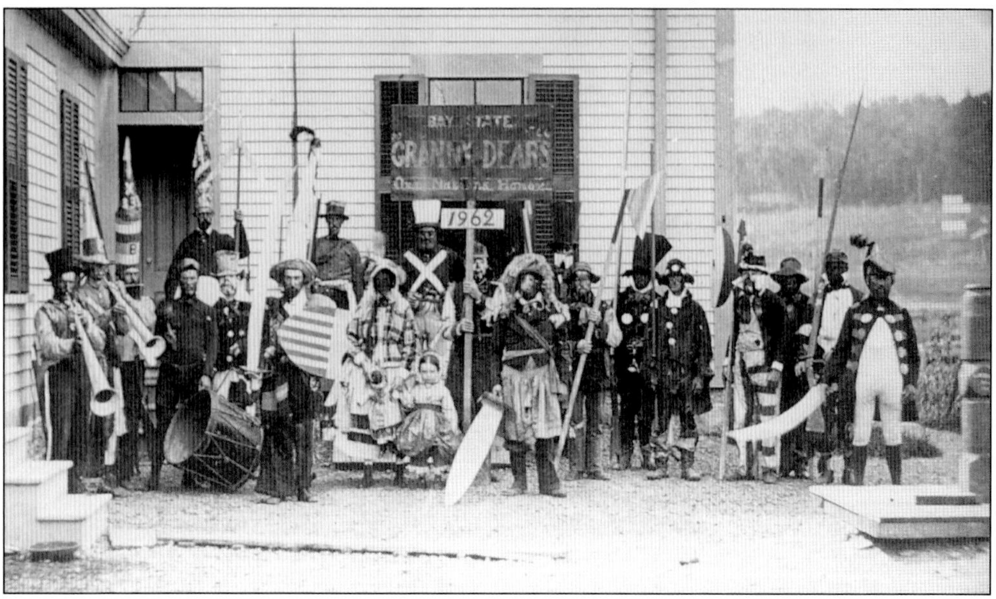

The parade leaders of the first Fourth of July parade in Corry met behind the George H. Coney residence on Washington Street after the parade in 1862. "Bay State" was a nickname for Massachusetts, and "Granny Dears" sounds suspiciously like Grenadiers, (British Grenadiers fought the colonists in the Revolutionary War). They may have been spoofing the Colonial British troops.

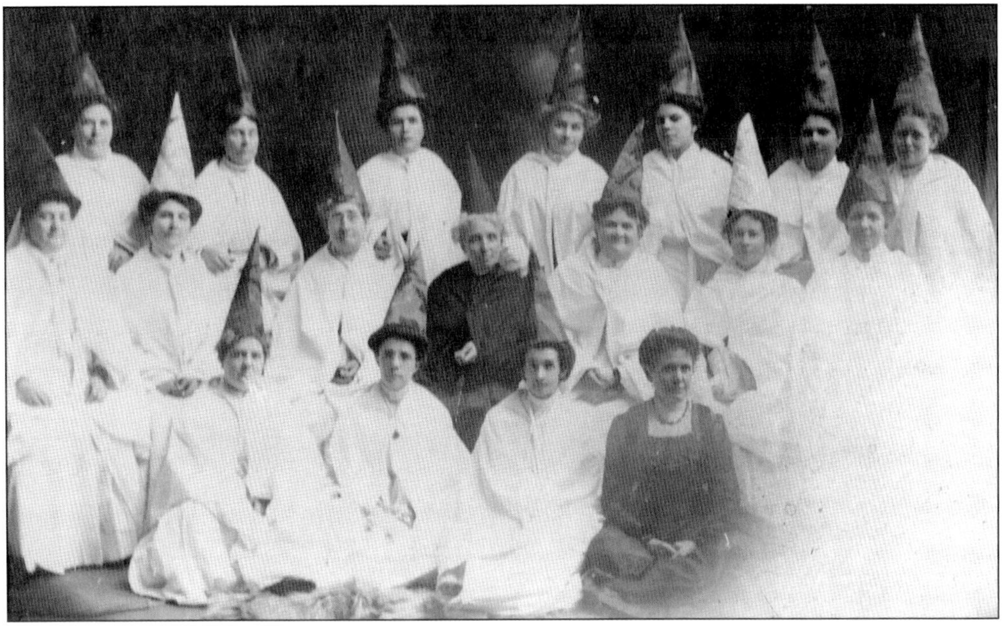

Ladies of the Maccabees, Hive 44, was organized on February 22, 1894, in the Starbird Hall on the corner of Center and Washington Streets. Starting with 54 beneficiary members, it grew to 210 with 32 social members in 1913. They held many events, and social times were every other week after the meetings. The guard team of 16 members was one of the best drill teams in this part of Pennsylvania.

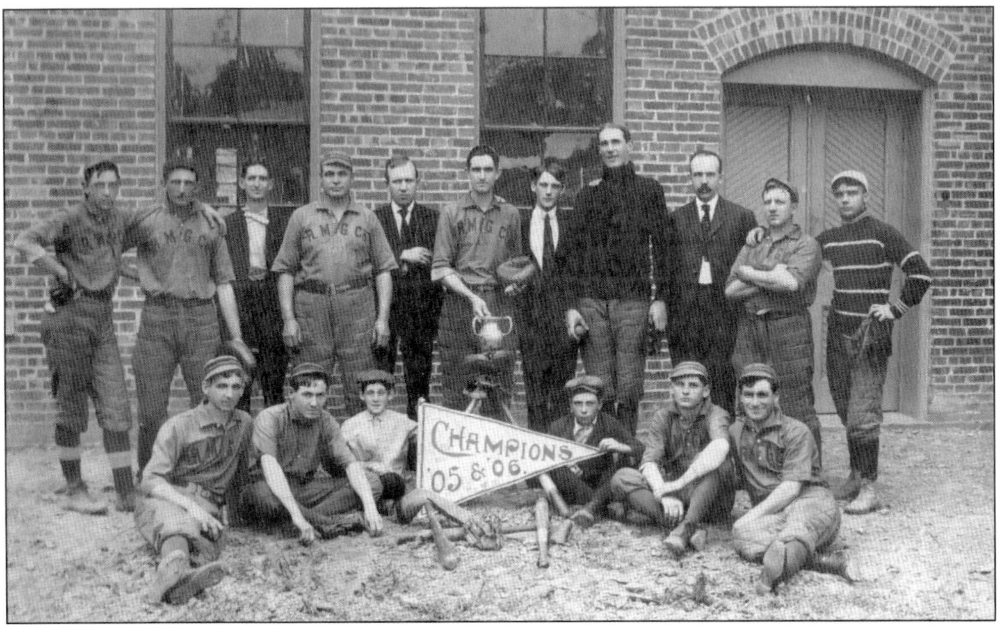

In the spring of 1905, a few local baseball enthusiasts met in the chamber of commerce office on Main Street and organized the Corry Baseball League. The first four teams were the Raymond Manufacturing Company, Kurtz Brass Bed Company, Municipal Club, and Corry High School. The diamond was located on Washington Street with a grandstand and bleachers. Raymonds won the first trophy, which was donated by D. Warren DeRosay.

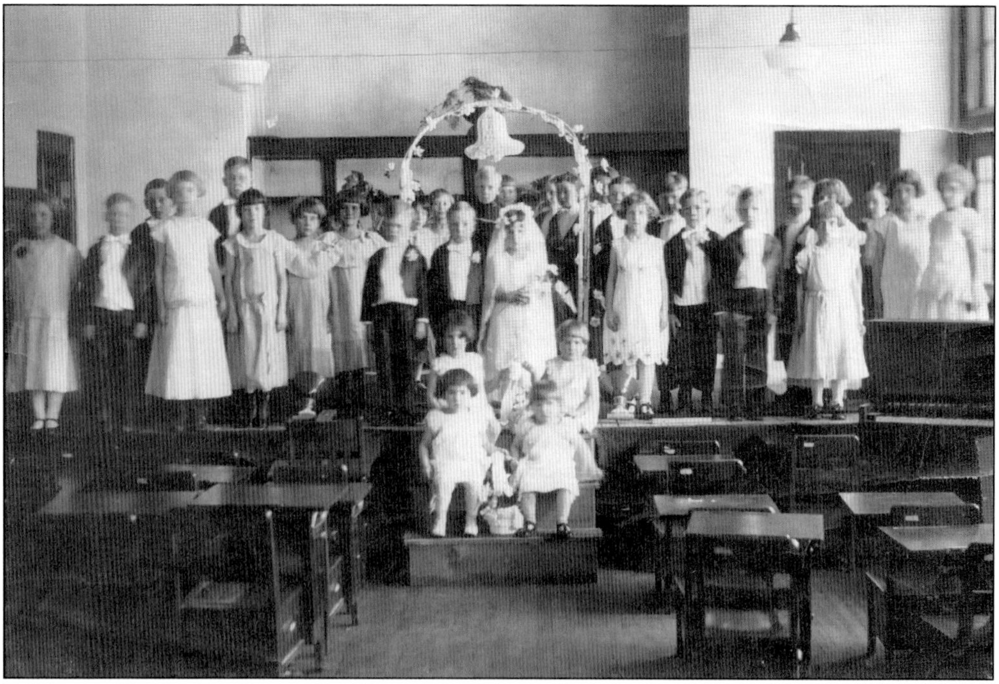

Gen. Tom Thumb married Lavinia Warren (both little people) on February 10, 1863, at Barnum's American Museum in New York. P.T. Barnum turned the wedding into a huge celebration. It was an expensive, lavish affair and became a fanciful legend. The fascination of the wedding still carries on to this day. Churches and schools put on plays for fun and fundraisers, including the Harding school in 1925.

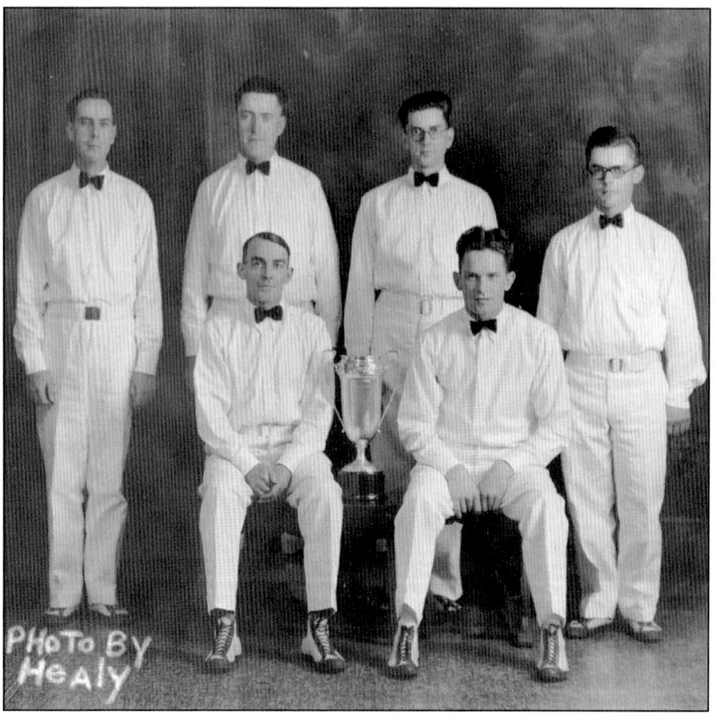

First aid is always an important part of the work day for gas and electric companies, and serious training became a friendly competition. The winners of the Northwestern Region of Pennsylvania received a sterling silver trophy to be displayed in their office until the next year. The champions in 1929 were from the Corry Penelec office. Pictured are (standing) J.R. Dearing (captain), E.H. Miller, A.L. Young, and Dorr Clark; (sitting) H. Rouscher, and C.C. Anderson. (Author's collection.)

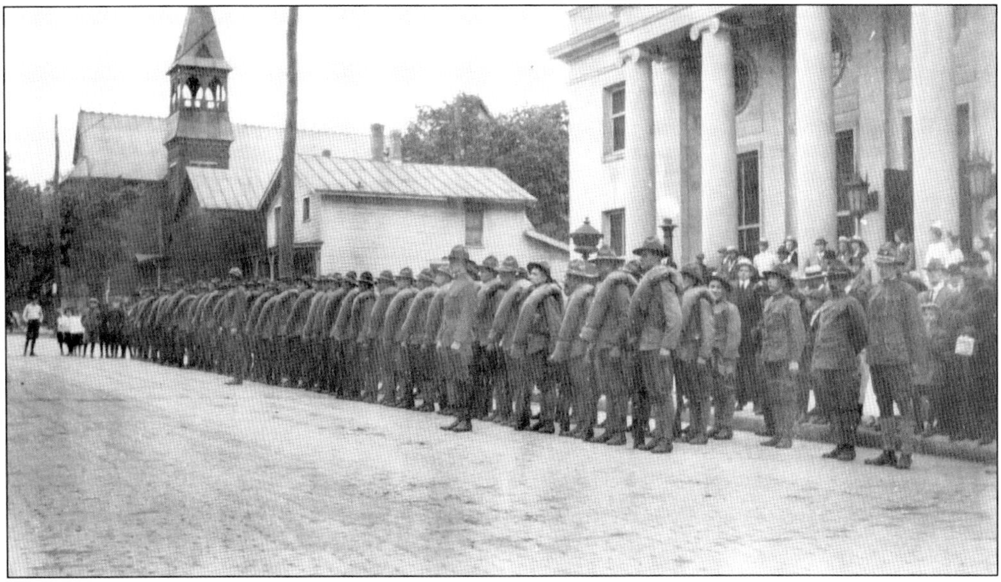

During World War I in June 1916, a tremendous crowd gathered at the Corry Depot to see Company A, 16th Regiment, leave for state mobilization camp at Mount Gretna, then possibly a long service in Mexico and anywhere they may be needed. The greatest gathering that Corry had ever witnessed watched as Captain Brown marched the company of 80 men from the armory on the corner of Maple Avenue and Washington Street, then west on Washington, and South on Center to the Federal Building. After saying farewell to their family and friends with a lot of cheering and weeping, and the train with the Erie Company cheering them on and singing in the first two coaches, they boarded the special troop train and headed for the war.

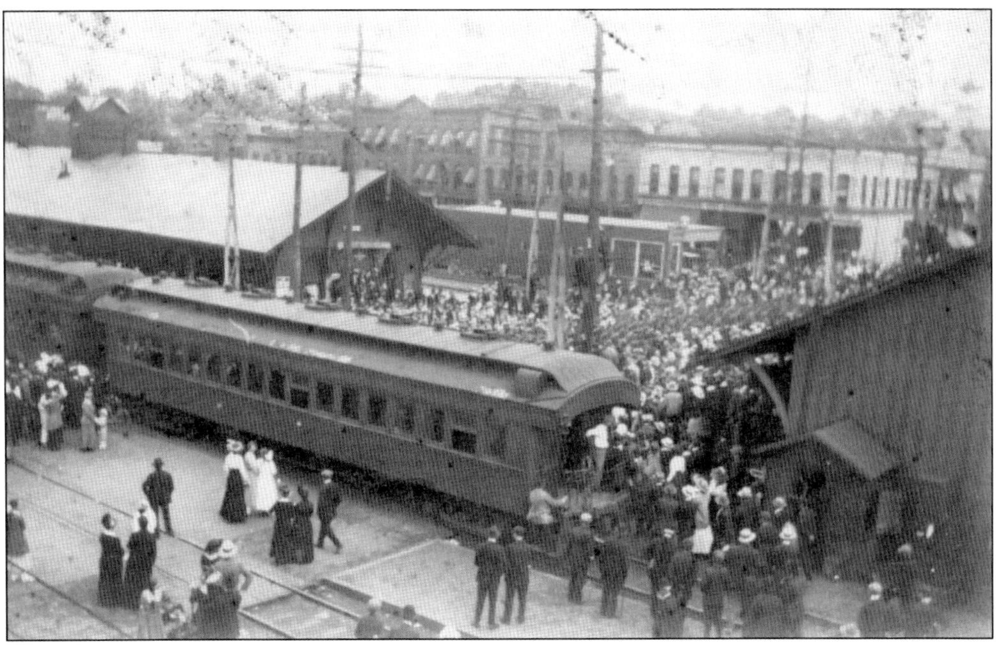

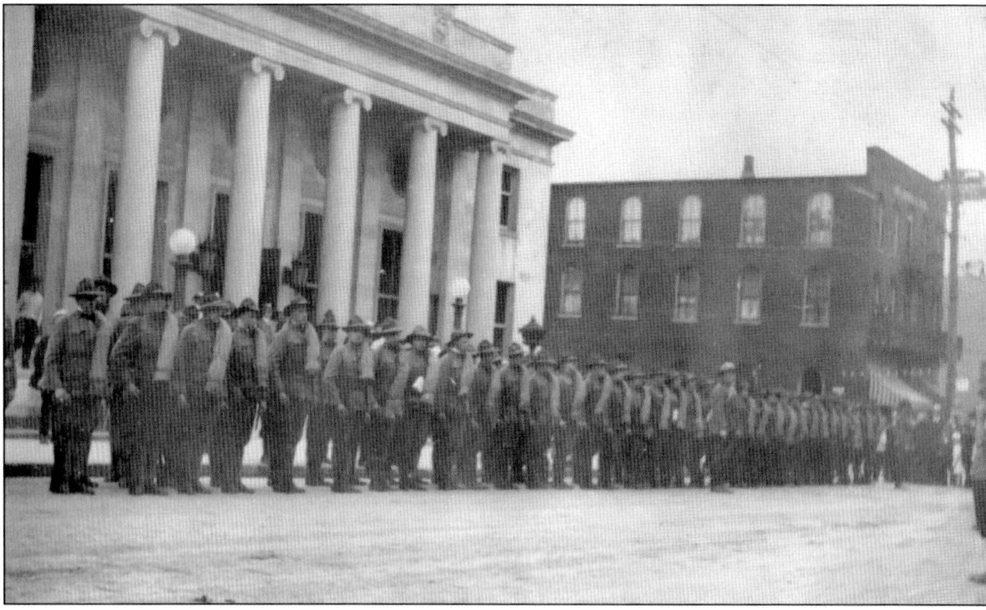

In June 1916, when 80 members of the National Guard Company A from Corry left for mobilization camp at Mount Gretna, the officers were as follows: R.W. Brown, captain; Jack Richards, lieutenant; Wallace Wolman, first sergeant; P. Dean Hyde; Harry Haenel; Charles Keefer; Joseph Barnhart; and Perry LaPaze, all corporals. The rank and file of the company won the respect of the community. Every single man answered the mobilization call, and Thursday morning found every member ready to report at the armory. This was not the case in a few other towns, where some members did not report for duty. Company A left home intact and with many new recruits.

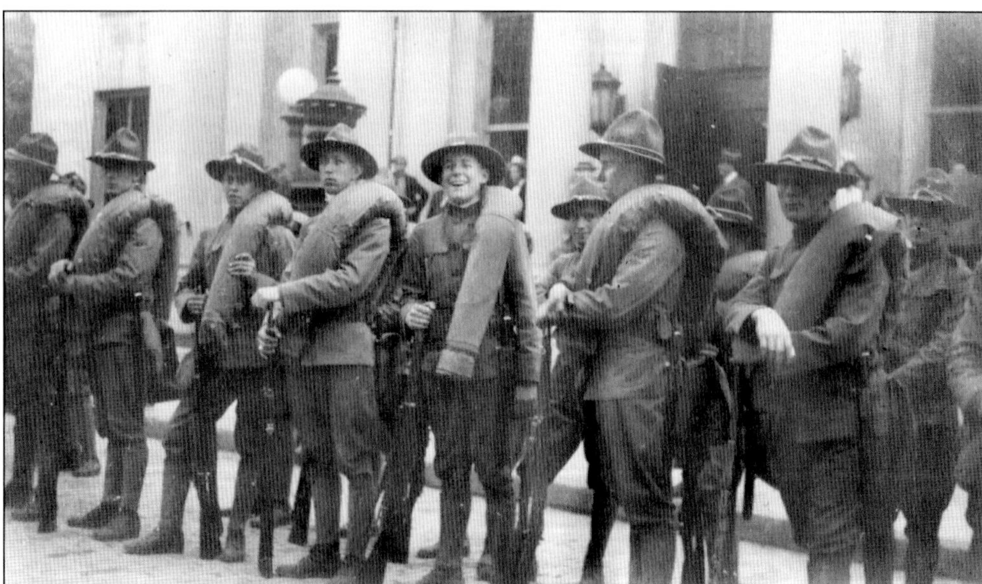

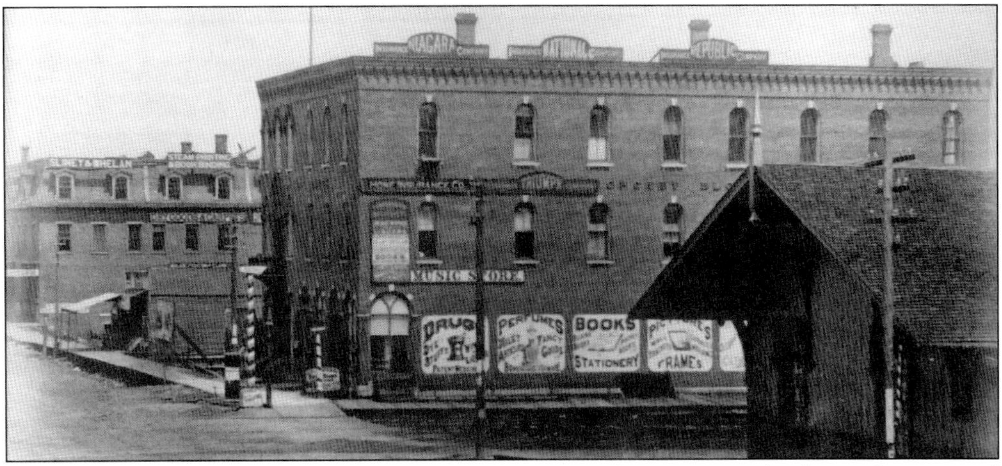

This was a rare sight in 1870: no one on Center Street and no trains at the depot. On a typical day, there would be dozens of trains stopping to transfer goods and passengers from one train to another, local citizens running errands, and travelers shopping while waiting for the next train. The Crosby block was on the east side of Center Street, next to the railroad tracks. It burned in 1875. (Courtesy of the Corry Fire Department.)

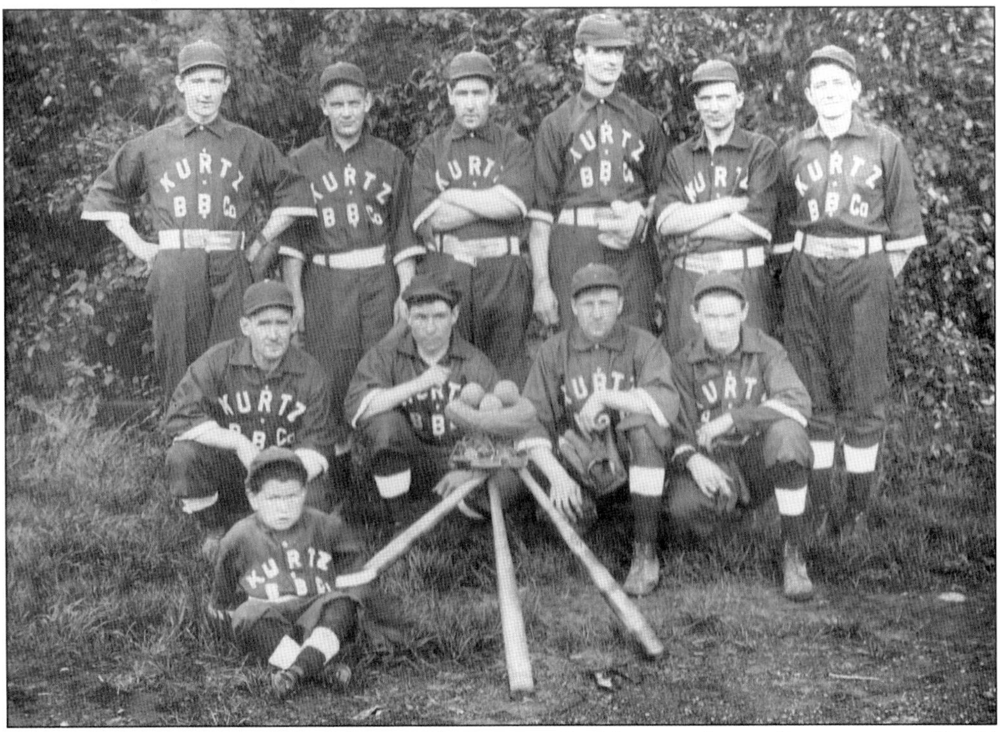

In 1913, crowds would gather in front of the Traction Building on Center Street to enjoy World Series baseball games as they happened. The *Journal* set up a bulletin board that showed the scores, and a direct wire connection was run to the balcony so that local fans could enjoy the game play-by-play. A man with a megaphone announced each play as it came over the wire. In bad weather, local merchants would let their awnings down to give the crowd shelter while watching the game. The local manufacturers organized their own teams and played good-hearted, but serious, baseball games at a ball diamond east of town.

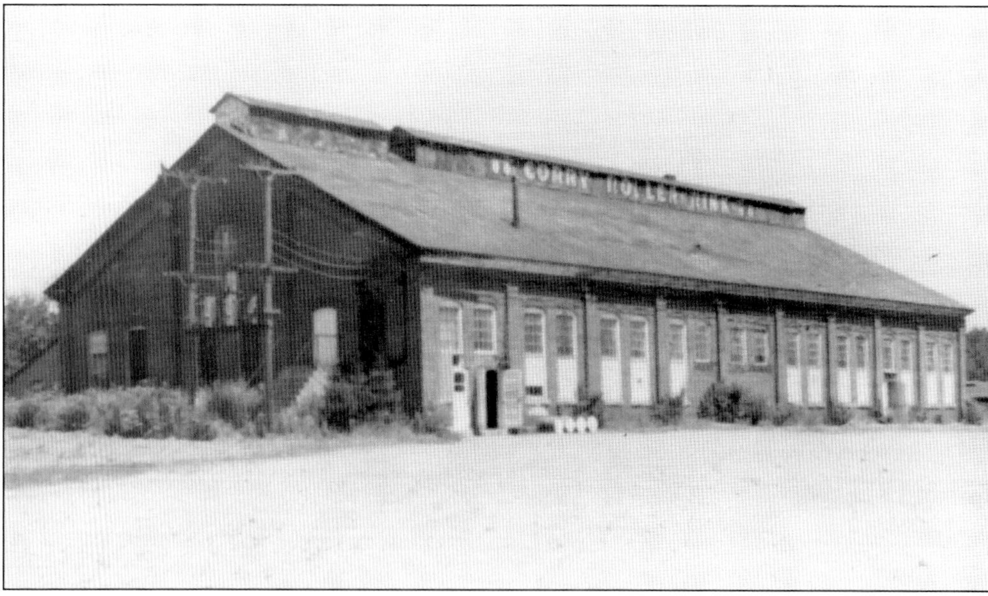

Waclark Titanite Explosive Company built this structure in 1909 on 20 acres of land north of Corry on Main Street. After the company closed, it became a popular roller-skating rink for kids to meet and have fun. It then became home of Erie Plastics, and when the plastics moved to a larger plant, it again became a roller-skating rink.

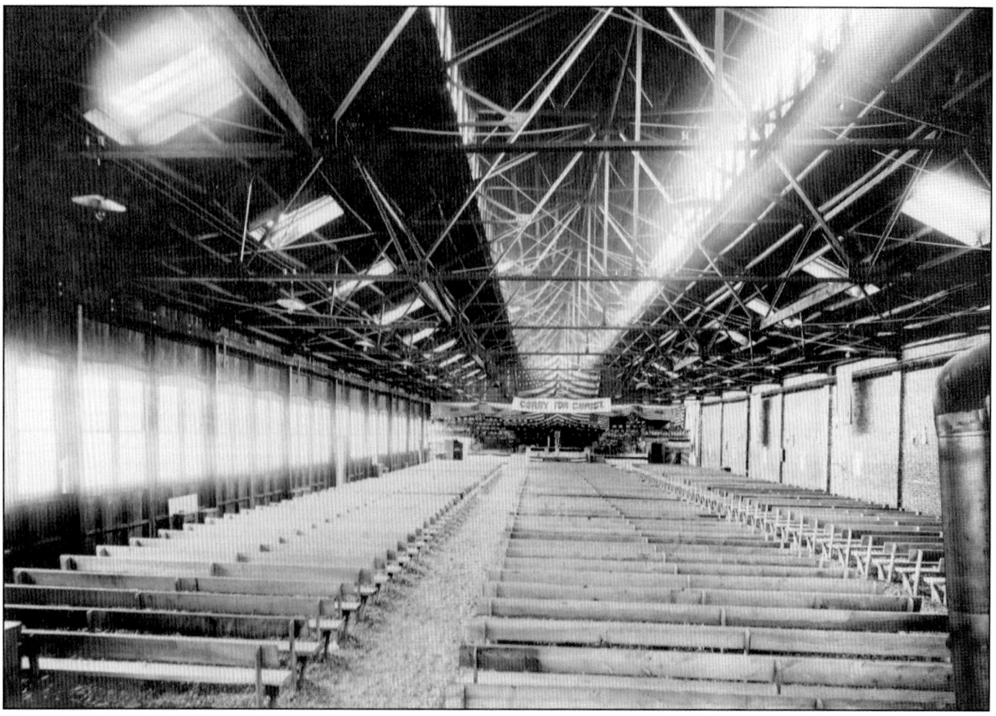

The United States Radiator and Boiler Company moved to Corry in 1905 and was located along First Avenue between Washington and Main Streets. They built a huge union meeting hall that was loaned to various groups who needed a larger place to gather. Corry for Christ was one of the bigger groups to use it.

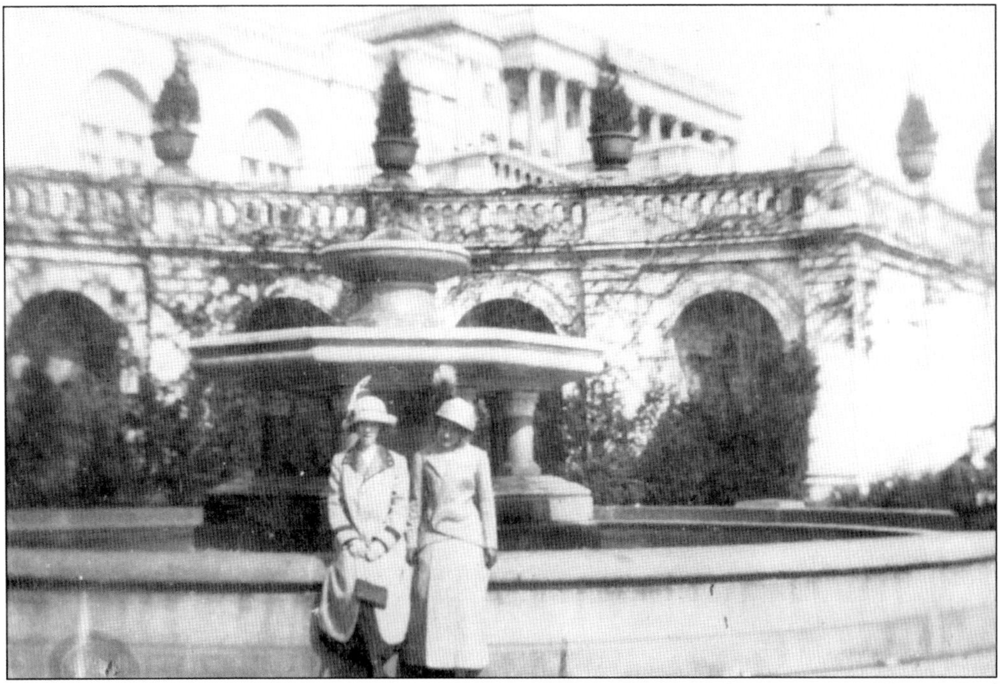

In 1913, the senior class at Corry High School went on a trip to Washington, DC. They visited the White House, the Capitol, and Arlington Cemetery. They even met Pres. Woodrow Wilson when he greeted them at the White House.

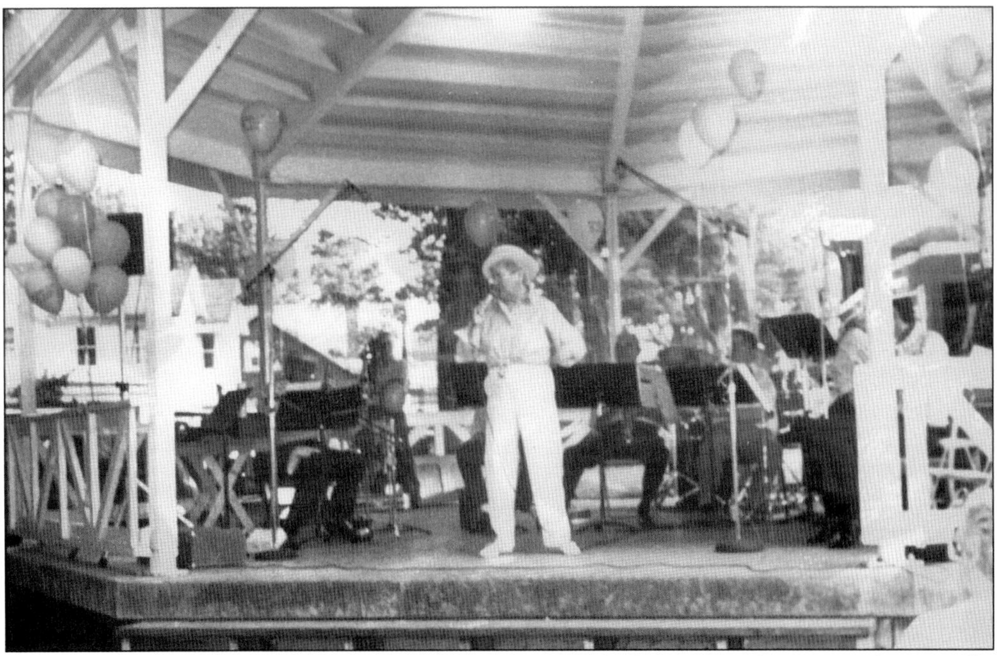

Gertie White was the owner of Reed Shop, a women's clothing store that was in business for years on Center Street. In her younger days, she was a singer with big bands, which were popular in the 1940s and 1950s. She traveled around the country entertaining crowds with show tunes. Gertie was also a fantastic artist with oil paints.

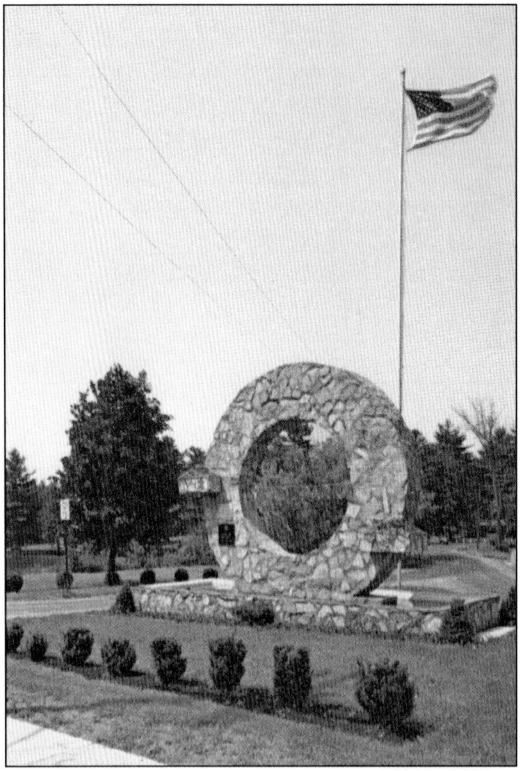

Glenn Mead owned a parcel of land known as Collin's Woods on West Wayne Street. His vision was that it should become a public park, so on Thanksgiving Day 1940, he gave the property to the City of Corry for that purpose. Mead Park Pond's actual name is Alice Lake, named after Mead's mother. In 1944, Mead bought the connecting land, known as Francis's Grove, from Sarah Francis for $1. Mead also gave this land to the city on Thanksgiving Day 1947, thus doubling the size of the park. He gave his entire estate to the park association for improvements and maintenance of the park. He was a member of the Corry Rotary, so a Rotary symbol was built at the entrance to the park in his honor.

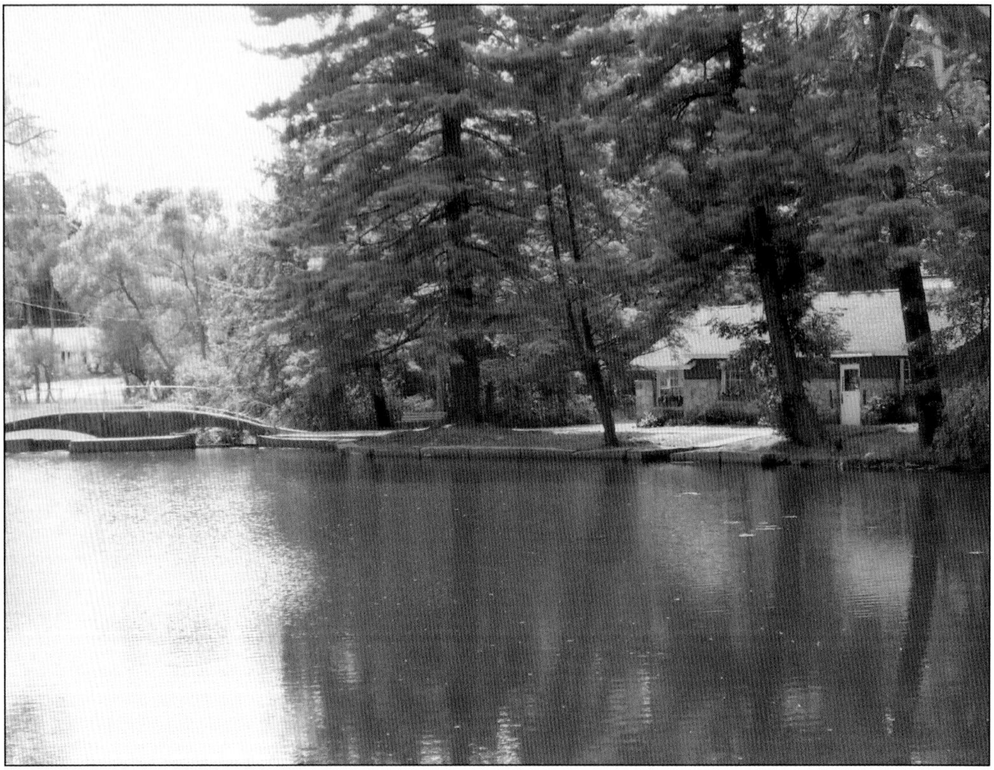

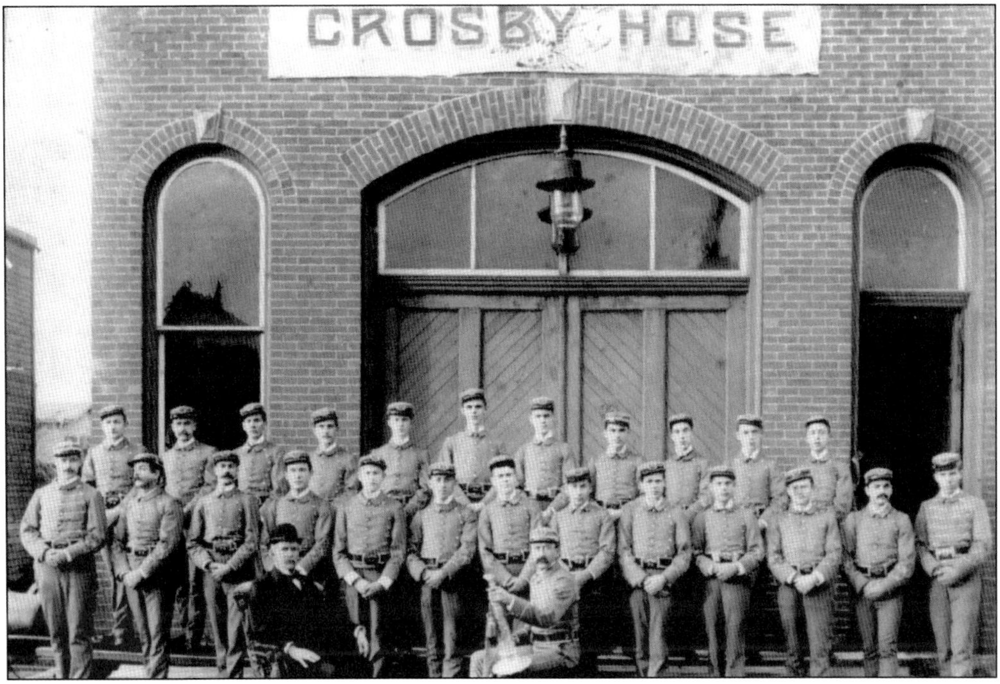

In 1890, H.A. Penrose called a meeting of men from around Pennsylvania that were interested in saving hunting animals and stocking fish. On August 22, 1890, Penrose called the meeting of the Corry Rod and Gun Club to meet at the Crosby Hose Fire Company. This was the initial meeting that started the Pennsylvania State Sportsmen's Association and the Pennsylvania Game Commission.

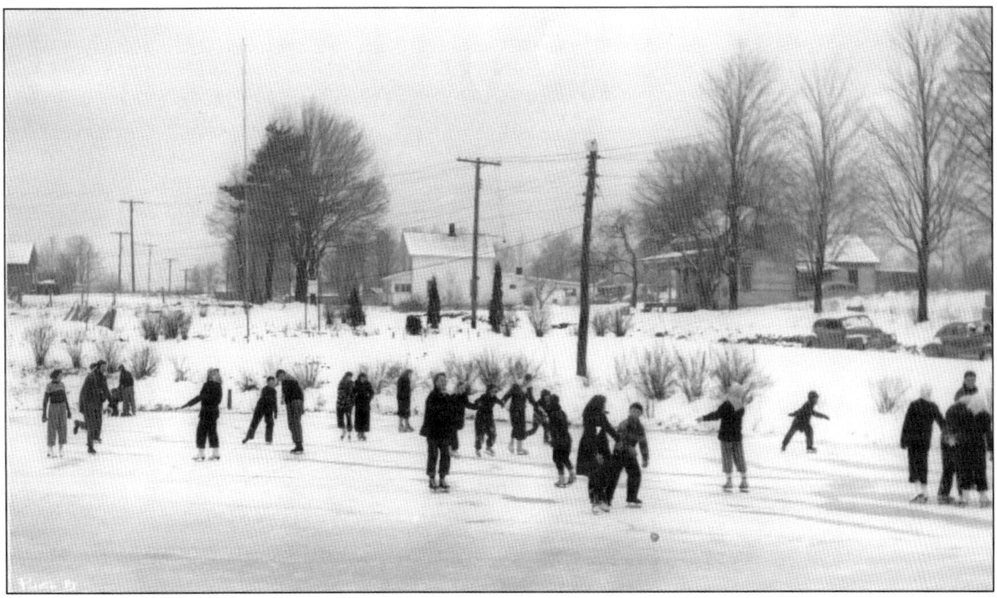

Corry had an ice-skating rink in 1930 on the Whitely property on the north side of Columbus Avenue. It was possible to flood the entire ravine just south of the pond. There was another ice-skating rink at Bear Creek near Howard Sheen's residence across from the corner of Wayne and Raymond Avenues, until the skating rink was moved to Mead Park pond (Alice Lake) in 1941.

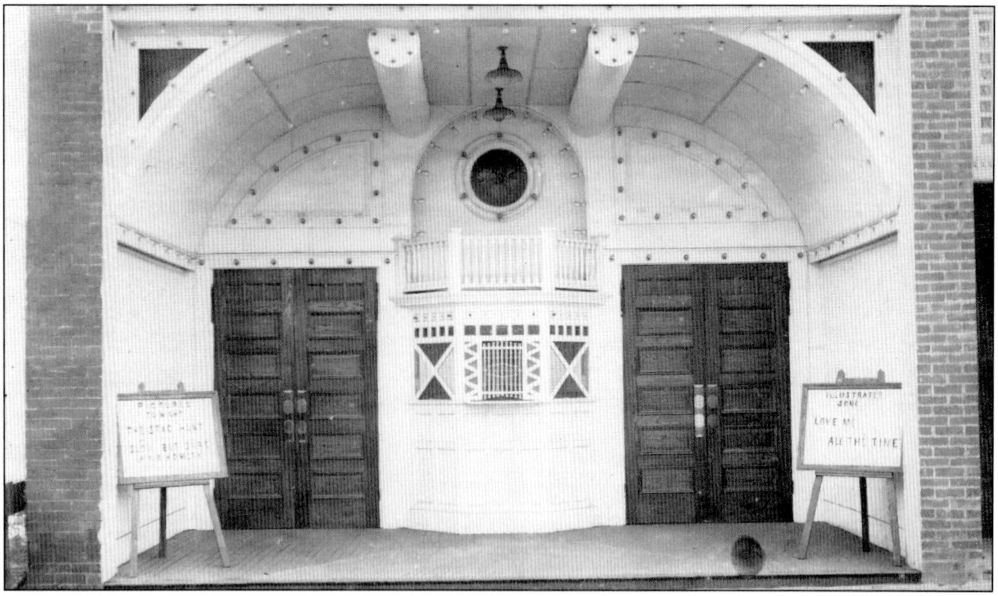

AmuseU Theater was located in the Traction Building at 32 North Center Street. It was one of the most popular institutions in the city, opening in 1907. Equipped with the very best in motion picture machines and comfortable opera chairs, the venue played the very best in motion pictures and illustrated songs. The front of the building featured an impressive blaze of electric lights. It closed in 1909.

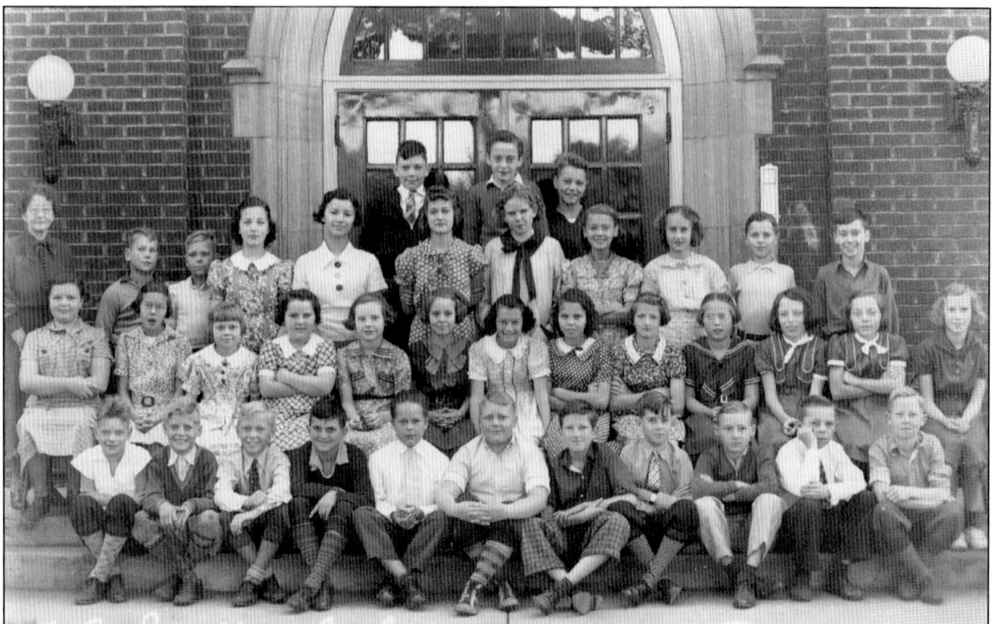

This building on Wright Street served as the junior high school until 1954, when the new junior/senior high school was built on Pleasant Street. The building then became home of Wright Street Elementary School for decades, until it was torn down and replaced by the new elementary school that extends from Wright Street to Wayne Street.

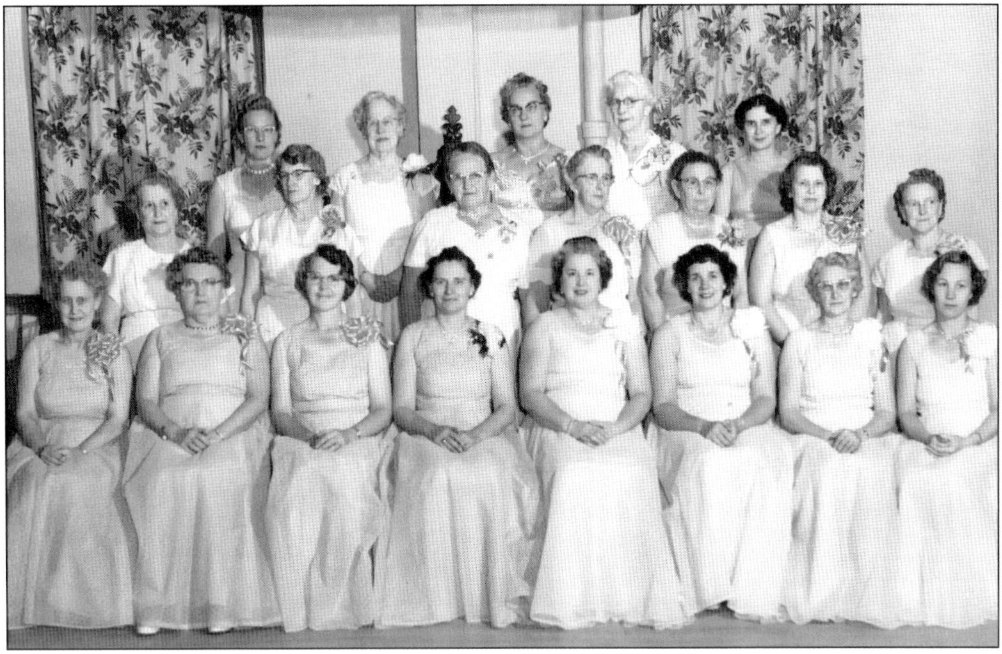

Lady Franklin Rebekah Degree Lodge No. 140, IOOF of Corry was instituted on June 10, 1884. The order was socially inclined with a spirit of helpfulness. In 1913, there were 80 members that met on the first and third Tuesday of each month in the IOOF Hall. An efficient degree staff conducted candidates through the mysteries of the degrees. The lodge continued until about 1960.

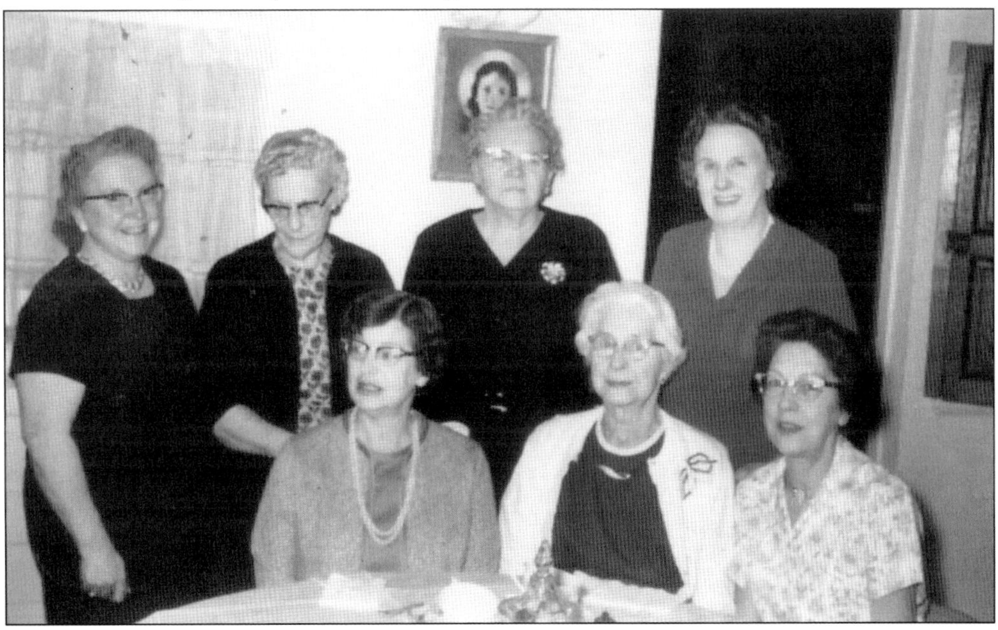

One afternoon every month, the "Birthday Girls" would take turns hosting a birthday party with lunch and homemade birthday cake. The ones that had a birthday that month would receive gifts. It was a good excuse to keep in touch with friends. Pictured from left to right are (sitting) Marilyn Denton, Bernice DeJean, and Ann Young; (standing) Doris Loveland, two unidentified women, and Mildred Orn.

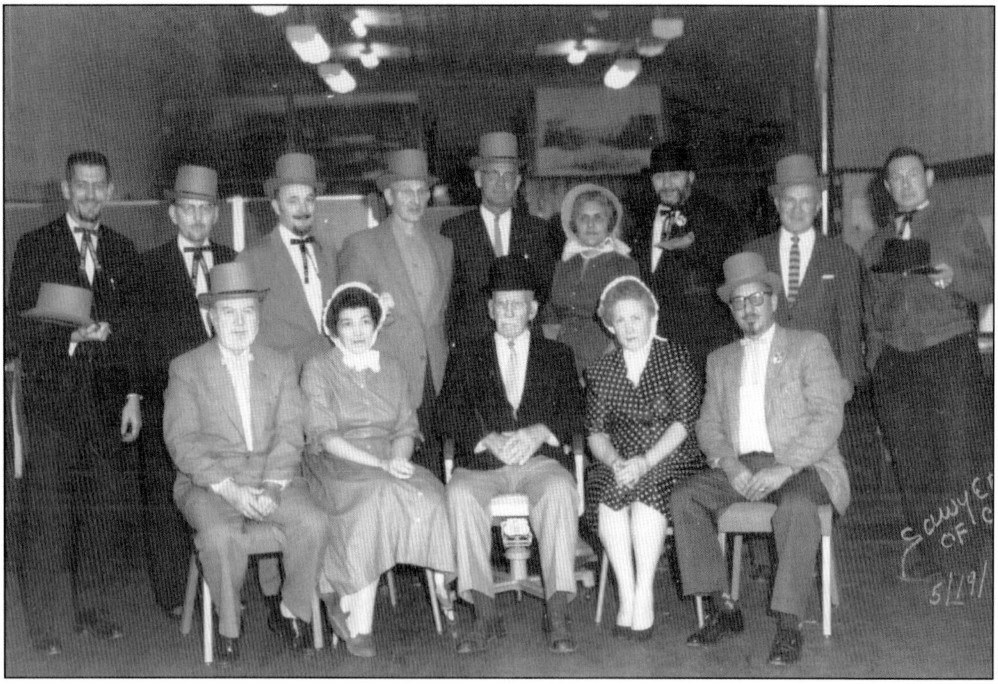

This was the centennial planning board at the headquarters in the former Cherry Hardware store on West Main Street (now a parking lot). From left to right are (first row) Victor Orn, Florence Grice, F.E. Whittlesey, Helen Nichols, and Stewart (Doc) Long; (second row) Bill Armitage, Stanly Anderson, Bob Tunnel, Guy Abby, Mayor Fred Kinley, Philena Follett, Frank Grice, Dallas Smiley, and Kirk Sawyer. (Courtesy of Bob and Ruth Ann Grice.)

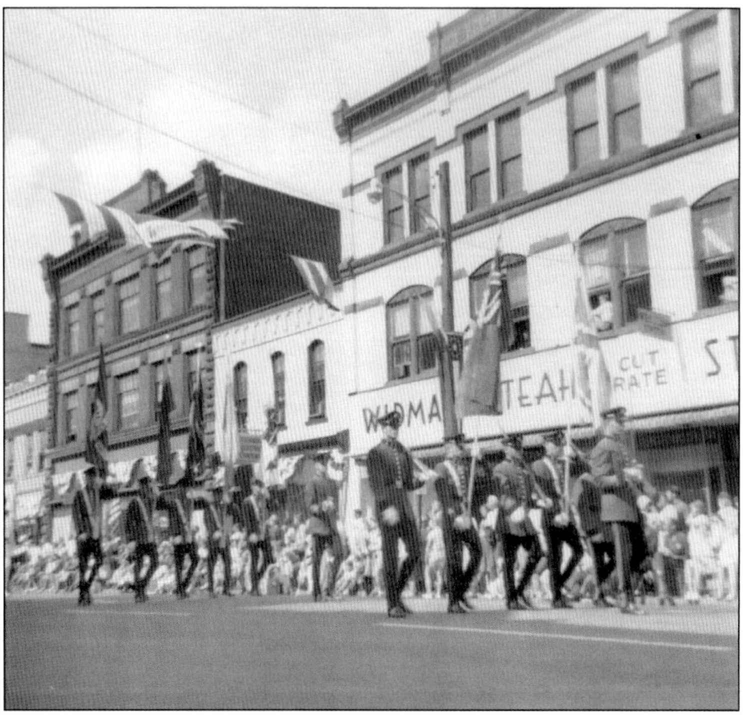

By the time the centennial celebration started, all men were expected to have grown a beard or have purchased a button releasing them from the obligation. If a man was caught without one or the other, they were put in a pretend jail until they bailed themselves out by buying a button. There were prizes for growing the longest or craziest beard or moustache.

Florence Grice had a big part in organizing both the centennial and the 125-year celebrations. The whole town was decorated with quasquicentennial flags and red, white, and blue swags. Grice is pictured standing in front of her house on Church Street dressed for the part. She also was a member of the Corry Historical Society and spent many hours helping to set up the Corry Museum. (Courtesy of Bob and Ruth Ann Grice.)

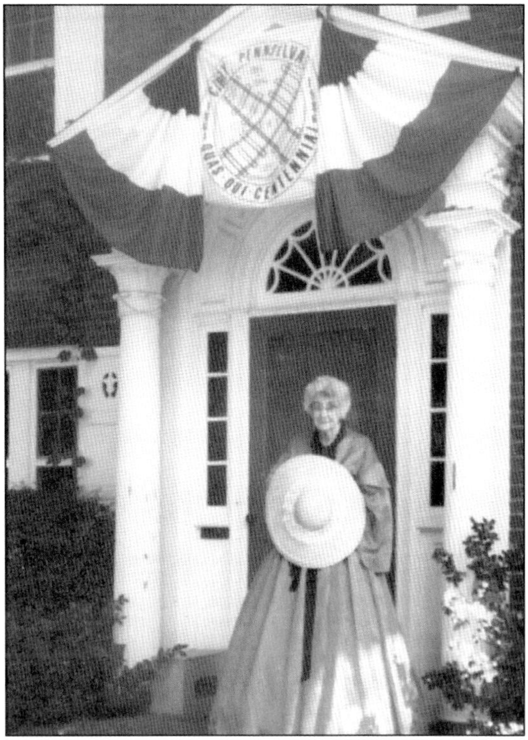

The year 1986 was the quasquicentennial for Corry, celebrating 125 years since becoming a city. During the big celebration, people dressed in 1861-era clothes, had a beard-growing contest, and a large parade. They also had old-fashioned contests, such trying to catch a greased pig. Someone custom-made a bomb-sized firework and published it as the "big boom"—it rattled every window in town. (Courtesy of Mike Magoon.)

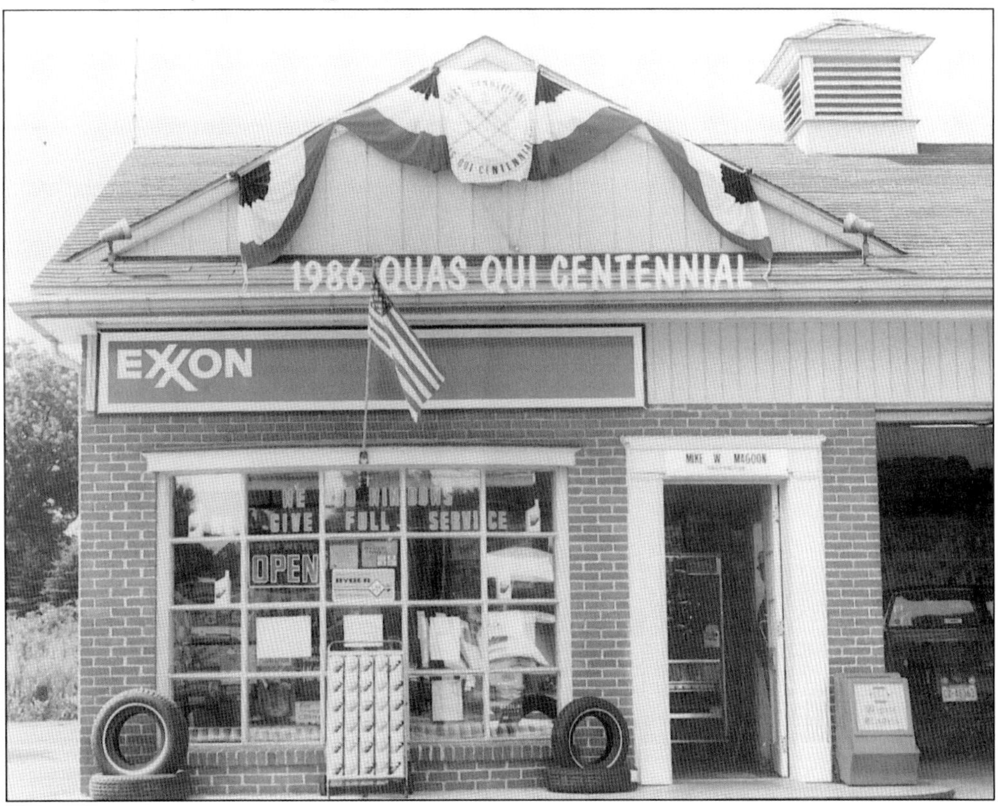

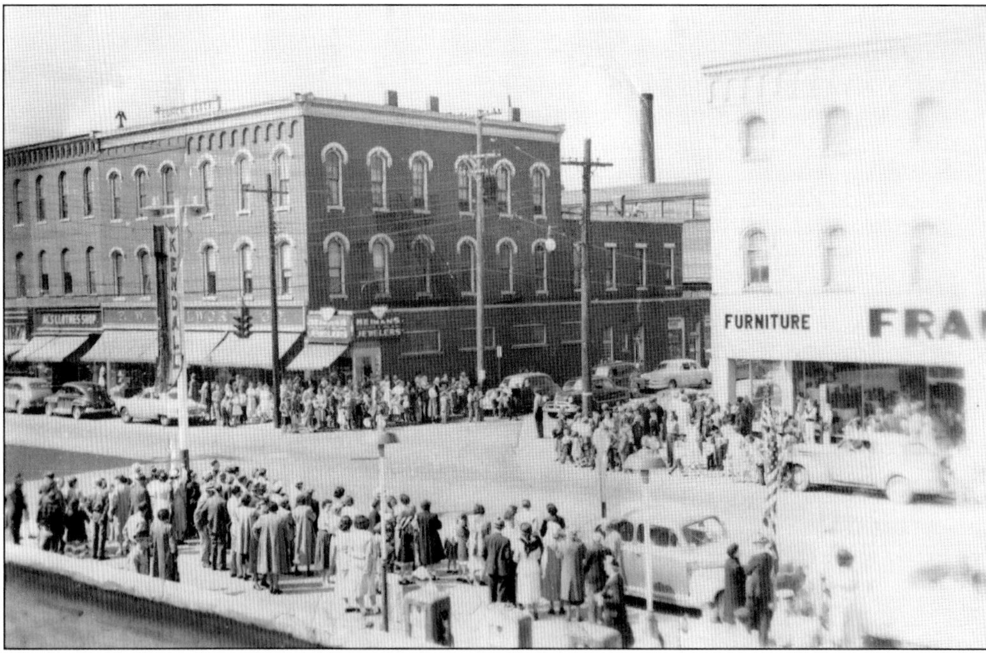

The crowd is pictured waiting for the centennial parade to start in 1961 at the corner of Center and Washington Streets. Woolworth's, Franz Furniture, Heiman's Jewelry Store, and Al's Clothing Store were still in business at that time. The photograph was taken from the roof of the Charger gas station.

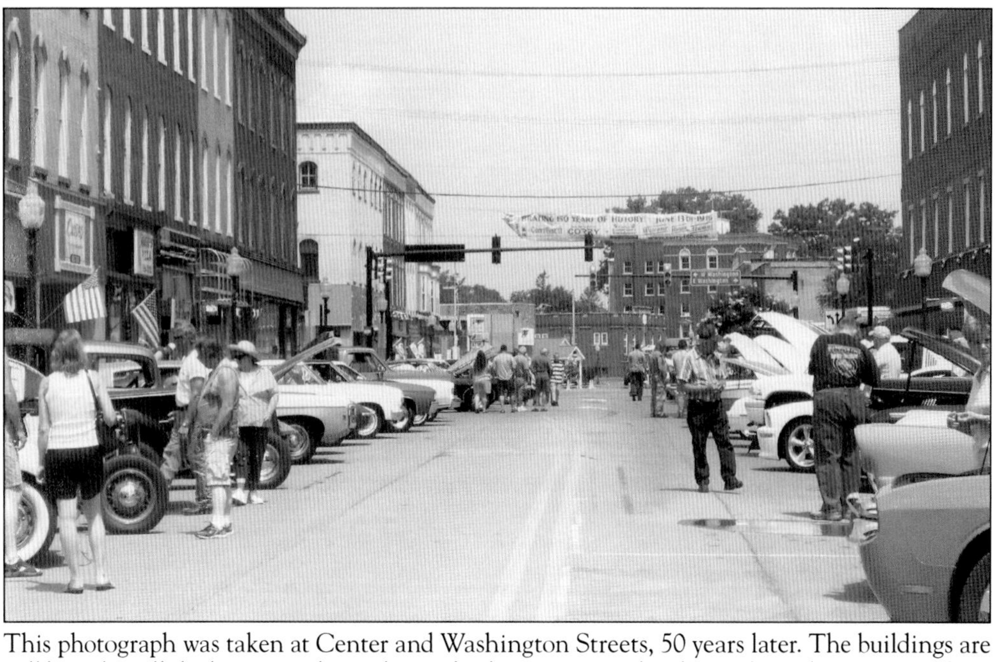

This photograph was taken at Center and Washington Streets, 50 years later. The buildings are still here, but all the businesses have changed. The Corry Hotel is the Higher Education Building, the old library is a restaurant, the Woolworth's store is empty, and Murphy's store is a large antique store. The Charger gas station has been replaced with senior housing. Center Street was closed for a car show during the sesquicentennial. (Author's collection.)

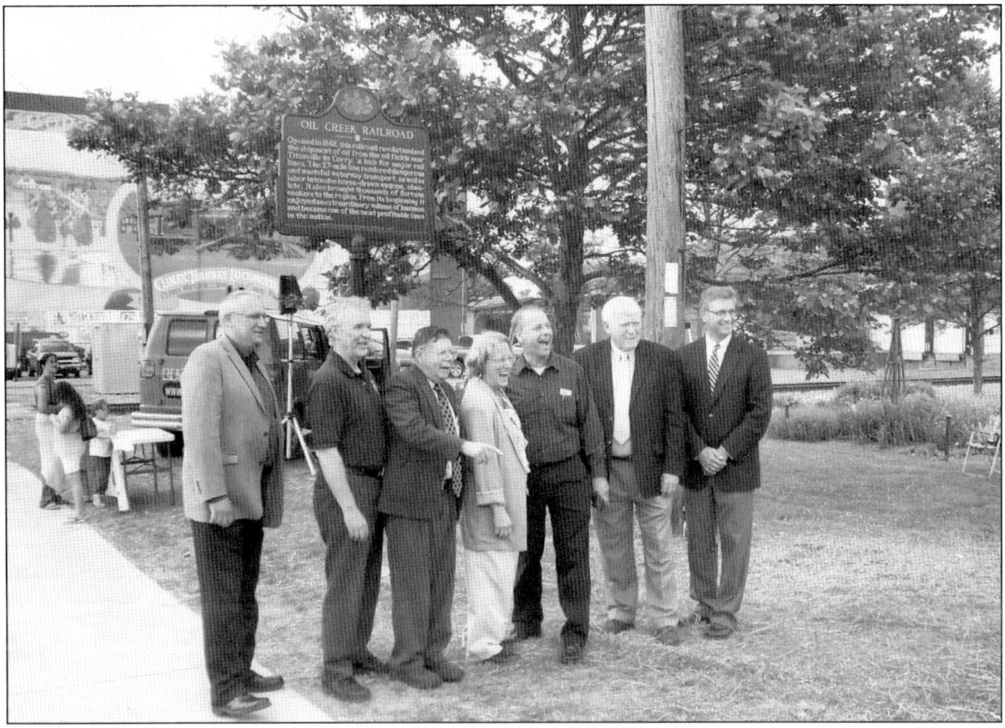

Pictured is the unveiling of Corry's fifth historical marker in June 2011. The presentation was made by the following: Carl Belke, president of the Western New York & Pennsylvania Railroad; Steve Bishop, executive director of the Corry Higher Education Council; Ken Springirth, rail and transit historian and author; Susan Beates, curator and historian of Drake Well Museum in Titusville; Scott Sanford, Corry's mayor; James Nystrom, Titusville's mayor; and Jeff Kidder, representing the Pennsylvania Historical and Museum Commission. (Author's collection.)

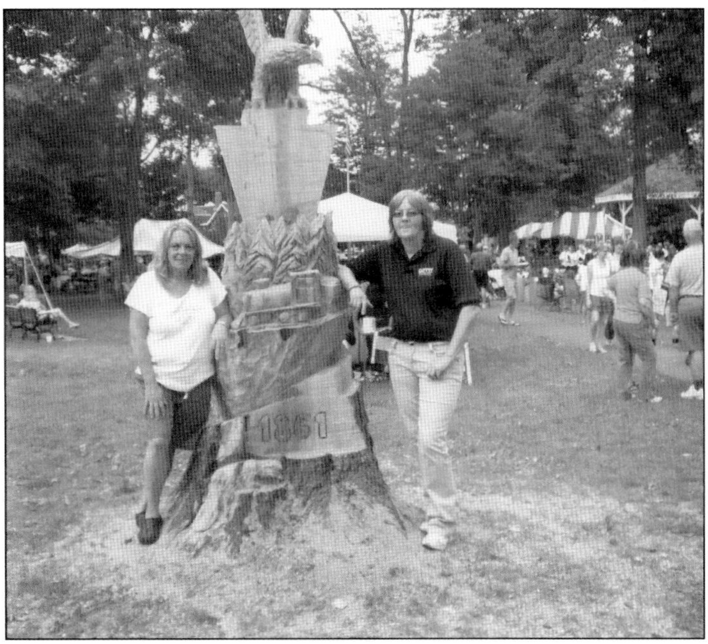

Just before CorryFest, one of the old maple trees needed cutting in the city park, so city workers cut it high enough to be carved. During festivities in the park, which included music, food, and craft venders, Scott Dow, a local artist, demonstrated carving with a chainsaw. No one knew what he was going to carve until the sculpture started to form. Pictured are Kathy Nielsen and author Jan Bemis. (Courtesy of Valerie Desmond-Lilley.)

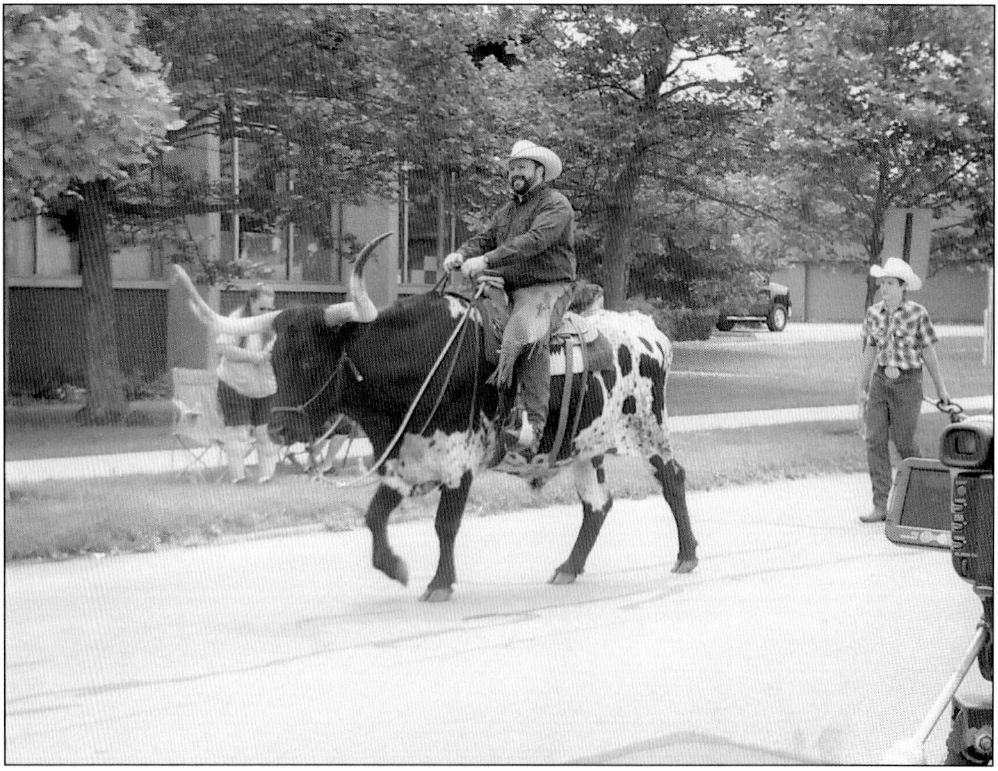

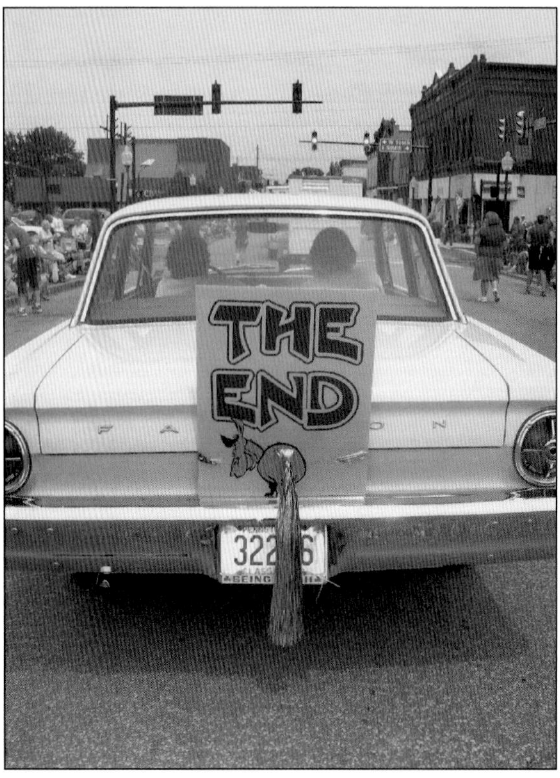

Matt Cox, minister and director of Miracle Mountain Ranch in Spring Creek, rode his steer from the high school to the elementary school in the 150-year celebration parade through all the noise and crowds. He then went to the city park and delivered a sermon called "Sermon on the Mount" while seated on the steer. The sermon also included his horse, dog, and rope twirling. (Courtesy of Joe Royak.)

Jill Hall is pictured driving her dad's 1965 Ford Falcon in the sesquicentennial parade. Passenger Jan Bemis is throwing candy to the crowds that were along all the streets from the high school down Pleasant Street, Center Street, and Raymond Avenue to the parking lot of the new elementary school. It is a CorryFest custom for the organizers of the parade to be the last ones in the parade. (Courtesy of Steve Sears/*Corry Journal*.)

Ten

The Climax Locomotive

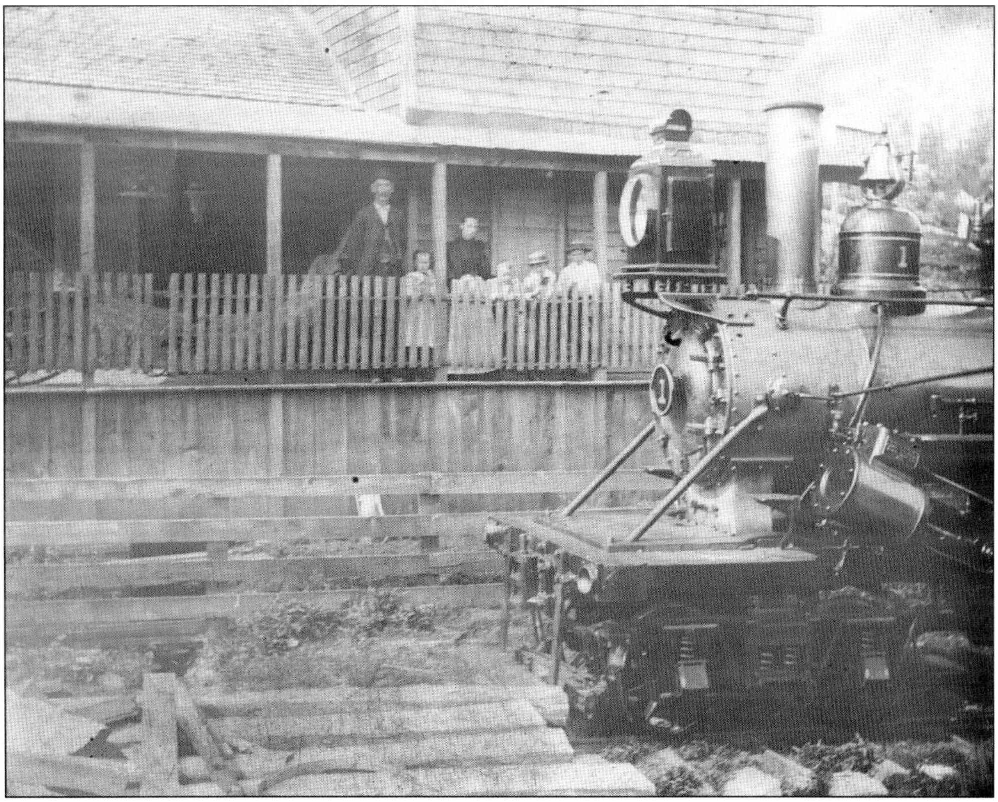

One of Corry's greatest accomplishments in the early 20th century was the Climax steam locomotive, the name meaning the height of success. It was well designed with constant improvements and well built. The factory workers took great pride in everything they built. It was also affordable—many were sold for short hauls around log yards as well as across the country on poorly constructed railroads.

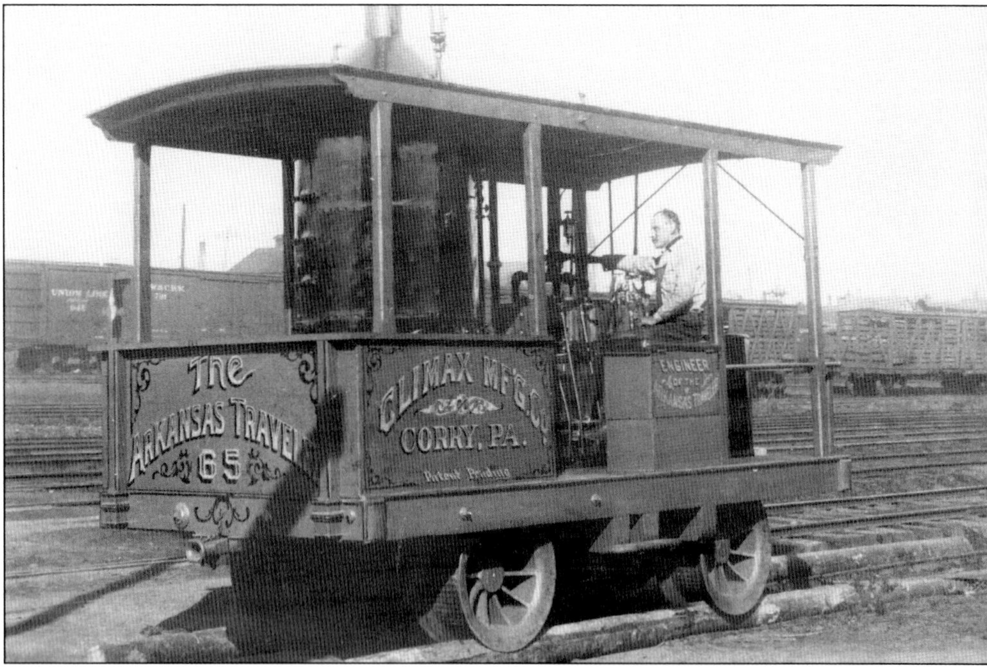

One of the most successful Corry plants by 1913 was the Climax Manufacturing Company, which was located on West Main Street between Second and Fifth Streets along the tracks. G. Yost constructed the plant in 1868 for the construction of Climax mowers and reapers, which for years were some of the leading harvesting machines.

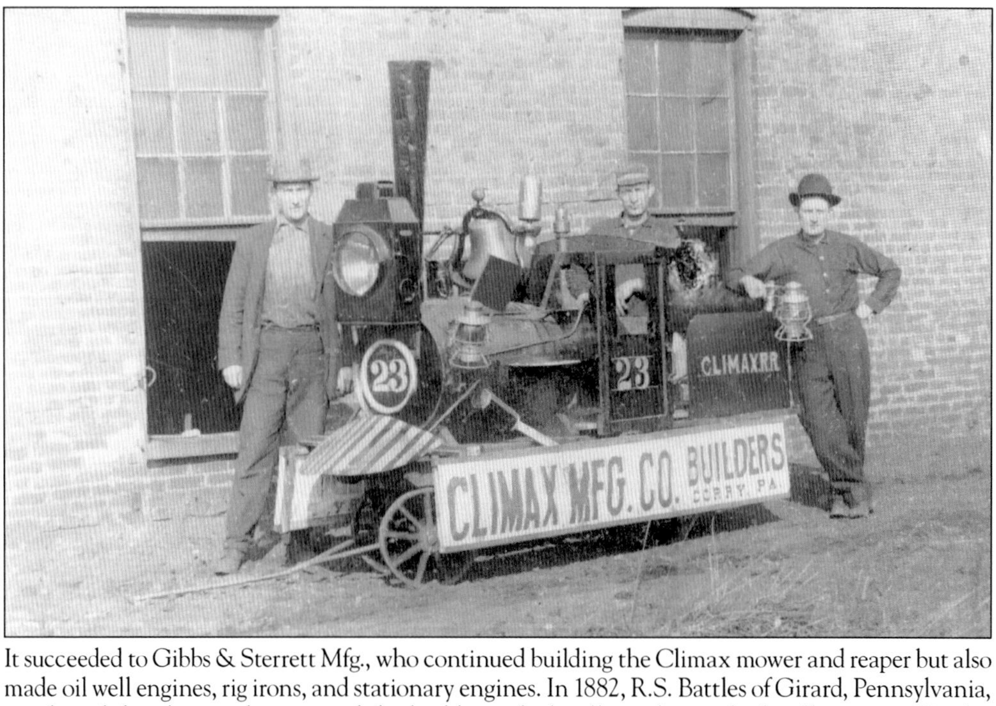

It succeeded to Gibbs & Sterrett Mfg., who continued building the Climax mower and reaper but also made oil well engines, rig irons, and stationary engines. In 1882, R.S. Battles of Girard, Pennsylvania, purchased the plant and continued the building of oil well supplies and oil well engines. He also commenced the construction of the Climax, geared locomotives, and logging cars.

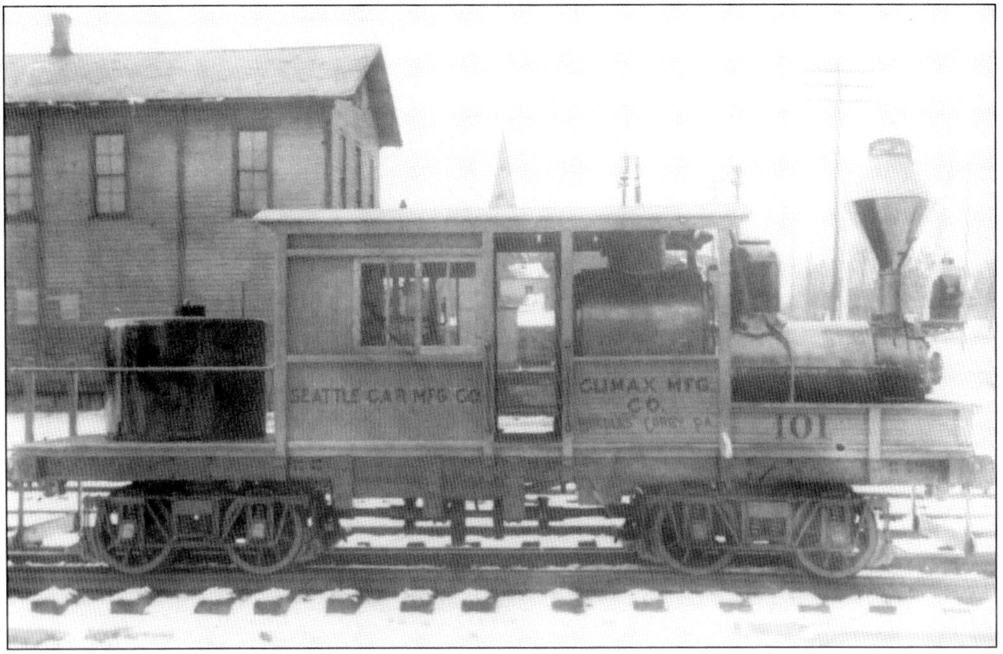

The demand for the locomotives and logging cars increased to such an extent as to take the entire output of the plant. Battles continued to operate the plant until his death in 1904. At that time, the company was incorporated and enlarged. New machinery was added, including electric cranes and pneumatic tools.

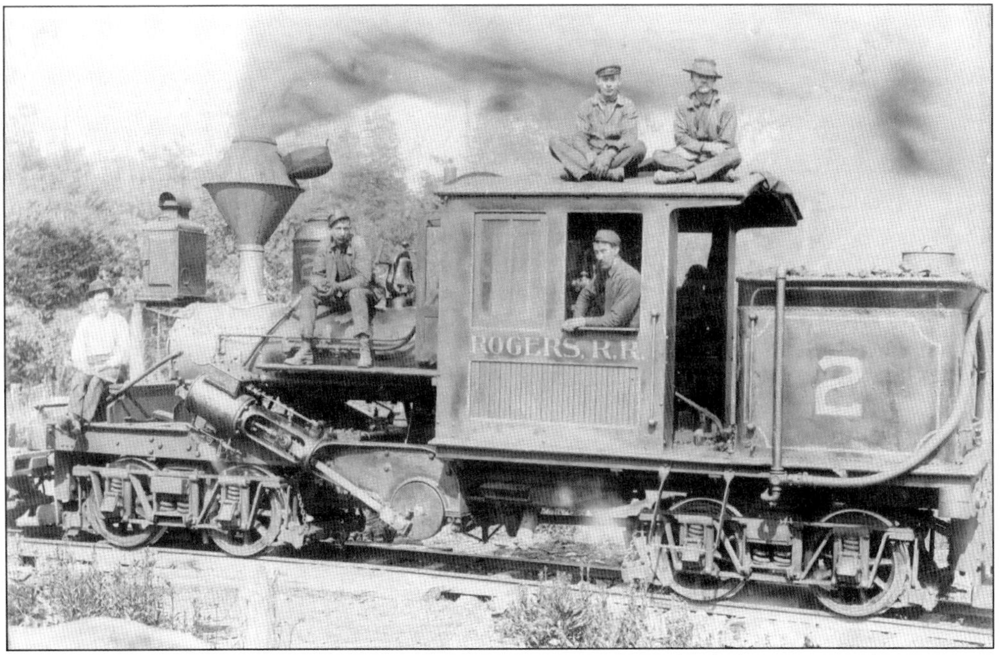

The Climax locomotive was exhibited in 1905 at the Lewis and Clark Centennial Exposition in Portland, Oregon, and won its highest prize, the Gold Medal. It also won at the Jamestown Ter-Centennial at Norfolk, Virginia, in 1907. It was rapidly gaining a great reputation for being well built and dependable.

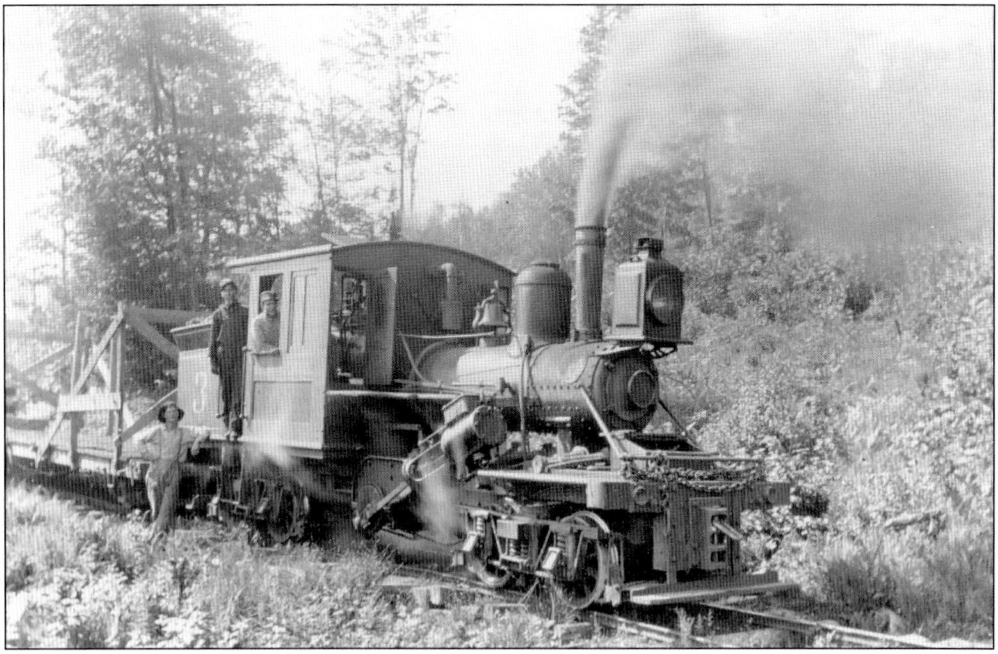

The Climax-geared locomotive was the only geared locomotive to have the boiler mounted in the center of the main frame, which allowed it to apply power to the center of each axle. The two long-stroke horizontal engines, with which each locomotive is equipped, are attached one on each side of the frame.

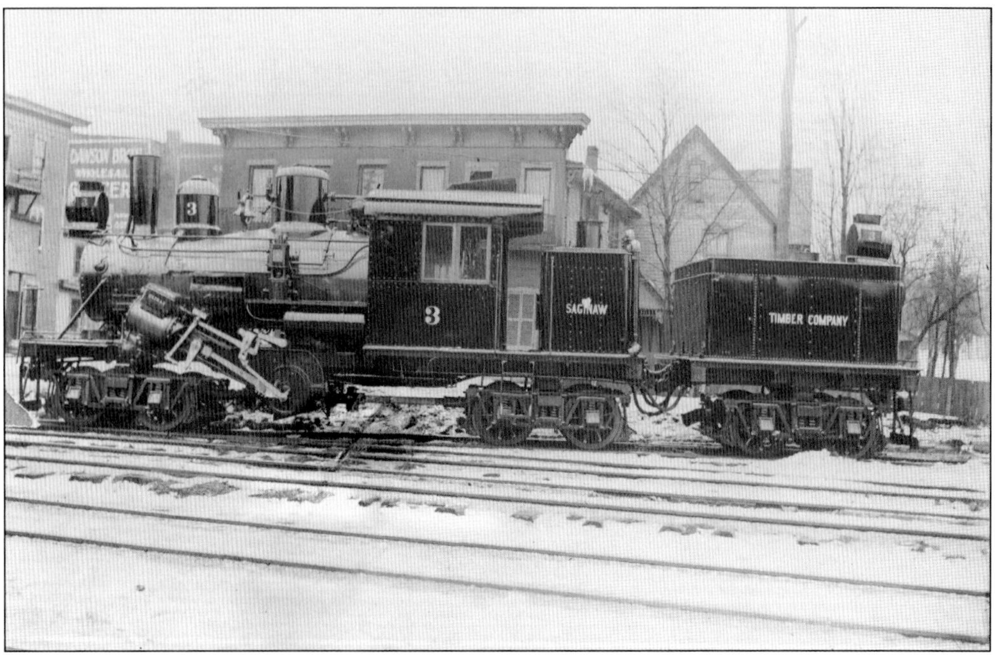

The horizontal engines are connected to a crankshaft, where there is a master gear transmitting the power with a longitudinal shaft to each axle gear through to trunk pinion. This transmits the traction effort to each axle through longitudinal shafts and universal couplings, transferring the power to each wheel equally, a Climax exclusive.

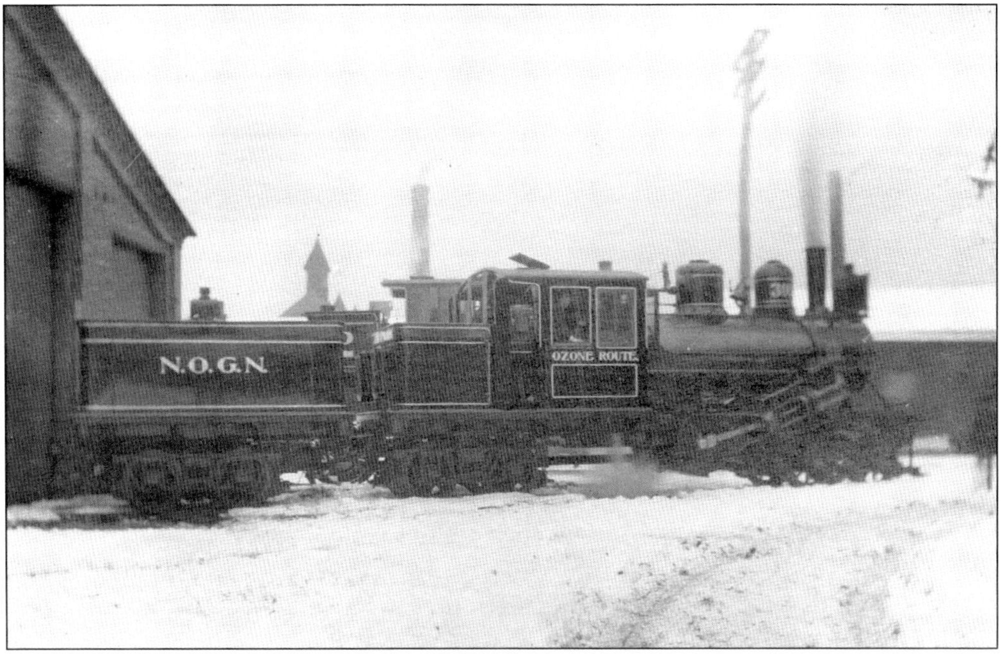

These locomotives were especially built for steep grades, sharp curves, and rough and uneven track—no grade was too long for them. The Climax could negotiate sharper curves with less resistance than any other geared locomotive because of the short, rigid wheelbase and the application of power to the center of each axle through the longitudinal shafts and universal couplings.

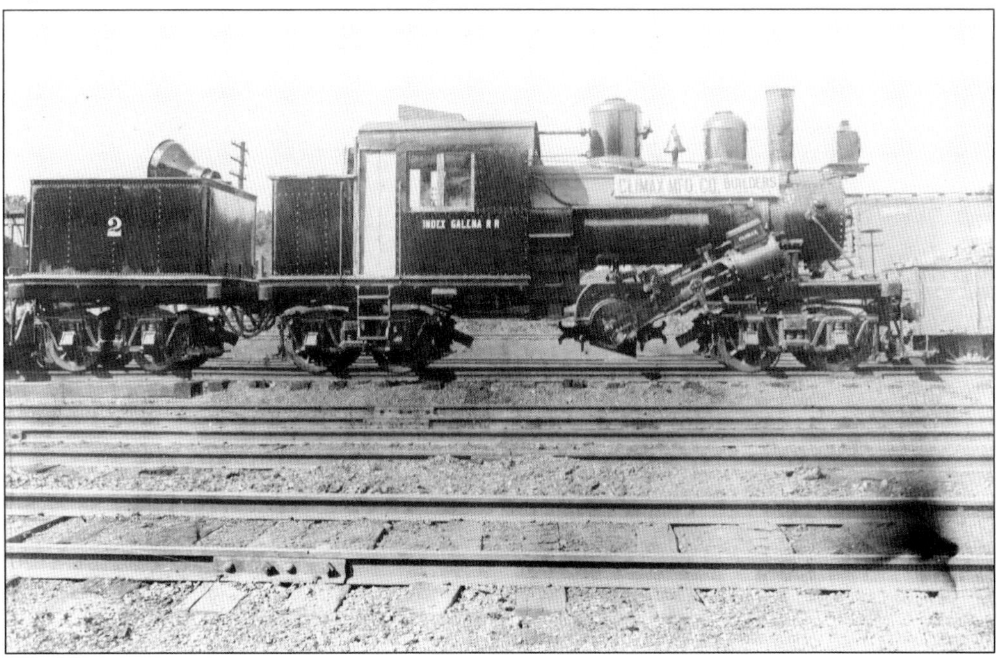

Besides logging, Climax engines were also used by coalmines and other types of mining as well as industrial plants for switching, sugar cane plantations, and wood chemical plants that made charcoal. Contractors also used them for earth moving, and short-line railroads used a lot of them, even using them on passenger trains where the grade was too steep for other locomotives.

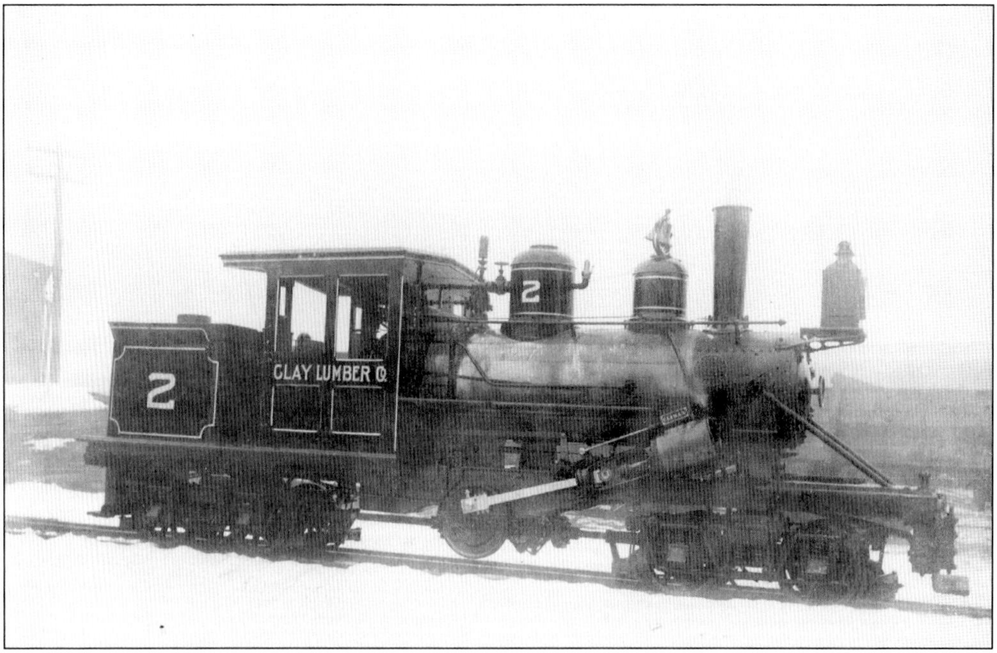

Climax-geared locomotives were built from 1888 to 1928. They could run on the lightest rail or uneven roadbed, and could even run up a 16 percent and over grade or negotiate a 50-foot radius curve. They were built to run on steel, wood, and pole tracks. Climax built 1,050 locomotives of varying sizes from seven tons to 100 tons.

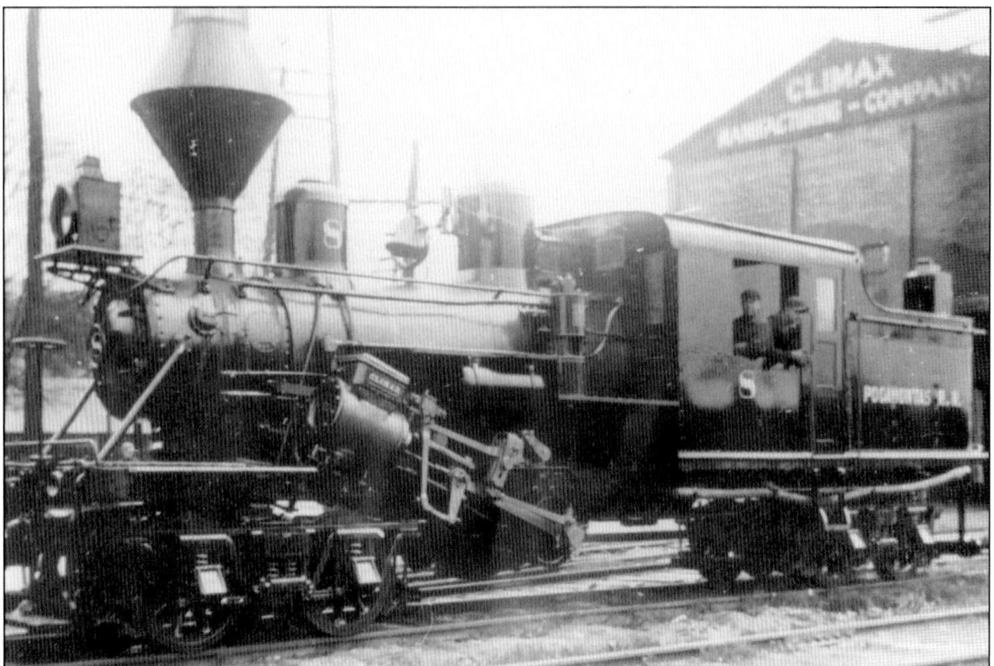

The horizontal type is divided into two classes. A Class B had two trucks with eight driving wheels and weighed from 20 tons to 60 tons. The Class C had three trucks with 12 driving wheels and weight ranging from 70 tons to 90 tons. The Class C has a separate set of trucks for the tank.

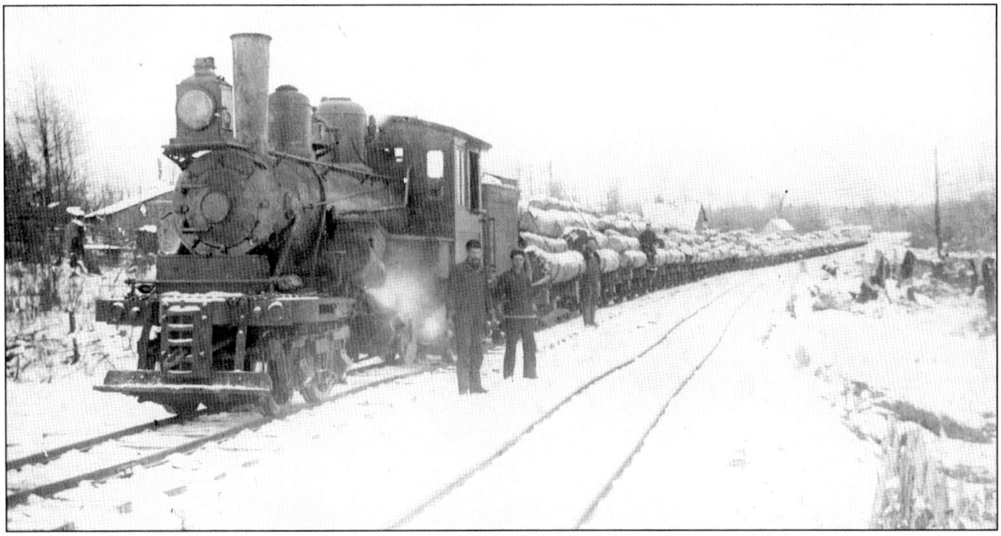

All Climax locomotives were built by the Climax Manufacturing Company, later renamed Climax Locomotive Works. An agency and service facility were established in Seattle, Washington, to sell and maintain locomotives for West Coast buyers. Production began in 1888 and continued until 1928. About 20 locomotives survive in North America, and five are operational. Two survive in Australia, with one on display and one under restoration. Seven class B locomotives were delivered to New Zealand; four of the seven survive today. Three are being stored, and one is under restoration. One Climax is being restored for use on a scenic railroad in West Virginia and is expected to be in operation by 2016.

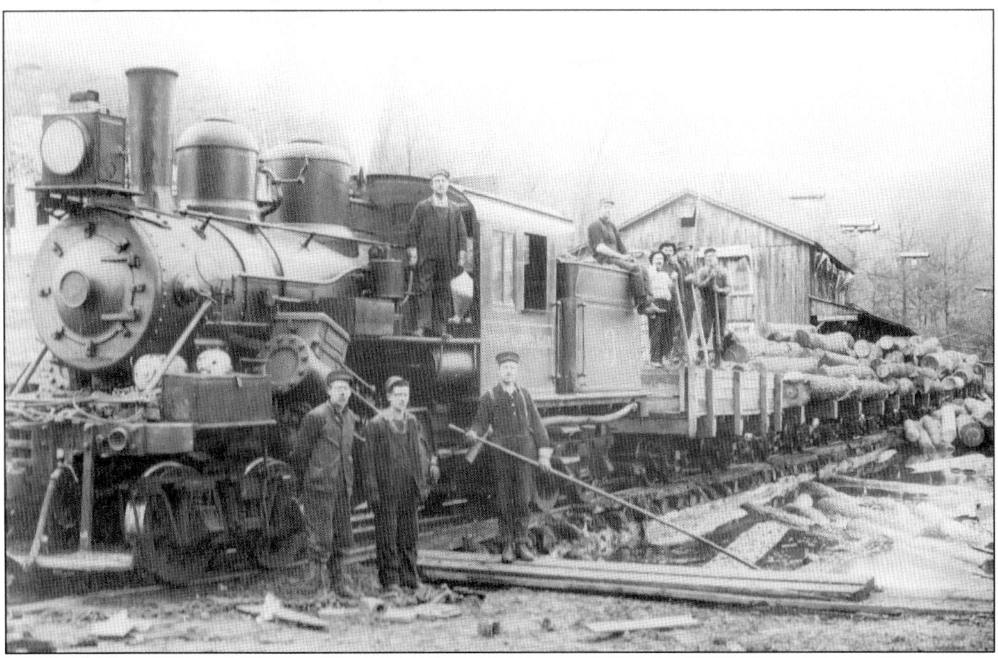

Climaxes were built in three classes: Class A was small—generally under 17 tons, with a frame similar to a flatcar and a wooden boxcar to protect the crew from the weather; Class B looked more like a regular locomotive, weighing between 17 and 60 tons; Class C was the biggest, with a three-truck design. "Ferdinand" from the *Thomas and Friends* cartoon is a Climax Class C.

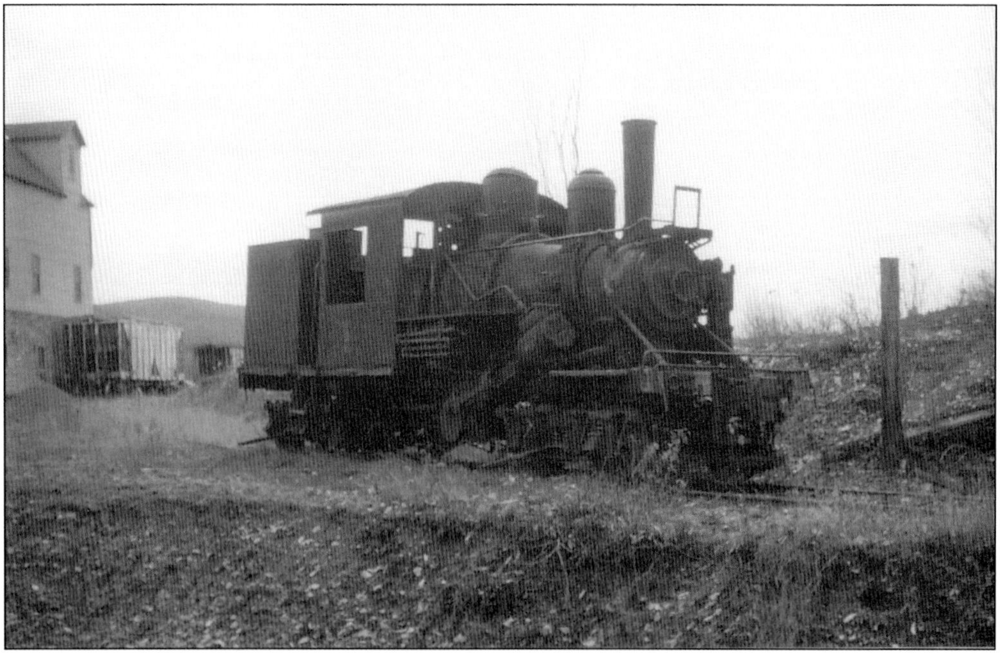

Hoping to save an important part of Corry history, a group of businessmen spent months writing letters and searching for a Climax engine in good enough condition to restore and display. In 1959, they traveled to Oneonta, New York, where they found one that had been abandoned. After looking it over, they decided to buy it and bring it back to the town where it was built.

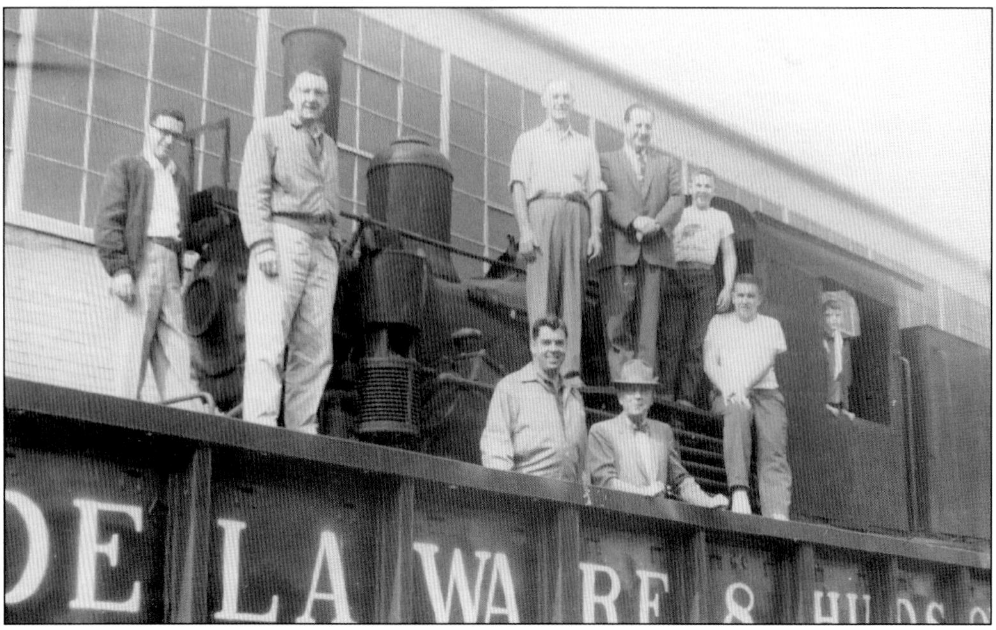

The Corry Group bought a retired Climax locomotive in January 1960, and with great effort and planning moved it back to Corry on a train. Pictured from left to right are (first row, lower) Armour Hillstrom and Sidney Eston; (second row, beside and on the train) Angie Carbone, Dick Rossbacher, Walter Casler, Frank Grice, Tom Grice, Bob Grice, and ? Casler with the train when it was delivered in front of the Corry Jamestown building.

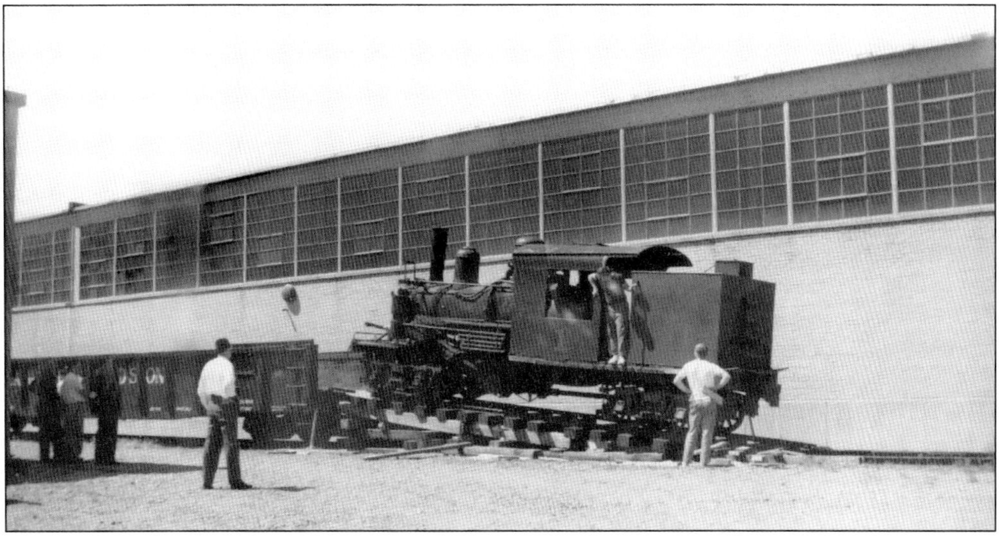

In 1960, a group of citizens bought a retired Climax engine to preserve one for posterity. The locomotive they found was a 30-ton standard-gauge Climax. It originally left Corry on March 20, 1927, for Barclay Chemical Company in Laquin, Pennsylvania. It was used on a two-mile track to deliver carload lots to various industries on its line until 1956, when diesel locomotives replaced it.

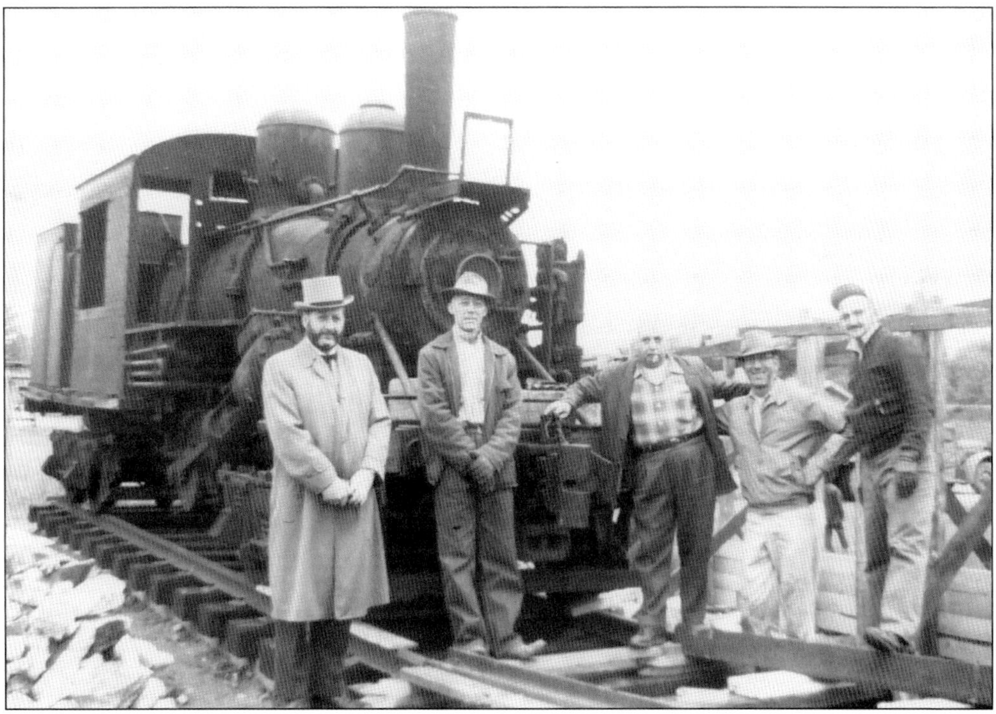

Pictured from left to right are Frank Grice, Walter Caster, Phil Zalzneck, Norm Edingek, and unidentified. The engine was eventually trucked to Mead Park and set on rails, and the building was constructed around it. It was refurbished to look as it did when it originally left the builders 34 years earlier. Even though the museum has constantly grown since 1961, the Climax engine remains the center of attention and is the symbol of Corry.